Advance Praise for Grassroots Marketing for Authors and Publishers

"Shel is the ultimate frugal marketer. If you don't want to spend a lot of money marketing your books—but you still want to sell a ton of books -- read his book. He provides lots of doable ideas that don't cost a lot of money but can produce great results."

—John Kremer, editor, Book Marketing Update
and author, *1001 Ways to Market Your Books*

"Dynamite stuff! I have even more respect for you as a knowledge-able colleague after reading Grassroots Marketing for Authors and Publishers! The 'Google' chapter alone is worth the price of the book. And the real-life marketing plans stimulate think-ing and present strategies any author or publisher can modify for their own books."

—Marilyn Ross, CEO, SelfPublishingResources.com, book coach,
speaker, author*The Complete Guide to Self-Publishing/Companion,
Jump Start Your Book Sales,* etc.

"It's clear that Shel Horowitz not only wants you to be one of the rare successes in a very crowded book marketplace, but that he knows what he's talking about. Practical and frugal suggestions on every page that will get your book noticed—and bought!"

—Rick Frishman, co-author, *Guerrilla Marketing for Writers,
Author 101,* etc., and CEO, Planned Television Arts

"A brilliant potpourri of marketing tidbits and little-known tricks of the book publicist's trade."

—Fern Reiss, author, *The Publishing Game* series

"Plan ahead. Determine the location and size of your market be-fore your write the book and buy this book now—it will show you how—and much more."

—Dan Poynter, author, *The Self-Publishing Manual*

"Shel Horowitz is one of the most creative and frugal Publicity Hounds I know. His book is jam-packed with ideas, tips, marketing examples from other successful authors, and even some fun and quirky ideas that will make your books fly off the shelves. The many bulleted 'to do' lists will keep you on track and on budget."

—Joan Stewart, PublicityHound.com

"In Grassroots Marketing for Authors and Publishers, Shel Horowitz presents a marvelous array of real-world book marketing strategies based on his decades of professional experience. His insight will help every author and publisher to sell more books. After all, selling more books is what successful marketing is all about, and that's what Shel's book is clearly all about! I was so impressed that I took the unprecedented step of urging Shel to co-publish with us."

—John F. Harnish
Special Projects Director, Infinity Publishing

"One of those books that becomes a required purchase for new and not-so-new publishers (alongside Kremer's 1001 Ways, Poynter's Self-Publishing Manual, and Reiss's Publishing Game)."

—Thomas Nixon, SmallPressBlog.com

"Outstanding toolkit! Every author can profit from these practical, low-cost tips and techniques to sell and promote their books!"

—Marisa D'Vari, author of *Building Buzz:
How to Reach and Impress Your Target Audience* and four other books

"In a world full of self-publishing, self-help, self-proclaimed gurus, Shel Horowitz walks the talk. I see his books mentioned everywhere-in cyberspace and on my colleagues' bookshelves. Now, he shares the secrets of how he makes it happen. You should inhale every one of Shel's ideas on how to market your book."

—T.J. Walker, Author, *Media Training A-Z*

"Shel Horowitz scores an unerring bullseye with every chapter of this book. He accurately steers authors through the pitfalls common in publishing, and accurately assesses the bewildering array of options available to authors. With common sense, pragmatism, and a crystal-clear writing style, Shel keeps an author focused on the truly useful activities; methods that long experience has shown will increase sales and visibility-and gives sound advice on which ones to avoid. If you retained the top three consultants in book publishing, and picked their brains at a cost of tens of thousands of dollars, this book is what your notes would look like after a week. I plan to give a copy to all authors, and make reading this book a requirement for any prospective author who submits a proposal to Elite Books in the future."

—Dawson Church, Ph.D
Publisher, Elite Books

Shel Horowitz is a generous, highly experienced marketer of books and general items. Known for his focus on ethical marketing, the author has put together an essential reference book for the independent press and self-publishing industry. With over 170,000 new books being published a year, it has become extraordinarily difficult to get seen among the crowd of other books and publishers. Shel's book gives practical guerrilla marketing ideas and procedures that give the little guy at least a chance of getting seen and bought in the market place...If you are thinking of writing a book; if you have even been fortunate enough to have been accepted by a major publishing house, you will find all the marketing aspects you will be expected to use to maximize book sales. We rated this book a high four hearts.

—Bob Spear, Heartland Reviews

Grassroots Marketing

FOR

Authors and Publishers

Grassroots Marketing

Marketing

FOR

Authors and Publishers

Shel Horowitz

AWM Books — Hadley, MA

Grassroots Marketing for Authors and Publishers
©2007, Shel Horowitz

Book Cover Design: MyLinda Butterworth
Interior Design: Day to Day Enterprises
Editor: Virginia Schulman

AWM Books edition: - Hadley, MA
ISBN-10: 0-9614666-3-4,
ISBN-13: 978-0-9614666-3-3

Infinity Publishing edition: - Haverford, PA
ISBN 10:, 0-7414-3469-5
ISBN 13:, 978-0-7414-3469-2

Printed on recycled paper—Green Press Initiative
Printed in the United States of America
10, 9, 8, 7, 6, 5, 4, 3, 2, 1

Library of Congress Control Number:, 2006909008

Publisher's Cataloging-in-Publication Data

Horowitz, Shel.
Grassroots marketing for authors and publishers / Shel Horowitz.
p. cm.
ISBN 0-9614666-3-4 (AWM Books)
ISBN-13 978-0-9614666-3-3 (AWM Books)
ISBN, 0-7414-3469-5 (Infinity Publishing)
ISBN-13, 978-0-7414-3469-2 (Infinity Publishing)

1. Books--Marketing. 2. Marketing. 3. Book industries and trade. 4. Booksellers and
bookselling. 4. Authors and publishers. 5. Publishers and publishing. 6. Authorship-
-Marketing. 7. Self-publishing. I. Title.

Z283 .H675 2006
381.45--dc22   2006909008

Published jointly by AWM Books - Hadley, MA
and Infinity Publishing- Haverford, PA

Dedication

To my wife's parents, Susan and Stanley Friedman, with thanks for more than two decades of friendship and support.

Table of Contents

Acknowledgements

Special thanks to the entire past and present membership of the PMA-L (now defunct), Smallpub-Civil, Pub-Forum, and Self-Publishing discussion lists (from whom I've learned so much over the years!)—and to all those who've put their knowledge into book form and are listed in the Appendix—especially John Kremer, Dan Poynter, Fern Reiss, and Marilyn Ross for their indispensable resources on self-publishing. Without all of you, this book wouldn't have been possible, because I'd still be a greenhorn.

In alphabetical order within sections, and with apologies to anyone I've missed.

For reviewing the MS (or sections) in advance: My wife, Dina Friedman, always my most thorough critic. Also Brian Jud, Aaron Shepard, Jacqueline Church Simonds

For input on the cover and/or salesletter: Susan Alcorn , David Ambrose, Greg Babic, Meg Bertini, Jay Brown, Virginia Brucker , Alan Canton, Andrew Chapman, Anita Chiappori, Caryn Colgan, Joseph Cosentino, John Culleton, Michele DeFilippo, Pam Fenner, Sheyna Galyan, Bob Goodman, Peter Goodman, Marion Gropen, Simon Grose-Hodge, John Grossman, Ron Gurfinkel, Dee Hamilton, John Harnish, Joseph Harris, Rick Hibbard, Kyra Hicks, Barbara Hudgins, Tordis Ilg Isselhardt, Leila Joyner, Barry Kerrigan, John Kremer, Mary Ellen Lepionka, Don Lessne, Mayapriya Long, Dick Margulis, Pete Masterson, Gus Maximus, Rita Mills, Peg Nichols, Tom Nixon, Maggie Parkhurst, Dan Poynter, Dee Power, Sheila Ruth, Michelle Shane, Walt Shiel, Jacqueline Church Simonds, Lisa Smith, Nancy Smith, Isaac Starr, Cathy Stevenson, Melinda Thompson, Bridget Watts, Mike Wickham

For permission to use their material or their stories, and/or connecting me with other sources: Ned Barnett, Larry Baxter, Mary Doyle Brodien, Joyce Brooks, Virginia Brucker, Jack Canfield, John Paul Carinci, Alex Carroll, Stephanie Chandler, David Chananie, Dan Cullen, Linda Delgado, Paulette Ensign, Arlene Evans, Catherine Franz, D. Dina Friedman, David Hall, Charles Hayes, Ivan Hoffman, David Horowitz, Ruth Houston, Larry James, Brian Jud, Stacey Kannenberg, Mike Kelley, Lorraine Kember, John Kremer, Betsy Lampé, Gary Lehmann, Ted Lish, Jill Lublin, Dave Marx, Curt Matthews, Barbara Meislin, Sheree Paris Nudd, Charles Patterson, Angie Pederson, Diane Pfeifer, Douglas Pfeiffer, Yvonne Phillips, Dan Poynter, Dominique Raccah, Laura Ramirez, Yardenna Rand, Fern Reiss, Lorna Rubin, Sheila Ruth, Pam Schwagerl, Connie Shelton, Ed Smith, Jonathan Somich, Ratanjit Sondhe, Joan Stewart, Cathy Stucker, Kent Sturgis, Kristie Tamsevicius, Jack Thomas, Dorothy Thompson, Rita Toews, Linda Urban, Carol White, Ernie Zelinsky

My production staff: Virginia Schulman for copyediting, and for the long, entertaining debates about what to capitalize, what to hyphenate, etc. For another wonderful cover and interior and index: MyLinda Butterworth. For coding the website and double-checking all the URLs (and for her years of tireless support as my Webmaster and virtual assistant): Michelle Shaeffer. For falling in love with the book, putting together an innovative co-publishing deal, and assisting in many phases, John Harnish of Infinity Publishing.

For providing me with direction about what to include:
Ned Barnett, Joyce Brooks, Janice Campbell, Paulette Ensign, Ted Fuller, Kathleen Gage, Barbara Gonzalez, David A. Hall, Stacey Kannenberg, Michael Kelley, Paul Marriner, Sheree Parris Nudd, Angie Pedersen, Yvonne Phillips, Laura Ramirez, Janet Reinhold, Dorothy Thompson, Irene Watson, Carol White

For giving me a bonus to use as a sales incentive: Kenrick Cleveland, Sean D'Souza, Dan Janal, Brian Jud, Yanik Silver, Jacqueline Church Simonds

PART I

Creating a Marketable Book

Chapter One

The Marketing Plan—and Marketing Stunts

- *Structure your plan*
- *Real-life marketing plan examples*
- *Out-of-the-box marketing stunts*

Your book is not a cookie—so don't try to get by with cookie-cutter marketing. Because every book, author, and publisher is different, each book needs a unique marketing plan—one that harnesses the author's and publisher's strengths and vulnerabilities.

As examples, radio won't be the best choice for an author with a very thick accent or a major stuttering problem. If the author is a charismatic speaker who electrifies audiences, emphasize live presentations. But if the author has physical disabilities or other restrictions on travel, some of the many Internet selling tools might take center stage.

In some genres (among them science fiction, mystery, and romance), a well-established fan culture holds frequent conferences and media events. Those options aren't present for business books, but business authors can conduct corporate training—while environmental authors can speak at topic-oriented (as opposed to book-oriented) conferences.

The possibilities are limitless; it's a matter of filtering and sifting from the forest of possibilities to figure out the best match for your particular situation. When you have a coherent plan, the results can be quite gratifying, as they've been for Lorraine Kember of Perth, Australia, self-publishing author of *Lean on Me: Cancer through a Carer's Eyes* <http://www.cancerthroughacarerseyes.jkwh.com>, whose multifaceted nonbookstore strategy made her book profitable within six months, as she reports:

I have now sold around 2500 copies—none of these through book shops. My sales have come from public speaking, media coverage through newspapers, television and radio and from my website. I spend hours each day on the Internet marketing my book to organizations all over the world. I also spend a great deal of time promoting my website and requesting reciprocal links. This has been very successful as my site is now rated high by Google and I have an above average link rating. As a result of my tireless endeavours I am now receiving book orders from: America, United Kingdom, Canada, India, New Zealand, Australia and have even received an order from Singapore.

How to Structure a Marketing Plan

Talk to a dozen publishing and marketing consultants; you'll probably get between 10 and 20 models for creating a book marketing plan. Later in this chapter, you'll see some examples. Meanwhile, let's talk about the elements of a good plan. It should:

- Identify the various audiences likely to want your book (not only one reader at a time, but also in quantity)—and explain why they'd be interested
- Demonstrate to decision makers (such as acquisitions editors at publishing houses, distributors, or sources of capital) the book's possibilities for success
- Recognize the strongest selling points for this particular book in its chosen market—often expressed as benefits to the reader
- Examine how best to reach those target groups: what they read, watch, listen to, attend...and how to use those identified contact points to hook into those prime prospects; what sales channels will likely work to reach these specified audiences, and how to market effectively through each channel
- Suggest various subsidiary rights or spinoff possibilities
- Match up the author's or publisher's interests and skills (and budget!) with the techniques most likely to generate sales

- Figure out the most effective ways to market, with the least expense for the most return—whether or not these ways follow the conventional wisdom

If bookstores are a major part of the marketing mix, it may even be helpful to do two versions of the plan: one to show the book trade, and a broader one for your own use that sees bookstores as merely one element in a successful multipronged campaign.

And if you're approaching agents or traditional publishers, incorporate the key aspects of your marketing plan directly into your book proposal.

Actual Marketing Plan Samples

These two actual marketing plans that I drew up for clients are very individualized, and that's deliberate. I didn't want to give you a more generic example precisely because I really want to get you thinking strategically about why your book is unique, and which promotional strategies are a good fit with your own skills and interests. If you need help constructing your marketing plan, contact me.

You'll find a third example, focusing entirely on bulk sales, at <http://www.grassrootsmarketingforauthors.com/bulkmarketingplan.html>

YARDENA RAND: SNAGGING A DISTRIBUTOR

I prepared this marketing plan for the author—a first-time publisher with a very classy coffee-table book—to show to distributors. For a number of my clients, I have prepared two different marketing plans: one that aims at distributors, wholesalers, and bookstores, and one aimed directly at the author or publisher, focusing more on direct sales. My name does not appear on this one because it was designed for the audience she wanted to reach, not for her.

Fairly few of my clients tell me the results, but Yardena was nice enough to keep me informed:

> I wanted the plan to focus on the traditional book trade because I
> needed to entice distributors (with only one title, I need a distributor
> to get national coverage). I sent packets out on a Friday to three

distributors and by Wednesday morning, I had heard from one of the biggest in the industry, Biblio, accepting my book! Thanks so much, Shel. I couldn't have done it without your expertise and your help!

Marketing Plan for
WILD OPEN SPACES:
WHY WE LOVE WESTERNS

By Dr. Yardena Rand
ISBN 1-932991-44-1

SUMMARY:

Fifty-seven million American adults are Western movie fans. The genre touches something deep in our collective imagination—and the genre's appeal crosses every possible demographic and psychographic category.

This book is designed to appeal to three distinct audiences:
1. The lovers of Westerns themselves
2. Their friends and family, who either want to understand their loved ones' obsession, or who are buying gifts for them
3. Academics using the book for classes or research in film studies, American civilization, popular culture, communication/mass media, and other disciplines

The author is a trained marketer and tireless promoter who was able to get press in some 45 newspapers during the research phase (including the *Miami Herald, Kansas City Star, Minneapolis Star-Tribune,* and *Rocky Mountain News* (Denver's major paper), and numerous placements in smaller papers targeted toward the American West (e.g., in Billings, MT, and Casper, WY). As a result of this publicity, in the pre-Internet days, she was able to develop and interview a research base of 1052 fans of Westerns. She will promote this book extensively in print, electronic, and online media, as well as through personal appearances in both pop-culture and academic settings. She will also enlist the 1052 interviewees as active promoters within their own networks, most of which should drive sales directly to the retail channel.

She's also a highly qualified researcher, with a doctorate in American Civilization from Brown University, and a high-level market research career for entertainment industry clients including Disney, the History Channel, Home and Garden Television, Arts and Entertainment, Bravo, and American Movie Classics, as well as well-respected corporate clients in the technology sector, among them IBM, Cisco Systems, and Sprint.

The book is written in an approachable, accessible style, to appeal to non-academic audiences, extensively using direct quotes from the fans themselves—but it's also designed to pass muster with academics who demand rigorous research and professional-level analysis. Thus, it should be a strong seller both in general-interest bookstores and in college/university textbook stores.

One of its greatest attractions for mainstream audiences will be its stunning collection of 110 photos, including stills and publicity shots from many of the great Westerns, featuring such legendary actors as John Wayne, Jimmy Stewart, Debbie Reynolds, and Kevin Costner.

General Interest Bookstore Appeal

WILD OPEN SPACES offers top-notch production values and a creative layout from one of the foremost book designers working in the industry: Mayapriya Long of Bookwrights, Charlottesville, VA. With consistent use of white space, art, and pull quotes, as well as the riveting quality of the included photos, the book is easy to read and eye-catching. It will lend itself well to window and in-store displays, especially when tied to seasonal events (and there are many to which the book can be tied, including, of course, birthdays of famous Western actors and directors), as well as author/participant appearances.

Since the book will be marketed heavily as a gift item, the author will explore premium placement/visibility options such as end-caps in the October-December shopping season.

WILD OPEN SPACES has received endorsements from several significant authors in the field, including Vine Deloria, Jr (*Custer*

Died for Your Sins) and John G. Cawelti (*The Six-Gun Mystique*). The author will continue to actively pursue prepublication reviews and hopes to get at least one big-name movie star who has acted in/directed Westerns.

It's the kind of book whose cover draws the reader, whose subject forces the reader to open the book, and whose beautiful execution generates a reader who says, "I have to have this," and heads for the register, credit card in hand.

Additionally, the author will drive traffic to bookstores through a concerted publicity and marketing program (details below).

Library Appeal

The wide popularity of books on the movies (over 61,000 listed on Amazon) make this a much-requested subject in public libraries, and the additional benefit of verifiable scholarly research will appeal to academic libraries. The author will include libraries in her appearance itinerary.

Regional/Geographical Appeal

Certain areas of the country should be especially receptive to both library and bookstore sales, as well as other distributor-oriented channels such as gift shops in museums, national parks, and entertainment-industry retail stores. These include areas with vast population and many tourists, such as Los Angeles (movie capital), San Antonio (the Alamo), Houston, St. Louis, Chicago (Museum of Broadcast Communications), New York (home of television and live theater), and Washington, DC (Smithsonian Institution), as well as pretty much all of the 19th-century frontier lands, which include most of the United States except the easternmost states and Hawaii.

Academic Bookstore Appeal

For academic audiences, the key point of interest may be the statistical research that documents Westerns' wide appeal beyond the traditional view of the beer-swilling, politically and culturally conservative, working-class middle-aged white male, and the accompanying narrative that explains the appeal to women

(1/3 of the audience), people of color, and other audiences that don't meet the stereotype. Rand demonstrates that the Western fan mix is demographically almost identical to the wider population: the fan base includes people in every occupation, every cultural background, every economic class. Can feminists love cowboys? Of course. Is it possible to sip vintage white wine and nibble caviar in a 5th Avenue penthouse while watching William Holden in *The Wild Bunch?* You betcha. And is there still a place for the farmhand, the construction worker, and the truck driver to face down the bad guys at High Noon? Oooooh yes.

The author will seek both course adoptions and inclusion on Recommended Reading lists, and she will also pursue impulse sales from college students, staff, and faculty in college bookstores. She will market to professors in such areas as Film, Communications, American Studies, and Popular Culture, and if success warrants, will expand to Sociology, History, Psychology, and Literary Criticism.

MARKETING AND PROMOTION PLAN

Direct Mail to Drive Bookstore Sales

- Co-op flier mailings to bookstores and libraries through Publishers Marketing Association and/or Florida Academic Press
- Postcard and/or flier mailing to targeted special-interest bookstores at museums, national parks, and relevant attractions
- Fliers and letters to all 1052 interviewees, thanking them for their participation and offering strategies to promote the book
- Selective mailings to professors of relevant courses, seeking textbook adoption or at least adding to Recommended Reading list for classes (an effort that could be widely duplicated if initial results are positive)

Media Publicity

- Minimum of three ads in *Radio-TV Interview Report* tied to specific timely events, to generate 30-100 radio interviews
- Fax or e-mail blast to major newspapers

- Books/press kits to appropriate major national TV and radio talk shows
- First- (prepublication) and second-rights (postpublication) excerpts sales efforts and/or review/feature promotion focused on national magazines with large circulations (including *USA Weekend, Parade, Reader's Digest,* those covering the entertainment industry—*TV Guide, People, Us*—but also some unexpected places, such as *Redbook,* where the finding that women love Westerns may be a good publicity hook
- Prepublication galley/ARC review copies to book trade (*PW, LJ, Kirkus,* etc.) and major national reviewers (*New York Times, Washington Post, Village Voice, New York Review of Books,* etc.). Also to top reviewers at amazon.com who review books on popular culture, and to small-press-oriented review outlets such as *ForeWord, Midwest Book Review* (postpublication, final copy), *Independent Publisher...*
- Ongoing subscription to PR Leads <http://snipurl.com/la5x>, which provides contact for journalists seeking story sources
- Donate copies for fundraising giveaways at top-ranked PBS and NPR stations

Author Appearances

- Bookstores and libraries
- Academic conferences (already confirmed for National Popular Culture Association and American Reception Study conferences, 3/05 and 9/05)
- Writer's conferences
- Book-industry trade shows and public festivals including BEA (Book Expo America), NEBA (New England Booksellers Association), New York Small Press Fair, and assorted regional shows
- Fan gatherings within the Westerns community and the general movie-making industry
- Tie-ins with Hollywood events such as studio tours

Online

- Dedicated website for the book, set up as a portal site for all fans of the genre and related activities: the website will provide information about Western fandom (e.g., cowboy action shooting, rodeos, film festivals, chuckwagon cook-offs, dude ranches, national parks, Old West towns, Wild West days, etc...will collect e-mail addresses for newsletter that will provide notification of author appearances and other marketing events (as well as valuable content on its own)...will offer interactivity through reader forums and potentially other devices...will offer enough rotating content that the search engines rank it highly...and, of course, will promote the book extensively, with excerpts/photos from the book, reader and press reviews, a pressroom including interview questions, etc.

- Author will make certain excerpts/articles available for use on high-traffic websites, e-newsletters, and print publications catering to the target audience
- Author will regularly post favorable reviews, Listmania entries, etc., on amazon.com, all of which will identify her as the author of WILD OPEN SPACES.
- Author will encourage others to post favorable reviews on amazon.com
- Author will identify and join at least five high-traffic, highly relevant Internet discussion groups, and will post with signature linking to the website and listing the book by title and ISBN

LARRY BAXTER: REINVENTING A DEAD BOOK

This is an example of a plan directed toward the author, covering far more than bookstore strategies. I was hired to write a marketing plan for a well-written, highly original novel hidden in some really terrible packaging. I flat-out told the author that he needed to republish and start over. He followed my advice and produced a beautiful book worthy of the contents. The Eppie Award mentioned here is an award series for e-books, <http://www.epicauthors.com/eppies.html>. And PMA, which is mentioned throughout this book, is the largest trade group of independent publishers; the initials used to stand for Publishers Marketing Association.

Marketing Plan for:

THE MAYAN GLYPH
Prepared for Larry Baxter by Shel Horowitz

Key Audiences

Good news—this book can find an audience in a wide range of markets, many of which are quite easy to target. This document may vastly expand your thinking about what's possible.

Bad news—this may come as a shock, but I am not sure that you've identified the right core audience. While you will certainly sell a few to tourists visiting Cancun, I see those sales as supplemental—and probably involving difficult-to-obtain cooperation from gift-store owners whose English is limited, whose business practices don't necessarily conform to U.S. norms, and who would need (but not necessarily welcome) a lot of handholding to market the book. Not that you shouldn't try there, but I would establish a solid sales record of a few thousand copies before I approached them.

Whom can you go after instead?

- Tourists/ecotravelers specifically interested in Mayan ruins. This would include a good-sized subset of the Cancun/Cozumel tourists—but also people flying into Mérida to see Palenqué and of course, Uxmal and Tulum. Target this market and forget about the beach-and-tennis crowd. It also would have reach into visitors to Oaxaca, Chiapas, and Guatemala/Belize. Travel agents offering tours focused on pre-Columbian civilizations and/or ecotourism will help reach this market, and there are many other ways to reach them as well. And remember that many of these areas receive large numbers of tourists from outside North America—specifically Europe. While non-native speakers of English would probably prefer books in their own language, many travelers from the United Kingdom, South Africa, Australia, New Zealand, Belize, and much of the Caribbean use English as a primary language.
- Anyone who has ever participated in an archeological dig,

especially those who have done so in the Americas south of the Rio Grande.

- Large chunks of the scientific/medical and academic communities: epidemiologists, pathologists, archeologists, anthropologists, historians, MD general practitioners, engineers/inventors (largely due to your own activities in these areas rather than the content of the book—can appeal on the "one of our boys wrote this book" slant), teachers in departments/courses such as Spanish, comparative culture and civilization, ancient history, pre-Columbian civilization, native peoples, epidemiology of infectious diseases, art history. The high quality of your research will be another asset in these markets.

- Other nontraditional travelers can be reached through hostels, educational institutions, Doctors Without Borders (bit of a long shot), religious missionary organizations, U.S.-oriented Spanish-language immersion programs in at least Mexico and Guatemala, native English speakers teaching English as a foreign language in those countries...

- Literary agents, who can pursue foreign translation and book-club rights. I would think some publishing house in Mexico would want this book! In addition to a nice chunk of money, foreign translation sales add greatly to your prestige as you market the book through other channels (as will your Eppie award). A good foreign-rights agent may also be able to get you other, probably much smaller, sales to markets that export a lot of travelers to Mesoamerica— Germany and Japan, for instance. Book clubs for travelers, mystery/suspense readers, police procedurals, etc., are all possible. Yes, you can approach them yourself, but you probably want to delegate this, especially since the copyright is already no longer fresh as the book world (rather idiotically) defines it. Once again, a good track record in other channels will make book-club sales much more likely, and success in landing even a single club deal will ripple through all the rest of your marketing. Both the foreign and book-club sales would have been easier to go after before publication, but they are still worth pursuing.

However, they can be a time sink, and it makes a lot of sense to use an agent, who only gets paid when a sale is consummated.

Proposal: Relaunch Book under Your Own Imprint

Since you've done only P-O-D, have no distribution channel other than Amazon, and have essentially no copies in the marketplace—we have the opportunity to relaunch the book as if it were a new title. If I were you, I'd take $5000 or so from that $30K marketing budget to get the interior and cover professionally designed (please don't tell me that you think you did this already; the production values do not compete in today's retail marketplace), and another $5000 or so to do a traditional offset run of 2000 or 3000 copies. I'm guessing you're spending at least $6 per book right now, and probably more like $8-$10; with that price structure, you can't distribute the book through any wholesale or retail channel. Working from today's printing prices, you should be able to do offset for no more than $3 per copy, and quite probably a good deal less. (The ideal price would allow you to still make a profit at 70% discount off list price, yet still be priced within the range of competing titles by unknown authors.) The remainder of this marketing plan is based on the assumption that you do republish it more professionally. [Several paragraphs specific to this author's situation have been deleted here.]

Retail Channels

- General-interest bookstores: They will only be a significant channel if either you build a lot of demand through constant media appearances, an active program of author events in-store, or—the best option—using these two types of events to build each other. The reality is that traditional bookstores will not be your strongest channel, and they'll be frustrating to deal with.
- Book-trade specialists: mystery/crime, art, cultural history, even science fiction/fantasy (yes, I know, it isn't that kind of a book, really).
- Specialty retail. Museum gift shops: A great big YES for

any art and archeology/anthropology museums with a good pre-Columbian collection. Also some store chains like the Museum Store, 10,000 Villages (and a gazillion similar stores that are independently owned) that are not located in museums. Science and nature stores. Any store that sells replicas of ancient artifacts. Texas-specific or centric stores (I'm sure they exist). Oh, yes, and it's certainly worth a try to get the resort hotels in Cancun to stock it, though I think this will not be your strongest market.

Other Sales Channels

- Corporate special sales: drug companies, organizers of relevant scientific and medical conferences, makers of scientific equipment—especially any brands mentioned in the book, travel agents, tour operators, hotels within 50-100 miles of Uxmal, airlines, any companies that sell toy Mayan pyramids or pyramid construction kits, law-enforcement organizations, anyone working on the issue of bioterror (e.g., think tanks and research institutes, Homeland Security bureaucrats), etc.
- Catalogs: there are probably dozens of appropriate ones that could sell your book over the Net and via mail order.
- Book clubs: science, mystery, history, Discovery Channel, QPB, BOMC.
- Republication in other countries, as noted above.
- Reseller program that could involve many, many websites, newsletters, conference organizers, professional organizations, etc. As one example, visit <http://www.ancientamerican.com/bookclub.htm>

Creating Buzz in These Communities: Internet, PR, Advertising, Author Appearances

INTERNET

- New website for the book: cover, synopsis, first couple of chapters, endorsements, order form, schedule of author appearances, a press or media room with photo and sample questions (and eventually, a list of media that have covered you), outbound links to the Mayan sites you sent me, an article or two about Mayan history and culture, maybe some photos of Uxmal—and some reason for visitors to give you their e-mail address (newsletter, some kind of monthly contest). I made a quick preliminary check and did not find sites for larrybaxter.com, mayanglyph.com, or themayanglyph.com, which means they are probably available. I'd recommend obtaining your name and at least one of the others. Your name has the big advantage of being pretty difficult to misspell, so I'd use it for radio interviews. Both domains can point to the same place, at least until you publish a different novel. You should also register the name of your publishing house. Domain names are around $8 or $9 apiece for a year, so getting several is no biggie.

- Identify as many relevant, high-readership discussion groups as you can, starting with the most relevant and working outward. I found these to get you started: Cities of the Ancient Maya [since closed]—looks like a good one to start with: 100 members, lay-oriented, archives are open to the public Timewavezero2012 <http://groups.yahoo.com/group/timewavezero2012/>—a bit off the track, very metaphysical/New Age—but with 598 members, it might be worth your while 2012 Theories <http://groups.yahoo.com/group/2012-Theories/>—similar. 406 members and probably a good deal of overlap with the previous one Spiritual Prep 2003 <http://groups.yahoo.com/group/SpiritualPrep2003/>—another similar one; 706 members—check if it's still active before getting involved, since the group name contains the year 2003 Mayan Studies <http://groups.yahoo.com/group/Mayan_Studies>—only 73 members and academic in tone—but these may be important people who can bring your book to wider audiences Aztec Culture, even smaller <http://groups.yahoo.com/group/AztecCulture/>

Sign up for two or three of these at a time. Read the posts for a week or so, then send an introductory post that talks about your book, and includes a "signature" that you'll use at the end of every post. Then look for at least one or two posts every week on each group that you can respond to, helpfully and informatively. This will draw traffic to your website over time, and thus sales. Plus if some of these people like your book, they will have a lot of influence and will recommend it to others.

I could find you dozens more, in general archeology/ anthropology, infectious disease (where you want lay audiences)—but first see if you like the method. It is extremely powerful, but not for everyone. The ideal group has 500 or more members (some have many thousands), a manageable number of posts including some that you can learn from and some that you can respond to, and a high ratio of good content to idle chatter. Many are available in digest form, which means you get all the messages from a whole day in one or two posts, which you can print and read off-screen.

- Website traffic building campaign: optimization of pages, cross-link campaign, judicious use of pay-per-click advertising
- Write articles and excerpts that you can seed to other websites in exchange for a blurb and a link

PR/ADVERTISING
- Send galleys four months before the publication date to major publishing trade media
- Obtain blurbs from people in several of these industries, as many and as high-powered as you can get
- Develop both a general media mailing list and specific lists in niche markets
- Create and distribute at least one press release a month, with different angles and audiences; archive all the releases on your website, post to free distribution lists, and distribute to a targeted list. Follow up with top-tier media.

- Consider a subscription to PR Leads <http://snipurl.com/la5x>, which will send you notices of journalists looking for story sources that match your keywords.
- Consider an ad campaign in *Radio-TV Interview Report* <http://snipurl.com/oun8> to go after talk shows.
- As your budget starts to increase following sales, it may be time to hire a full-service publicist.
- Small-scale paid advertising to publications in specific niches, testing thoroughly before committing significant resources.
- Attempt to sell first or second serial rights to magazines (another place your literary agent will help).

AUTHOR APPEARANCES

The more you can do, the more books you will sell. Don't just show up and sign. Give readings and talks. Think widely and broadly, e.g.:

- Bookstore and library events (no pay, and with bookstores, they will take commission).
- Regional events in Boston/North Shore area, throughout Texas, Mexico—all places where the book has a strong hook.
- Professional conferences—perhaps on the theme of working science and research into a work of fiction. Epidemiology, archeology, and conferences on the craft of writing, for starters. Can get paid for some of these.
- Once sales start rolling, go out on the college circuit, where you can get paid.
- Talks in elementary/high schools—little or no pay but their parents are often receptive book buyers.
- Travel industry events.
- Local, regional, and national book fairs.
- Radio, as much as possible.
- TV, if you're comfortable with it. If you're not comfortable, a great place to get some practice is Brian Jud's "The Book Authority" show in Hartford. He'd probably be especially interested in how you took it over and rereleased it under your own imprint.

DISTRIBUTION

Once you've redesigned the book and gone with your own imprint, you have to figure out how to get the book into stores. Most large distributors don't want to work with unknown one-book publishers without a solid track record. But there are some options, and if you can get a distributor, it removes much of the hassle (though also quite a bit of the per-unit income). If not, there are always wholesalers, but they have their own challenges.

In descending order, here are some options:

- Try to get accepted by Midpoint or Small Press Distribution or the one or two others that take individual titles.
- Apply for the PMA small press distribution program through IPG (Independent Publishers Group).
- Sign up with Biblio, an imprint of NBN (National Book Network).
- Use Book Clearing House or another well-regarded fulfillment service.
- Find a publisher to distribute for you.
- Join one of the PMA mailings to qualify for free listing with Baker & Taylor (a wholesaler, not a distributor).
- Use a network of smaller wholesalers such as the distributors (lower case).
- Use independent publisher representatives (but they won't talk to you until you're moving serious quantities).
- Forget about the bookstore market and do all your own fulfillment (NOT advised!).

Notes: It is possible to get insurance against your distributor going bankrupt (happens more often than you'd guess). The distributor or wholesaler should insure your books against damage by fire, flood, etc.

Be sure your budget allows for returns; you may get 25–50 percent of your inventory back, and you'll have to get rid of them at a discount through your website or other direct sales.

Be sure you have your marketing ducks in order well in advance of distribution. If you can get the books to move out the door of the stores, they will stay sold and may even get reordered. Otherwise, most stores will only give you 30 to 90 days on the shelf.

One-Book Marketing Stunts

Unique books lend themselves to unique marketing. I'm reproducing these ideas not because I expect you to duplicate them; the whole idea, after all, is that they worked only for one specific book. Rather, try to duplicate the creative process of coming up with something that works for your book and your book alone, that you can incorporate into your marketing plan.

Note that last phrase: these types of techniques should not stand alone but be part of a larger and comprehensive plan.

Why am I putting these in a section on marketing plans when they're really more like marketing stunts? Because a well-thought-out plan incorporates even the crazy stuff, if it works. Often a hare-brained idea gets "legs," and successful authors adapt the ideas that work to their future marketing.

FUND YOUR PRINT RUN WITH A CUSTOM EDITION

Mike Kelley, publisher of Lonetree Press, produced a collectors' edition of *Violent Night* by Byron Justice. The hand-sewn hardback in assorted colors netted $3000 profit, which he used to cover much of the cost of the trade paperback edition.

SELL A BOOK, SELL A HOUSE

I'm a great believer in getting paid to do your own marketing, but Gary Lehmann, self-published author of *Investing in Rochester*, takes the concept a lot farther than I ever did. He got licensed as a Realtor and specialized in selling fixer-uppers for revitalization projects. Then he wrote up his method for buying and fixing up old houses in Rochester, NY (complete with contacts for local regulatory and advisory agencies), set up as a periodical (magazine), with a date rather than an ISBN, and published two runs of 350 copies each. He got a magazine distributor to get them into grocery and drug stores throughout the county (which pretty much sold out the run), priced the book at only $10 (his unit cost was $3), split the profits with the distributor—and sold a whole lot of houses to people who had bought the book!

Chop Your Book in Half

Ernie Zelinsky received 25 defective copies of his book on creative thinking, *The Art of Seeing Double or Better in Business*. As he was trying to fall asleep one night, he got the idea to cut the books in half. Following one of the processes in his book, he jotted down the idea.

A week later, he was trying to think of better ways to get in front of his target audience (corporate Human Resources people), and he saw his note. So he had his printer chop those books in half. Then he wrote a letter explaining that he had sent half a book to get the recipients' attention, and that his book was about innovation as a tool to increase productivity in business.

> I am happy to report that this idea was so stupid that it paid off big time! Sending the half-books with the letter resulted in several orders for ten books, which further led to sales of several hundred books as well as several seminar presentations for one client. The extra revenue from this crazy idea totaled between $15,000 and $20,000.

Ernie then told the media, garnering two feature articles that led to more gigs and sales.

For his latest book, *How to Retire Happy, Wild, and Free*, he made a PDF of the top half of the book, and gives it away free at <http://www.thejoyofnotworking.com>; he thinks this is a big part of why he's sold 25,000 copies in less than two years.

Create a Holiday or Annual Event

My client Charles Hayes, who writes books about self-education, has gotten a lot of mileage over the years for his annual Self-Education Week; when I was promoting my own book on frugal fun, it benefited from the publicity around my now-discontinued International Frugal Fun Day.

Starting a holiday is easy, and plenty of authors have done it. Just send the information to <http://www.chases.com> and <http://www.celebratetoday.com>, a year or two ahead.

Once you have your holiday, most media will not know or care that you instigated it. But you can send out press releases about National Whatever Day, focused on how your book is timely for the holiday and can help readers to receive your key related benefit.

And once in a while, these holidays even take off and become part of the culture, like the annual Great American Smokeout smoking-cessation day. Of course, it doesn't hurt that a major nonprofit organization is behind it!

START A MOVEMENT

A year after publication of *Principled Profit*, I launched a ten-year campaign to get 25,000 signers on a pledge about business ethics, each of whom would inform at least 100 other people. You can see (and sign) the Pledge at <http://www.business-ethics-pledge.ORG>. While I have plenty of other reasons to undertake this campaign, my expectation that it will sell more books and generate more speaking gigs certainly helps with my willingness to put in the fairly significant time this effort requires.

When the ethics pledge was hosted on the commercial PrincipledProfit.com site, a fairly consistent 20–25 percent of pledge signers bought the book. We've only just moved it to the .org site. In early results, a lot more people are signing, but fewer signers convert to book buyers. However, about 80 percent are subscribing to my newsletter (up from less than 10 percent), so I'll have many chances to convert them later.

PARTNER WITH A HIGH-TRAFFIC RELEVANT WEBSITE FOR A SPECIAL EVENT

In April 2006, I happened to receive a press release announcing a partnership between romance imprint Dorchester Publishing and Internet dating site cupid.com, to organize speed-dating events in New York, Washington, D.C., San Francisco, Atlanta, and Chicago. The publisher is coming in as a major sponsor, lowering the cost of participation to attendees by 30 percent, and offering book giveaways as well as—is this perfect or what?—dating tips from some of its best-selling romance authors.

Quoting from the press release:

"Our purpose in forming this partnership with cupid.com is three-fold," says Dorchester VP and Editorial Director Alicia Condon. "First and foremost, it's a wonderful opportunity for us to participate in helping people make real-life connections. Second, we hope to re-educate readers about the romance genre, which has long been stigmatized and shuffled to the back of bookstores. And last but not least, it's a chance for us to foster reading among those in an age bracket that publishers have long had trouble reaching...Our hope is that if we put the books most likely to appeal to this demographic into their hands, that they'll take a chance on it and realize that reading can be just as entertaining as seeing a movie or watching TV."

Note to Self-Publishers and Publishing Company Owners:

A considerable amount of additional material is available to help you design and produce a marketable book, and get it into the bookstore system. Since that information is completely irrelevant to those publishing traditionally, I have put it into a supplemental e-book. Here's the Table of Contents:

Chapter 1: Determine Your Audience, Find Your Market
Chapter 2: Which Technology Should You Use?
Chapter 3: Find the Perfect Title
Chapter 4: Covers: Marketing from the Outside In
Chapter 5: How to Get into the Stores: Distributors and Wholesalers

If you bought this book directly from me, it was included in the price. If you did not receive the download instructions, please contact me for your copy. If you bought the book elsewhere, you may purchase the supplement for US $9.95 by visiting <http://www.grass rootsmarketingforauthors.com/buysupplement.html>

Chapter Two

What's Your Publishing Strategy?

- *Plusses and minuses of the four main publishing methods: traditional, self-publishing on your own, self-publishing with help, subsidy/vanity*
- *Which is right for you?*

Planning your publishing and marketing is a key element of success as an author or publisher—yet it's the element that many people leave out entirely. And then they're surprised when their books hit the market and drop with a thud. So this chapter will provide at least a skeleton of guidance around the four most common ways to turn a manuscript into a finished book.

Who Will Publish the Book—And How?

You've got four primary ways to get a publisher, and each has strengths and weaknesses. Each is right for certain types of books, and totally wrong for others.

Traditional Publishing
Self-Publishing on Your Own
Self-Publishing with Help
Subsidy/Vanity

Traditional Publishing

For over a hundred years, most books found their way into print when a publisher bought the right to publish from the author, brought the work into print, and coordinated not only the production but most of the marketing.

And this is still the dream of many authors. They want an agent, an advance, a contract with a major house, and a glitzy book tour.

They expect a publisher to work hard for them, and turn their book into a best seller.

This is great, if it happens. And it does happen, even for first-time authors—at least the part about landing a publisher. My wife, D. Dina Friedman <http://www.ddinafriedman.com>, managed to sell one book to Simon & Schuster and another to Farrar, Strauss & Giroux in 2004, with publication in 2006. But she started approaching agents and big houses 18 years earlier.

The unfortunate reality is that it's gotten much, much tougher to sell a book to a major publisher. Large publishers are deluged with submissions; many of them won't even open the envelope unless it comes from a reputable agent. And agents are almost as tough to land as publishers; Brian Hill and Dee Power, co-authors of *The Making of a Bestseller*, report that the average literary agent receives about 4680 submissions per year—and accepts 11 of them![1]

Even when you succeed, you may end up wishing that you hadn't. Things are especially tough for the "mid-list" author, who won't be a superstar but could comfortably sell a few thousand copies a year. I was a mid-list author like that; in 1991, I found an agent who quickly sold my book, *Marketing Without Megabucks: How to Sell Anything on a Shoestring*, to Simon & Schuster, which published it in 1993. But less than two years later, the firm discontinued the book and sold the remaining inventory back to me.

These days, a book doesn't even get close to two years to prove itself. The window is usually between one and six months; about three months is fairly typical.

And the publishers want to see a "platform": they want to know that you have the capacity to sell a whole lot of books, through your newsletters, websites, speeches, networks, and so forth. That's the most important part of a nonfiction book proposal, these days.

Platform is a major factor in fiction as well, although it's secondary compared to the publisher's sense of whether the book will sell well in its established markets—and that's not the same as literary quality.

Another thing traditional publishers often want to see is a marketing budget/marketing plan. Right in the proposal, they want to see how much of your own hard-earned bucks are going into promotion, and how effectively you intend to spend it. Yes, this used to be the publisher's job. Shifting this onto the author takes away much of the incentive to go through traditional publishers. But take hope: Catherine Franz of <http://www.abundancecenter.com> says you can ask the publisher to match your marketing investment.

Unless they've targeted you for success and paid an advance of at least six figures—and those are extremely rare—large mainstream publishers do little or no marketing for you; for the most part, it's up to you, the author. So if you want a glitzy book tour, you can probably expect to set it up and pay for it yourself.

Once you have a publisher, you may find that the realities are not what you thought. Even back in 1993 when my Simon & Schuster book came out, the publisher's marketing effort was minimal. The company got a dozen or so print mentions, of which three were significant (*Library Journal* and the *Christian Science Monitor*, plus my hometown local paper), set up exactly two radio interviews for me, and reimbursed me $30 to send out some press releases that I wrote, and for which I researched the media list.

I also had to edit out 80 pages of the manuscript without additional compensation, because I was told, "It's too long and we can't find any fat to cut." This would have been a bit less annoying if I hadn't asked, at the time we negotiated the contract, what the page count meant in terms of words. The answer I received then was "Write what you need to, don't worry about it."

Worse yet, I've begun to hear stories from big-publisher authors that their publishers are actively sabotaging their marketing efforts. As one among several examples, I've heard of a children's-book author who requested a review copy for the producer of a major TV show where he had contacts, and was told in no uncertain terms that they weren't going to squander their limited number of slots with that show on a mid-list children's author!

Some publishers have very unfriendly clauses in their contracts, in some cases even claiming the right to recoup an advance from the author if a book doesn't earn it back. Don't sign such a contract no matter how badly you want to get published! If you get an offer, join the National Writers Union or the Authors Guild, and use the contract review service to identify and negotiate out dangerous clauses.

Another friend of mine published two genre books with Harper Collins. She spent more than her advance to promote the books, was pressured to churn out the second book extremely quickly, and then was just about completely ignored by the company.

But for every Simon & Schuster, Harper Collins, or Random House, there are dozens of smaller publishers, with fewer resources but typically more commitment to your book. These can be a joy to work with, and may try much harder to get publicity for you and support you through other marketing efforts—but even here, it's ultimately the author's job.

My next traditionally published book was with a house like that, Chelsea Green. They've been a joy to work with in every regard (except the size of the advance!), and I'd happily work with them again if I had a book that was right for them. Even so, the marketing support, while better than Simon & Schuster's, was limited—but this book is still in print after six years, has earned out its advance, and now generates a royalty check every six months.

And then there are the economics, which are very strange in publishing. When you and a publisher agree on a contract, you get an advance against royalties. The contract will specify that royalties are earned either on net or list. Net is what the publisher receives after wholesalers or distributors or retailers take their cut; list is the stated cover price of the book. Typical terms for a first-time author might be 6 percent of list or 10 percent of net. If you're a good negotiator, there may be an "escalator clause" that raises the royalty rate after a certain quantity of books have been sold.[2]

If the book has a list price of $20, every book sold would earn back $1.20 at 6 percent of list. If royalties are figured on 10 percent of net, that would mean the same $1.20 on copies sold directly to bookstores at 40 percent discount, 90 cents on copies sold to wholesalers at 55 percent off list, and 70 cents if sold through distributors at a 65 percent discount. However, many contracts call for reduced royalties on copies sold at greater than a 50 or 55 percent discount, which could make earning back your advance a very difficult proposition.

In round numbers, let's say that every book earns the author a dollar toward paying back the advance. Thus, on a $10,000 advance, the author will need to sell 10,000 copies to earn back the advance and begin to generate more income. But most books don't sell anywhere near that much.

Does this mean the book is a money-loser? Not at all. The publisher might have invested about $25,000, total—paying not only your advance but also the expenses of editorial, design, production, and marketing. On a $10 average net sale per copy, that means the book will be profitable after 2500 copies, not counting any revenues generated from subsidiary rights.

As an unknown author, you can probably figure on an advance somewhere between $5000 and $25,000 from a major publisher. Occasionally someone does a whole lot better, like Christopher Paolini, teenage author of *Eragon*, who took his self-published book and his healthy sales record (built on incessant and highly dramatic author appearances) to Random House for big bucks and big promotion.

If you've used an agent (which is almost essential for the top-tier publishers), 15 percent comes off the top. So if you got a $10,000 advance and earn a dollar a book, you actually collect only 85 cents—and you have to sell 10,000 copies before you see another dime.

So with all this craziness, why do people still strive for the famous publisher?

- Credibility: it really does open doors to have a publisher that everyone's heard of.
- Distribution: Getting books into stores is a major challenge with other publishing methods; the biggies have it all in place. In the pre-Internet days when I published a book with Simon & Schuster, I got fan mail—actual postal letters—from India and the Philippines!
- Subsidiary Rights: It's easier to get foreign rights, book clubs, film options, and so forth—though it's certainly possible to get these with other types of books. In fact,

the book *Legally Blonde,* which was turned into a movie, was originally published through one of the subsidy publishers. My self-published *Principled Profit* has been sold to publishers in India, Mexico, and Nigeria, and in a corporate sale to Southwest Airlines (a better track record on subsidiary rights than any of my three traditionally published books).

- Size of Advance: Big publishers usually pay substantially more than small publishers to acquire a book. And of course, if you self-publish or use a subsidy house, you actually have to spend money.
- Professional Services: At least some publishers still provide professional editing (although more and more of them will refuse a book that isn't sufficiently "clean" to begin with). And of course, you don't have to worry at all about learning the intricacies of book layout, printing, and all the rest of the nitty-gritty involved in creating a book. For writers who just want to write, it's very seductive.

Self-Publishing on Your Own

With self-publishing, you're fully in control. You decide on everything, from the date of publication to the look of the cover to the offers you might include on the last page. You get to keep the profits, and you get to build your reputation. At the same time, you're fully responsible. If there's a problem, it's your problem. If your distributor goes belly-up with 2000 copies of your book in the warehouse, it's your money down the tubes.

And if your book fails in the marketplace, it's nobody's fault but yours.

You are the publisher of record, the owner of the ISBN block (the group of numbers that identify every individual book and its publisher—this is the series of numbers on the barcode of every commercially published book in the world; it is required to sell in any bookstore, including amazon.com). In the U.S., the only legitimate way to obtain your own ISBN is through R.R. Bowker <http://www.isbn.org/standards/home/index.asp>, which is the official agency for issuing ISBNs. You can buy a single ISBN, though that's usually a very bad idea. If you plan to publish just one or two books, you may get by with a block of 10 numbers. Any more than that, and you'll want a block of 100 or more—because new editions, different bindings, supplementary products, and even e-books are supposed to get their own individual ISBN. Thus, if you do paperback, hardback, and e-book versions of a single title, and then release a revised and updated second edition, you've already consumed six ISBNs.

Once upon a time, ISBNs were free. In some countries, they still are, but in the U.S., the price keeps going up. As of this writing (July, 2006), a block of 10 is $269.95, and a block of 100 is $914.95.

Note that people in the trade can tell what size block you bought, and a 10-ISBN block is usually considered the mark of a self-publisher.

Publishing successfully involves mastering a myriad of skill sets—or finding others who already have those skills. Those who try to do absolutely everything themselves from start to finish typically end up with a mess. But self-publishers can succeed very well, if they understand how to locate and contract for professional yet affordable vendors who can help with design, editing, production, marketing, and distribution.

There is a considerable learning curve. Fortunately, it's easy to find guides. Numerous excellent (and not-so-excellent) books are out there, along with Internet discussion groups, newsletters, professional trade organizations, and of course, consultants. I've listed some of the best ones in the Appendix.

Also, marketing and publishing will take as much time and money as you want to throw at them. Temptations to spend or even squander lurk under every rock and tree, and it requires discipline to budget appropriately.

ADVANTAGES OF SELF-PUBLISHING

- You have total control.
- Speed: You can typically get a book out much faster than a large commercial publisher can (although it still takes several months if you want a quality product). By running several processes simultaneously, you can drastically reduce time-to-market. My most recent self-published book was only ten months *from the time I wrote the first word* until

I had books in hand, and six months after I completed the manuscript. By contrast, every commercial publisher I've worked with has taken a year or more once the completed manuscript was turned in.

- Nimbleness/agility: You can pursue marketing opportunities and contacts as they come up, without having to go through channels, and you can be very flexible with decisions such as size of print run.
- You can be very creative in your marketing.
- You can lower costs, **if** you're a good shopper. If you already have an ISBN block, or choose not to have one, it is possible (but usually not advisable) to do a short-run book for just a few hundred dollars. More realistically, I spent about $5000 for all editorial/indexing, design, and production costs for a 3000-copy run of *Principled Profit*, and about the same for a 2000-copy run of another, larger book eight years earlier.
- You can get closer to the pulse of your audience: When you're the author, the chief marketer, and the publisher, you bring different perspectives. As you test your book in the real-world marketplace and interact with your public, you gain insights from all these roles that would be much harder to assimilate across a large organization with an absentee author. (This is not impossible with traditional publishing, but you have to work harder at it.)
- If you establish a powerful track record, you will find it relatively easy to sell the rights to a larger publisher, down the road.

ON THE MINUS SIDE

- Self-publishing can be overwhelming and time-consuming; you'll be juggling dozens of complex timelines and tasks, and if you drop the ball, there's no one to pick up the slack.
- Unless you'll only sell at your own events and through your own stores and websites, you need to understand how to create a book with production and editorial quality at least as good as books from major publishers.
- Distribution is a huge headache.

- In the U.S. at least, you'll need to buy a block of either 10 or 100 ISBNs, and they're not cheap.
- If you don't know what you're doing, unscrupulous or incompetent vendors will take your money and leave you little to show for it.

Self-Publishing with Help

The good news is that plenty of people have acquired this expertise; you can still self-publish without having to learn dozens of new skills, master all the timelines, and so forth. You still use your own ISBN, which means you are still the publisher of record. That's a very important identifier, as we'll discuss in the next section.

So you can have an expert guide you through the process, find you a copy editor, book designer, indexer, and printer (in some cases, for considerably less than what you'd pay on your own), help you submit to the appropriate registries, enter the right award programs, pursue foreign and subsidiary rights, troubleshoot all the production issues (and there will be issues, trust me), oversee the marketing, etc., etc.

The bad news, of course, is that it isn't cheap. Depending on what services you request and which vendors you work with, you will probably pay somewhere between $5000 and $30,000 to get your book ready for production, and then there's the actual cost of design and printing, on top of that.

Still, if you have the money, working with a consultant or packager can take away most of the headaches while leaving you in control, taking away the stigma of subsidy publishing, and producing a beautiful book that you'll be proud of.

Two examples from my own business: At the low end, I put in fewer than 10 hours of billable time to help a client understand the process and obtain affordable, high-quality vendors. At the high end, I worked in-depth with one recent packaging client for a year, starting by editing his manuscript. I wrote him two different marketing plans (one emphasizing trade channels and the other emphasizing nontraditional marketing), secured all his production vendors (copy editor, interior designer, cover designer, indexer, Publisher's Cataloging In Publication data

(CIP) provider, as well as book printers for galleys and the final offset run), showed him how to buy his ISBNs, listed him in *Books in Print*, got him his Library of Congress Preassigned Control Number (PCN, formerly called Library of Congress number), created letters for him to seek endorsements and sub rights, wrote various marketing materials for him including cover copy, vetted his choices of publicist and distributor, and provided extensive one-to-one consulting and advice. Compared to what he found on his own, I saved him about half what I charged him by finding better and more affordable vendors.

You'll find a list of reputable book packagers and publishing consultants—myself and others—in the Appendix. The list is by no means complete, but these are firms whose finished work I've seen, and they do a good job.

Subsidy/Vanity

It certainly sounds seductive: pay a few hundred to a couple of thousand dollars and have a finished book to market quickly and with minimal pain. Dozens of companies have set up shop to turn raw manuscripts into finished short-run books. You've probably seen some of them advertise: AuthorHouse, iUniverse, XLibris, Trafford, Lulu, Publish America (which does not charge a set-up fee but has, in my opinion, exorbitant per-book charges and a terrible seven-year exclusive contract), Infinity, Booklocker, PageFree, BookSurge, and many others. These are the "subsidy publishers," also referred to as "Print-On-Demand publishers" (not to be confused with P-O-D *printers*) or, incorrectly, "self-publishing companies."

And for some books, it's a fabulous solution; I have recommended subsidy publishing to some of my clients, when circumstances warrant that approach. For most, however, it's a poor choice.

You'll hear a lot of promises from these companies: that bookstores can get your book, that they can offer you various marketing programs, and so on. But here's the unfortunate reality:

Just because a book is listed in *Books in Print*, and a bookstore can order it, doesn't mean the bookstore *will* stock it. And the chances that they'll stock a subsidy-published book are even slimmer than with true self-published books. If bookstore sales are part of your marketing plan, you do not want a subsidy publisher.

Why?

- Insufficient quality control: Most of these places will publish pretty much anyone with an open checkbook. They do not require a professional edit and the books are often filled with grammatical mistakes and typos, they produce a generic interior and sometimes an equally generic cover (and some of the books look like academic textbooks from the 1970s—far outclassed by modern book design). Also, too many books would never find a traditional publisher because they just aren't good.

- Bookstore-unfriendly policies, such as short discount (20 percent, versus the standard 40–42 percent) and no returns.

- Higher-than-market prices that just can't compete with other titles. The economics of producing books in very short runs are very different than the economics of printing several thousand at a time.

- Lack of marketing support. For most of these companies, "marketing" means they list the book on their website and maybe issue a generic press release. After reading this book, you'll understand that marketing should go a whole lot deeper than that.

Add in a couple of extra disadvantages to the author:

- Author-unfriendly economics: If you start to sell quantities wholesale, you may find that you're buying your inventory for more than you can sell it for. Not good! In any case, you will pay a lot more per copy than you probably would through any other publishing channel. The low start-up costs are only the most economical option if you only plan to run very few copies; the high per-copy costs more than offset the savings on as little (from some subsidy houses) as 15 copies.

- Stigma: The name of your publisher does matter. While a traditional publisher's imprimatur offers cachet, a subsidy house means, to industry insiders, "There's a very good chance that this is crap."

- Lack of control: With many of these companies, *they* set the price. *They* set the discount and return policies. *They* own the ISBN for your book, which means they are the publisher of record, no matter how often they claim that you're "self-publishing." In true self-publishing, all of these items are directly under your control.

To be fair, some companies (Infinity, Lulu, and Booklocker among them) offer the option of using your own ISBN and imprint. If you take advantage of this option and use these companies as a way to get the production services without the learning curve, then they actually can be called "self-publishing companies." Of course, you can get the same results (and usually more cheaply) by hiring a P-O-D printer on your own, but working with a subsidy house definitely shortens the learning curve—and the hassle factor.

I have an insider perspective on this: for two and a half years, one of the largest subsidy publishers was a client of mine. I did the newsletter, and I was always trolling for success stories (I profiled one in every issue). For every real marketing coup I was able to highlight, there were five or six where the accomplishment was only getting a newspaper clip or a few minutes of TV air time.

So why would anyone want to publish a book this way? There actually are some situations where it makes a lot of sense. For instance:

- You have no interest in selling to bookstores and expect to sell primarily in markets that are not sensitive to price, such as speaking engagements.
- Your primary purpose in publishing is to have a few copies for family and friends, and you have no dreams of succeeding in the marketplace.
- Your goal is to be bought out by a traditional publisher, you see subsidy publishing as a way to free yourself up to hustle sales, and you don't care if you make any money as long as your sales record achieves your goal (however, if this is the case, I suggest going with a book packager, which will cost more upfront but allow you to recoup your outlay

much faster, and increase the likelihood of bookstore sales, awards, and other goodies).

For this book, I'm actually co-publishing with my own imprint and with Infinity, even though I'm an experienced self-publisher and had originally planned to simply do this book on my own. A number of unusual circumstances came together to make that a sensible decision. It all started when I approached a friend who's an executive at Infinity to see if he had any interest in a special-sales purchase for all Infinity authors. He decided that he really wanted to publish this book, and made me a deal that was simply too good to pass by. Since I do almost nothing in the bookstore channel, I thought that I could simply outsource all the bookstore side of the business and not have to mess around with the whole-salers, bookstores, and all of their hassles.

My friend noted that at least a few Infinity titles have gotten major reviews, and that the company's business model was sufficiently different from the larger players that it might not carry the same negative baggage.

And from my point of view, an extra advantage in this particular case is that it gave me hands-on experience with the only major publishing model I hadn't tried, and therefore more credibility to write and market a book on marketing for authors and publishers.

Interestingly, a number of the self-publishing gurus are outsourcing. My contact at Infinity happened to mention that they're printing the latest edition of John Kremer's *1001 Ways to Market Your Book* (under Kremer's own imprint). And Dan Poynter announced that the latest edition of *The Self-Publishing Manual* was produced by book shepherd Ellen Reid. If this method appeals to you, visit science fiction writer Piers Anthony's very comprehensive list <http://www.hipiers.com/publishing.html> to see feedback on any publishing company you're considering working with. You may also want to invest a few bucks in attorney Mark Levine's *The Fine Print* <http://www.book-publishers-compared.com>; I haven't seen this book, but those who have (including John Culleton, whose opinions on books for authors I greatly respect) say it's extremely helpful in comparing subsidy publisher contracts.

Chapter Three

Endorsements, Reviews, and Awards

- *Three key credibility builders for your book*
- *How to get them*

If you're an unknown author publishing with an unknown publisher (or worse, a publisher known for putting out junk), you can expect it to be tough to get people who know nothing about you or your book to take a chance and buy it.

Of course, you know that your book is terrific. And you probably have no problem saying so. But unfortunately, your endorsement of your own book doesn't carry much weight. You need objective voices: neutral third parties who say fabulous things about your book, or objective judges who will rate your book better than other titles selling against it.

We'll explore three of the major ways to build that third-party credibility:

Endorsements

Reviews

Awards

Endorsements

Call them endorsements, testimonials, or blurbs—whatever you call them, get at least a few for your book.

The best endorsements not only provide a well-known name, but also very specific information about what that famous reader came away with thanks to your product. It doesn't just say, "What a great book!" If it's a how-to or self-help, encourage testimonials that speak specifically to "what I learned" or "how I improved my life." If it's fiction, the blurbs should talk about the wonderful writing, the great story, the memorable characters, and so forth.

For instance, an ideal testimonial for a book on taxes for the super-rich might read something like this completely fictional example:

"Boy, do I wish I'd found *Tax Relief for the Rich* years ago! I brought Chapter 7 to my accountant and we figured out that just one strategy would save us $372,567 in taxes this year. Anyone who pays at least $1000 in taxes will save many times the purchase price. Go and buy it right now!"

—Henry Henry III, America's richest man

Or this, for a novel:

"I should never have started *Memoirs of a Werewolf* so close to bedtime—I stayed up half the night reading it! I couldn't put it down. The use of language is riveting, the characters are unforgettable, and I simply had to find out what happened. I'll be on the edge of my chair, waiting for Barbara Lewis's next masterpiece."

—Maryann Megaseller, best-selling author of *The Book You Have to Read* and many other books

OK, so what makes these two imaginary blurbs work so well? First of all, there's a celebrity factor. You would be very blessed to get endorsements in today's world from, say, Warren Buffett or John Grisham.

You'll notice both blurbs mention the book title, and the fiction blurb also names the author. So this builds brand awareness for both the book and the author when it's quoted in a magazine ad, for instance.

The nonfiction blurb offers these extras:

- A specific dollar amount—not rounded, but a believable actual number—that he saved by using the book.
- The specific chapter where he found that nugget.
- The notation that this huge savings stemmed from implementing just one strategy out of many in the book.
- The amazing admission that he used this material to educate his professional advisor, and then leveraged that education to realize the savings.

- A call to action that first qualifies the audience—those who pay more than $1000 in taxes (which happens to be everyone in the target market)—and then the time-linked command, "Go and buy it right now!"

For fiction, you want first and foremost a great read. According to the idealized fiction testimonial above, this book delivers with gripping writing, strong plot, and great characters. In fact, it was so compelling that it interfered with the author's sleep: a powerful psychological trigger, delivered with a slightly ironic touch (the mind is lulled into thinking she will criticize the book, and then comes the twist).

Of course, not every endorsement is going to be as strong as these, or from a famous name. Is it worth going after endorsements from "lesser" people, or endorsements that aren't quite as compelling?

Absolutely! There are a lot of folks out there who will be happy to lend their name; they may not be superstars, but they have the credentials to be taken seriously.

At a minimum, you should have two or three endorsements. At a maximum? I don't think there is a maximum. You won't necessarily put them all on your back cover or in the first few pages of your book, but you'll have them and can use them on your website (either in a big list or even in a rotating script so visitors see a different blurb with every visit), excerpt them in your press releases and newsletters, include a sheet of them in your press kit, and on and on it goes.

For my own book *Principled Profit*, I went after endorsements in a big way. The book went to press with 55 endorsements in the first few pages, and after publication, I still continue to collect them. If you visit <http://www.principledprofits.com/new-blurbs.html>, you'll see the complete list (there are 78 as of July 2006), nicely organized with a "jump menu" so you can click on any name and go immediately to the blurb. And some of these are big names in the field, such as legendary Internet marketer Mark Joyner. Just because I didn't get his endorsement until the book had been out for two years was no reason not to use it!

You don't have to be a marketing guru to pull this off. Part of my inspiration for collecting large numbers of blurbs was hearing Jacqueline Marcel, previously unknown author of *Elder Rage*, talk at a Publishers Marketing University session about how she got over 50 endorsements for her book. Even big publishers are catching on. Just as I was writing this section, I opened a package and found a review copy of a book published by Simon & Schuster's Pocket Books division. To my surprise, the first three pages were endorsements.

In the book itself, I watch over and over again as people pick it up and open it, and their jaws drop when they see the 55 endorsements. Some of them sit there and read them all before moving on to the content. And a lot of them buy the book.

My set of blurbs includes a number of people who are well credentialed. Among them (in alphabetical order):

- Sheldon Bowles, co-author of several books with Ken Blanchard of *One-Minute Manager* fame
- Jack Canfield, co-creator of the *Chicken Soup for the Soul* series (his blurb is on my back cover)
- Jim Hightower, progressive populist commentator
- Anne Holland, publisher of the hugely popular Marketing Sherpa website
- Jay Conrad Levinson, author of the original *Guerrilla Marketing* series
- Robert B. Reich, former U.S. Secretary of Labor
- Al Ries, bestselling author of several books on marketing and public relations
- Melanie Rigney, then-editor of *Writer's Digest* magazine

These eight demonstrate different ways to obtain an endorsement.

Sheldon Bowles showed up on an independent publishing list where I participate regularly. We corresponded several times and I helped him with various bits of advice, both on and off list. So, about two years later when I started going after endorsements, I dropped him a note.

> *Lesson:* **Be helpful whenever possible;**
> **be the kind of person others want to help.**

Jack Canfield and his co-author Mark Victor Hansen are both extremely generous with blurbs, if the book is suitable—but it can be challenging to reach them. In my case, I did have an edge. I had gone up to Jack a few years earlier while he was signing books at Book Expo America, introduced myself, and told him I wanted to pitch an idea for a *Chicken Soup* book. And he asked me, "Are you the same Shel Horowitz that sends me jokes?" Because I knew that he was on publishing consultant Dan Poynter's joke list, and Dan and I are on each other's lists, I said yes. We chatted briefly and he gave me his card.

By the time I wanted a blurb from him, his e-mail address had gone stale, so I simply e-mailed Dan and said that Jack had given me his address some time back but it didn't work anymore, and did he have the current one? He did, and Jack very graciously agreed. But because of Jack's generous spirit and mentality of abundance, I think I could have still gotten his blurb without that connection, by mailing postally.

> *Lesson:* **Ask people in your network to**
> **help you reach people.**

For Hightower, I actually used the contact form at his website (I did mention that I subscribed to his newsletter, which was true at the time).

> *Lesson:* **Use the contact channels the celebrity**
> **has already set up.**

Anne Holland is less known to the general public than Jack Canfield or Jim Hightower, but in the world of Internet marketing, her company is one of the superstars. Once again, I asked, using the publicly available address on her website, and once again I was able to say legitimately that I subscribe (I still do, and

I highly recommend Marketing Sherpa's newsletters). But what was interesting this time is that Anne actually hired me to do some copywriting shortly after the book was published, and then we collaborated to provide five copies of the book to her readers for her weekly giveaway, which meant I was getting publicity to her entire (very large) list.

> *Lesson:* **Asking for a blurb can lead to other collaborations.**

Robert Reich is a special case; he had run for governor in my state, and I had worked on his campaign; also, his sister is a personal friend who lives nearby.

> *Lesson:* **If you know celebrities, it doesn't hurt to ask.**

Jay Levinson is another public figure who is open and accessible, and likes to help younger writers. He used to be a frequent host of online chats on marketing, and I had saved his e-mail address (which still worked). He had actually endorsed my previous book, *Grassroots Marketing*, for which he was contacted by my publisher using the e-mail that I supplied, so it was easy to thank him again and ask him again.

> *Lesson:* **Be organized enough to keep track of good contacts when they drop into your lap.**

Al Ries came to me through B. L. Ochman, operator of a very active blog on PR. In the immediate aftermath of 9/11, B. L. was forced to evacuate her lower Manhattan apartment. When her landlord demanded to be paid for the months her apartment was uninhabitable, she turned to the discussion lists where she and I actively participated, and launched an Internet-based PR war until the landlord capitulated. I was one among many who wrote her a letter of support. When I approached B. L. for a blurb, she told me she knew Al Ries and asked if I'd like her to get him to blurb it as well. Of course I said yes!

> *Lesson:* **Accumulate good karma; sometimes you get to cash it in, and even if you don't, it feels really good.**

Melanie Rigney had been a co-panelist with me at a writers' conference; we had enjoyed each other's company, and each other's presentations, and she had even asked me about a writing project for the magazine.

> *Lesson:* **Speak publicly and get known and respected (and often, paid).**

It's worth noting a few other things, too.

- I got a large number of endorsements simply by posting on an appropriate discussion list that I was seeking blurbs. Those who responded are identified by name, title, business, and in some cases website. I don't just say Joe Smith, but say, for example, "Walt Boyes, principal, Spitzer and Boyes LLC, author, columnist, speaker."
- All the testimonials included in the printed book were collected by sending around an electronic file of the manuscript—thus, the expense to me was zero. However, I would have mailed paper manuscripts if key endorsers had requested them.
- I continue to collect testimonials; when someone says nice things about any of my books, I ask for permission to quote the statement. The answer is almost always positive.
- Have the decency to send each person who blurbs you a copy of the finished book. Not only is it the appropriate thing to do, it can also help your marketing. In fact, if you have an affiliate program, invite your endorsers to join it.

Some people will say no, or just not follow through, and that's okay. But on the whole, my batting average was extremely high, and yours can be, too, with the right book.

Keep in mind that once you've requested an endorsement, your endorser is aware of you and that may lead to other working re-lationships. For instance, you may be asked to blurb their books (which of course you should do if the book is decent).

I actually got a few hundred dollars to do a chapter for a Putnam/Berkeley anthology on simple living; the editor, Larry Roth, knew about me because I'd asked him for an endorsement of my book on frugal fun, *The Penny-Pinching Hedonist: How to Live Like Royalty with a Peasant's Pocketbook,* which I then plugged in the chapter.

FOREWORDS, ETC.

In the Supplement, I discuss the problem I had with my weakly titled nuclear power book. I talk about the better-titled book that more-or-less owned the category. But there was another major contender: *The Menace of Atomic Energy.*

Why? Because the top-billed author was Ralph Nader, known far and wide as a consumer advocate (this was decades before he ran for President).

If you can get the name of a popular author or other celebrity on the cover, or at least someone whose credentials are easily recognized, even if the person isn't a household name—with a blurb, as the author of a foreword, afterword, or, of course, as coauthor—you build immediate credibility in the marketplace. Many an obscure book has gained traction because the publisher used connections to get a well-known name on the cover. A foreword or afterword is the very best kind of endorsement and one for which you can ethically offer payment.

Reviews

For those in the know, reviews carry more weight than endorsements. The names might not be famous, but these are professionals comparing your book with the best-of-breed from every other publisher—or at least, that's the theory. People can get blurbs from their friends—but reviews from independent reviewers (at least the major ones) lend an air of objectivity.

You will be told over and over again that you can't get reviews on independently published books, that you won't get reviews once your book is more than a few months old, that only reviews in a handful of major publications count for anything, or that reviewers just love to insult authors.

In my experience, none of this is true—don't believe it!

I have gotten reviews and other press coverage on books that are quite a few years old. In fact, in January 2006, as I was writing this, I got a new review of *Grassroots Marketing: Getting Noticed in a Noisy World*; the book was published in May 2000. In 2003, my *Penny-Pinching Hedonist* book was written up in *Reader's Digest* and featured on the home page of MSN; it was eight years old and had just gone out of print (not a problem for me, as I had converted it to an e-book, and sold 60 of them thanks to the MSN mention). In 1999, *Bottom Line* did a three-page story about me and my marketing methods, and noted that I'm the author of *Marketing Without Megabucks* (*Grassroots Marketing's* predecessor)—which was written in 1991, published in 1993, and declared out of print by the publisher in 1995 (who sold the remaining inventory back to me).

These are just three examples in my own experience. I am still doing media interviews on all these subjects, and I still get reviewed.

So what's the magic secret? No secret at all. Find reviewers who work in your field and ask. Some of them will say no. Some will ignore you. And some will praise your book to the skies and then you can quote their reviews.

Major Prepublication Reviewers

When it comes to reviews, "Some are more equal than others." If bookstore and library sales will be a meaningful part of your marketing plan (and often even if they aren't), it's worth submitting to the major review outlets in the publishing industry: *Publishers Weekly, Library Journal, ForeWord, Independent Publisher, The New York Times,* and if appropriate, *School Library Journal* and *Kirkus.*

All of the above are "prepub" reviewers; they want to see the book well in advance of publication. Usually, you'll send a galley or Advance Review Copy (ARC—and please *don't* call it an Advanced Review Copy if you want to be treated seriously) *four to six months ahead of your publication date.* This is a firm date; these magazines will simply not review your book in their regular review columns if you wait until the book is published. And that doesn't mean running a few galley covers on your regular print run and pretending they're advance copies. If a prepub reviewer finds your book in stock on Amazon, for instance, you won't get the review.

Note that *Library Journal* has just announced that publishers who for some reason can't submit a galley can submit a finished book several months before it is available for purchase. However, I'd bet that those books will be treated like the ugly stepchild, and are less likely to be reviewed. There's no good reason you can't do galleys, so if prepub reviews are important, play the game.

Some have other requirements, as well. For instance, *Publishers Weekly* (PW) wants to know that you're doing 2000 copies or more and that you have a way to get books into bookstores. Follow each reviewer's current guidelines (posted on their websites) exactly. Yes, I know, this is silly, this is a waste of your resources, this throws a big monkey wrench into your production schedule—and I agree. But if you want to play in this particular sandbox, you have to do it the way the owners of the pails and shovels demand. Many authors and publishers decide not to bother, figuring that their chances are slim anyway.

And they're right; the chances are slim. However, it's not impossible. *Principled Profit* was reviewed in *Publishers Weekly*, and I know of many other independently published books that have been featured in one or more of these mega-publications.

Some experts say that a strong review in one of these can result in hundreds if not thousands of library orders. I have to say I didn't see that result. But for the rest of its life, I can say that my book was reviewed there, and that provides instant credibility in the industry.

There are other ways to get into these pages. I just sent yet another copy of *Principled Profit* to *Library Journal*, for an upcoming roundup on spirituality. Since the book will be three years old by the time the article runs, I actually called up the person coordinating that article and asked if my book would be considered. He said yes, so off it went. But it certainly helps if you can get a review that runs at the time of publication.

So...what exactly do you send the prepub reviewers?

First of all, either a galley or an ARC. A galley contains the interior of the book, but a generic plain cover that contains the information a magazine reviewer needs to determine if your book should be considered: title, author, publisher, contact information and/or website, publication date, price, distribution, print run (if it's 2000 or more), ISBN, final format and trim size (e.g., you might do 5-1/2" x 8-1/2" galleys in softcover even if the final book will be 6" x 9" and clothbound), shelving categories—*and* a brief outline of your marketing plan. Reviewers want to know that the book will be available and that it will be marketed; I suspect that my inclusion of this is what got me into PW. The galley may omit or have blank spaces for things like illustrations and the index.

An ARC is a bit more polished; it looks almost like a finished book, including a color cover. But the back cover includes a block with all the information you'd otherwise put on the front of a galley, and the front states that it's an Uncorrected Proof or Advance Review Copy.

When would you use one rather than the other? It seems that more and more books use ARCs—so if you have your cover done, that may be the better bet. Certainly if you've invested in a striking cover, it makes sense to convey that powerful impression—as long as you make it totally clear that it's an ARC and not a finished book. Another option is to do a galley but include a mock-up of the cover; however, the mock-up may get separated from your galley (unless of course, you include a small photo of the cover right on the galley cover). In my case, I wasn't even close to a final cover design, so I went with the galley.

Here's the galley cover I used for *Principled Profit*:

Front Panel:

PRINCIPLED PROFIT:
MARKETING THAT PUTS
PEOPLE FIRST
By Shel Horowitz

AWM Books, Northampton MA

Pub Date: June 30, 2003

UNCORRECTED PROOF

ISBN: 0-9614666-6-9

Categories: Marketing/Business Ethics

LCCN: 2003090557

$17.50 (US)

Final Trim Size: 6x9, 160 Pages

Available through all major wholesalers via Beagle Bay Books

Final Book Includes:

- Full index
- 16 pages of resources
- 55 blurbs, including Jack Canfield, Jay Conrad Levinson, Al Reis, Jim Hightower, Sheldon Bowles, Anne Holland of Marketing Sherpa, Melanie Rigney of Writer's Digest (all included in the galley)
- Full-color cover

Marketing Support:

- Extensive print and radio campaign targeting 150 outlets
- BEA presence
- Author appearances
- Dedicated website <http://www.principledprofit.com>
- E-mail campaign to reach 50,000 decision makers

Spine:

Horowitz: **Principled Profit,** AWM Books

Back Panel:

MARKETING/BUSINESS ETHICS

Forget Traditional Business Wisdom—Market Share Is Dead, Your Competitors May Be Your Best Allies, and Nice Guys Don't Finish Last

- Market share is irrelevant; the world is abundant and there's room for everyone to succeed
- You can actively profit from your competitors' success
- Honesty, integrity, and quality are far more important than quick profits—the Golden Rule actually WORKS in business
- As you create value for others, you build value in your own business
- The most important sales skill isn't even about selling

In his fourth marketing book, Shel Horowitz demands high ethical standards of companies that want long-term success in the 21st century.

Principled Profit: Marketing That Puts People First demonstrates many well-known examples of companies that did well by seeing their customers, suppliers, employees and even competitors as partners...and provides numerous practical ideas on marketing so everyone wins.

> "Shel Horowitz shows in *Principled Profit: Marketing That Puts People First* that not only do people *want* to change the paradigm toward cooperation and people-centered behavior, but that they can profit handsomely by doing so. I'm delighted to recommend this book."
>
> Jack Canfield, CEO, Chicken Soup for the Soul Enterprises, Coauthor, *Chicken Soup for the Soul at Work*

Please see inside front cover for over 50 other endorsements, including the author of *Guerrilla Marketing*, the editor of *Writer's Digest*, the president of bookzone.com, and one of the co-authors, with Ken Blanchard, of *Raving Fans*.

□□□

For either galleys or ARCs, it's usually best to do a run of between 25 and 100, using a digital P-O-D printer who is set up for ultra-short runs. In addition to sending to prepub reviewers, you can use these to get endorsements, interest book clubs, get your local media to notice the book, and so forth. I ran 100 and only used about 80, but I use the rest as giveaways when I attend local Chamber of Commerce events.

Along with your galley or ARC, fill out the packet with a press release that's good enough to quote verbatim (it often will be!), an author biography, a sheet about the overall series (if it's one of several related books), a mock-up for the final color cover if you have one (not necessary for ARCs, of course), and perhaps an author photo—or at least an offer to supply one. If you've had previous publishing success, call attention to it; my galley cites my three previous marketing books.

Once the final book is published, send a copy to these review outlets, some of which may hold off publishing your review until they know for sure you've actually gone to press.

Of course, there are many places to get media coverage beyond the book-review pages; we'll be talking about that in Chapter 7.

POSTPUBLICATION REVIEWS—BOOK TRADE

Some important review outlets want finished books. Among them is *Midwest Book Review*, which is the small publisher/self-publisher's best friend in the serious review community. MWBR actually *prefers* to give space to the little-heralded books that other reviewers have missed, loves to find gems amid the many terrible books that must cross that desk. The editor-in-chief, Jim Cox, participates regularly on the various self-publishing discussion lists, and commenting on one of his posts will knock you to the top of the pile.

The other big review market that wants finished books is *Choice*, which goes to librarians. It's certainly worth sending, but most of their columns are filled with offerings from major publishers.

POSTPUBLICATION REVIEWS—ELSEWHERE

Remember that you're newsworthy in your own backyard. You ought to be able to get some review coverage in local media, at least if you live in a smaller community without a lot of authors. My own community has writers under every rock and tree, and still I've managed to get substantial coverage of my books (though more often in the feature and lifestyle pages than on the book page). You should also be able to score some reviews in the press that covers your subject area. Local and genre reviews gave Mary Doyle Brodien a nice jump in sales for her second book:

> I would like to share an online review about my new book, *The Rosary Prayer by Prayer* <http://www.americancatholic.org/ Messenger/May2006/Books.asp>. The review also will run in the hardcopy edition of *St. Anthony Messenger Magazine*.

> More than 1000 copies overall have been sold since mid-December [she writes this in April]. A local paper ran a story on me, my son the artist, and the book and is responsible for hundreds of copies sold.

Also, use finished books to solicit reviews from major daily newspapers around the country, trade magazines, Internet review sites, and private reviewers who post on sites like amazon.com. It's a good idea to budget 100 copies or so to try to get coverage.

I have found that most genres have a few key people who review a lot of books and are pretty well known in their field. And that it is much, much easier to get reviews from these folks. They don't get asked that much, they often don't care about publication date or what publisher did the book—they just want to share great books with their readers. If you go to my review pages on my various websites (see Resources), you'll see the reviews I've gotten from people known in the worlds of marketing, book publishing, frugality, and ethics.

If you absolutely know that a particular reviewer in a genre publication should be covering your book, a little persistence (not enough to be pesty) may pay off. Learn from Carol White, self-publisher of *Live Your Road Trip Dream* <http://www.roadtripdream.com>:

> My very first press kit (professionally done and admittedly "slick") was sent to RoadTripAmerica.com. The owner took umbrage in my "Sample Book Review," "Appearance Options," and other pieces in the kit—and let me know about it in no uncertain terms. He said I needed to learn some humility—among other things! After some "humble" cajoling, he agreed to look at the book. I held my breath. The day he sent me the link to the review—I was afraid to open it. It was a beautiful, glowing review!
>
> Since then we have met, laughed about our rough start, and he has led me to some of my most important industry contacts. We continue to refer and support each other. He has been a great teacher and helped me stay focused.

PAY-TO-REVIEW

There are a number of places that charge authors or publishers to review. Personally, I'm not a big fan of this, not only because I'm frugal and would rather spend that money differently, but also because ethical questions are inevitable about the validity of a paid-for review. Also, I have never found it a problem to get actual reviews without paying.

If you find that you can't get reviewed for free no matter how hard you try, at least seek out review outlets known for not compromising their integrity just because the author or publisher is paying the bill. Two that come to mind are *Clarion Reviews* (formerly called *ForeWord Reviews*) and Bowker.

THE IDENTITY FACTOR

Some people claim that it's much easier to get reviews, especially major reviews, if your book doesn't appear self-published. I've never found my self-published status to be a problem, but when I sent galleys of *Principled Profit: Marketing That Puts People First* out to major reviewers, I did have my distributor actually mail them. (If I'd used a publicist, that would have been another choice.)

From that round of mailing, we got *Publishers Weekly* (only the online edition) and *ForeWord* but none of the other majors. Did PW choose to review because a trusted outside establishment sent the book? I doubt it—I daresay if I had sent it directly, I'd have been reviewed because the galley noted that there was distribution and sketched out the marketing plan. Of course, I'll never know for sure. But I do know that over a dozen respected reviewers covered the book from copies I sent directly.

Still, any indication (such as a distributor or a publicist) that the publisher or author is truly committed to a title can help sway a positive decision, because it shows the publisher takes the book seriously.

Some authors think they can get away from the stigma by having a different contact name. I'm not a big fan of this. It's so easy to check that sort of thing, and if the reviewers determine you're trying to inflate the size of your company, it isn't going to look good. Also, experienced reviewers know the difference between a 10-number ISBN and a 100-number block, know that most 10-blocks belong to self-publishers, and can easily check your website to see if you've got a staff directory or additional titles.

The stigma about self-publishing is slowly fading, and the best thing you can do, in my opinion, is to produce a top-quality product that competes well in the marketplace, demonstrate your commitment to the title, and give no reasons to turn your book down.

Awards

Even more than reviews, awards say, "This is a book worth paying attention to." Book awards are a lot rarer than book reviews, so they mean more. Awards not only allow you bragging rights, but also breathe new life into an older book; most of the awards are given out in the year following publication—and that gives you a chance to go back to the media with story ideas, put stickers on your book cover, and so on. Even being a finalist provides bragging rights, though obviously not as much as if you actually win. In fact, you can send out news stories when you're named a finalist, and then if you come away with the gold, silver, or bronze, another news release.

There are four tiers of awards (these are not comprehensive lists):

First, the immensely prestigious, internationally recognized awards like the National Book Award, the Pulitzer Prize, the Booker Prize, the Caldicott and Newbery Awards in children's literature, and of course, the Nobel Prize for Literature.

Second, widely known genre-specific awards including the Pushcart Prize, the Edgar, and the Nebula. Some of the contests where the prize includes publication fall into this category, such as the Walt Whitman and Yale Series of Younger Poets competitions in poetry.

Third, awards with a national following, among them the Ben Franklin, the Ippy (awarded by the online magazine *Independent Publisher*, the Eppie, NAPRA Award (Network of Alternatives for Publishers, Retailers & Artists, Inc., a New Age publishing trade group), Lambda Literary Award (for gay and lesbian titles), *ForeWord Magazine*'s Book of the Year, *Writer's Digest* Self-Published Award, and the D-I-Y Book Awards.

And fourth, all others—including awards given by regional publishing organizations, local schools or cultural institutions, business groups, and so forth.

While it doesn't hurt to dream, it's unlikely that an unknown author will achieve either of the top two tiers. But tier three is widely accessible. However, your book will be judged against some tough competitors, often including those published by large conglomerates.

What that means is your book has to match up. Its editorial content should be clearly presented, beautifully written, and absolutely error-free. Its production values—the look of the interior and cover, the quality of printing, the accuracy of its index—also have to shine. Otherwise, your entry fee merely buys a relatively expensive critique, at best.

As for the fourth tier, if you feel your chances are good, it's probably worth a shot. You can still legitimately claim to be an award-winning author, even if it's not an award you particularly want to brag about. In my own experience, people do sit up and take notice when I refer to myself as an award-winning author. This is what I've won:

- *Grassroots* was a finalist for *ForeWord Magazine*'s Book of the Year in the business category (tier 3 but not one of the three winners).

- *Principled Profit* won an Apex Award as the best book in marketing communication. This is an award for business communications in various categories (e.g., best brochure, best website) and is a fairly big deal in its industry (tier 3), but in the wider world of publishing, it carries very little weight (tier 4).

- *Principled Profit* also won Honorable Mention in the D-I-Y awards. Like the *Writer's Digest* program, this is tier 3, but acknowledges that the work is self-published (D-I-Y stands for Do-It-Yourself). For me, this is not a problem, but those who want to avoid being stigmatized as self-publishers wouldn't enter either of these awards.

A brochure I wrote for the Amherst-Area (MA) Chamber of Commerce, designed by a very skilled woman named Denise Plouffe, won an award for overall excellence from the regional Chamber of Commerce association based in a nearby big city. This makes me an award-winning copywriter as well as an award-winning author, but it is so far down in tier 4 that I don't use this credential very much.

CAUTIONARY NOTES

- In any contest or award, make sure to read the fine print. Adams Media recently ran a contest for best book proposal, but I chose not to enter, even though I have a proposal already written that met the contest criteria. The prize was less money than I would accept to write that particular book (a research-intensive project involving numerous contacts with celebrities, and therefore a lot of rejection and persistence)—and the grant of rights to the winning entry was so restrictive that I would have essentially given up all claim to the book if it became successful. So I wasn't willing to do that. I'll continue to refine my proposal and circulate it through other channels.

- Balance the cost of entering the award with the prestige of winning (including the cost of attending the awards dinner, if you plan to attend). I have never entered an award that cost even as much as $100, and there are some awards I wouldn't bother entering at pretty much any price, because they have no bragging rights at all.

PART II

Publicity

Chapter Four

Personal Networking
by D. Dina Friedman and Shel Horowitz

- *How people you know can help your book*
- *How people you don't know can become people you do know*
- *Leveraging those networks to sell*

What's a chapter on one-to-one networking doing in the publicity section? Because leveraging your contacts to sell books and using your contacts to reach other people's networks is what publicity is really about—and why it's one of the most powerful forms of marketing. It's the reason so many businesses claim that their best marketing is "word-of-mouth" (or "word-of-mouse"). Your job is to get the word about your book in as many people's mouths as possible, and networking is a key tool to accomplish just that. In this chapter, "I" or "my" refers to Dina, unless otherwise indicated.

There's an even more direct tie-in to publicity: if you network with the right people you can get lots of press. Shel has often been referred to reporters working on relevant stories by other sources who were part of his network. Sometimes, a friend highlights a media lead in the service they both subscribe to, and sends it to him to make sure he's seen it (and he has done the same). And of course, media people talk to each other. Many times, Shel has gotten a call or an e-mail from a radio producer, and when he asked how the broadcaster learned about him, it was from a note posted by another broadcaster.

Who Do You Know?

If you're a fiction writer or a poet, especially, you'll need the support of your friends and family to get the ball rolling. Whether you're self-published, or commercially published, unless you're one of the chosen few designated for best-seller status and a six-figure marketing campaign, your book is unlikely to be noticed by strangers, because there are simply too many books out there.

But people are more likely to buy your book if they know you, or know about you from others. And if those people love your book, and tell others about it, the momentum grows. It's a way of "creating the buzz." Commercial publishers do this all the time with the designated few. But the rest of us have to do it ourselves, in any way possible.

So, the first step: Make a list of anyone you know who might possibly buy your book. The key word is "possibly." Be as inclusive and exhaustive as possible. The parents on your kid's baseball team, the plumber, the dentist, people on your e-mail joke list—even those you've never met—members of any organization or club you've belonged to, as well as your family and close friends. Even if you think some people are unlikely to buy your book, keep them on the list anyway. They may tell a friend about it. Whenever you let people know about your book, ask them to tell their friends.

Here are a few of my "Who Do I Know" successes:

- My mother's cousin's wife, whom I've only met once or twice, has bought seven copies of my young adult novel about teenagers living in forest communities during the Holocaust, *Escaping into the Night*, as bar/bat mitzvah presents, and as donations to various day schools and synagogues. My father's cousin's wife, whom I've met about the same number of times, also bought multiple copies for grandchildren and other children of family friends.

- My good friend Mary Jo Maichack, a storyteller who performs widely at libraries throughout New England, wrote a letter to children's librarians praising my book and suggesting that they buy it for their library systems.

- An acquaintance whom I have not personally seen in several years arranged a speaking gig for me at a Jewish day school.

- A friend of my mother-in-law's, whom I had not met previously, put in a word for me at our local Holocaust education center. That contact led to several collaborations with the center director including a workshop for middle-school teachers on using the book in the classroom, speaking at the local Jewish Community Center book festival, and working together on a grant to pilot the book in the public schools. And now, he is passing the word to other Holocaust Centers around the region, and nationally.

Yes, I might have been able to arrange some of this myself, simply by calling the Holocaust Resource Center and the Jewish day school, and writing my own notes to children's librarians. But my batting average on cold calls to organizations where I have no personal connections is much, much lower. So use whatever networks you have and put them to work for you. It's called "power networking."

Shel has also had the good fortune to connect with a few power networkers with his Business Ethics Pledge campaign—a campaign that relates directly to his book *Principled Profit*. The single person responsible for more signatures, so far, than anyone else except Shel has put the campaign on his website and his newsletters, and also told numerous people. Thanks to him, Shel has a substantial number of signers in the capital markets industry—a niche that he would not have a clue how to reach on his own.

Niche Networking: Your Ideal Audiences

If you're writing a book on new treatments for tooth decay, you'll know that your audience will be mostly people in the dental field. But if you're writing a novel, a book of poetry, or some other general interest book, it may be hard to figure out who are the most likely groups of people who will be interested in buying your book. Don't fall into the trap of saying that your book is for everyone, because what you want to do is to format your marketing message to a specific target audience; depending on your target, the way you market the book will change. For example, I've picked the following targets for *Escaping into the Night*:

- The Jewish community: synagogues, day schools, religious school programs, book festivals
- Holocaust educators
- Librarians
- Teachers—especially middle-school teachers
- Book discussion clubs—especially mother–daughter book clubs

For each of these targets, my marketing message is slightly different, and highlights a benefit that is specific to that audience. When I address the Jewish community, I emphasize that my book covers a little-known aspect of the Holocaust, since this community is already inundated with Holocaust literature. For teachers, I focus on the book's suitability for middle-school students, its fast-moving plot, and the students' ability to relate to the main characters up close. This emphasis is based closely on what teachers and students have said to me about the book. I also offer teachers an additional benefit, referring them to supplemental materials, discussion questions, and teaching activities on my website. For book clubs, I offer a brief author chat by telephone or online.

For my second novel, *Playing Dad's Song*—a boy who has lost his father on September 11, 2001, and finally, two years later, is able to deal with his grief through music—I plan to target bereavement groups and music organizations. A friend of mine happens to be a national speaker on bereavement; he loves the book and plans to take it and show it around when he presents. Music teachers and organizations will also be particularly interested in a story about a boy who comes into his own after learning how to play the oboe. One local oboe teacher, who helped me with some of the details in the book, says she wants to get all her students together when the book comes out (in September 2006) and celebrate by having an oboe party!

Of course, you will make connections with your own book. Shel has a client with a lesbian novel with African-American characters. She actively markets to both African-American and gay and lesbian communities: approaching bookstores, media, Internet discussion groups, community events focused on books, community events with a different focus, the geographic communities where the book takes place, and so forth—and is far more successful with this approach than she would be if she were just trying to sell her wares in mainstream bookstores.

Two of the key things you'll want to do as you develop your marketing plan, then, are to identify the various niche audiences and figure out how to reach them—which often involves networking. Consider these factors, and others like them:

- The ethnic, cultural, religious, and interest-based subgroups that include you. If you are of African, Chinese, Latino, Norwegian, or English descent (among hundreds of others)...if you are Protestant, Catholic, Jewish, Muslim, Buddhist, Shamanist, Wiccan, or an unbeliever...if you are deaf, or blind, or have a walking disability, or have a chronic illness...if you are a liberal, a conservative, a Green, a Libertarian, there are communities for you...if you love to run, to swim, to golf, to play checkers, to knit sweaters, to invest in real estate, to eat organic foods...you—and your book—have an easy entry point into these communities. Whatever your subgroups, you can easily gain access (and be branded as an expert) to the relevant newspapers, radio shows, magazines, newsletters, blogs, chat groups, and other media—and you can participate in their events, as an exhibitor or speaker, you can write articles for them, you can provide resources for their educational programs, or you can simply participate and network.
- Any geographical community where you live now, used to live, or have relatives. Hint: The smaller the community, the easier it is to become known. So if you live in a big city like New York, break it down to something manageable, like the Park Slope neighborhood in Brooklyn. When *Marketing Without Megabucks* was published back in 1993, Shel even got Simon & Schuster to reimburse his costs for sending customized and carefully targeted press releases with headlines that started "Montclair Couple's Son", "Former Atlanta Resident," and so forth.
- Any school you've attended, even if you didn't graduate.
- All your business and professional organizations.

- Any nonprofits you're involved with, especially if you have a leadership position.
- The newsletter for your own place of worship.
- For fiction writers, any of the above that involve *the characters in your book or the locations where it takes place*; for nonfiction, any communities *relevant to your subject matter* (for practical applications, please look over the sample marketing plans in Chapter 1).

Spontaneous Networking

Never miss an opportunity to network! We often run into friends and acquaintances, and many times, they're interested in having a look. If you can sell your books yourself, make a habit of carrying a copy or two. Shel is still amazed at how often he shows someone his book and makes a sale on the spot.

It's also a good idea to travel with leave-behinds. I suggest postcards. Your book cover fills one side, nice and noticeable, and on the back, you can have a blurb, synopsis, ordering information, or whatever. You can even leave the back blank and run custom messages through your own laser printer, as long as it can handle card stock. Unlike a bookmark or business card, postcards are too big to be easily misplaced—but not so big as to be a burden to anyone. Shel and I carry our postcards everywhere we go.

Postcards also provide something to give when someone—and this may happen more often than you think—wants to help you by introducing your book to others. I printed 1500 postcards of *Escaping into the Night* in February, and by May I had distributed all of them—often in large batches to others who were willing to give them out. So I printed 1000 more.

And whenever I travel and we pass a library or bookstore, I show my books and leave a postcard, often with a short flier about the book that contains excerpts from reviews. But it's the postcard that usually attracts people. Assuming you have a good cover, specialty postcard printers provide a decently printed card at a very affordable price. At trade shows like Book Expo America, postcards can be extremely useful. They're compact and easy to carry, and you can use them to start a conversation.

Keeping in Contact

Of course, another way to build networks is to keep track of the people you meet. At every appearance, collect names and contact information for your print and/or electronic newsletter. If someone hands you a business card at a networking event, take a moment to jot a note or two on the back of the card so you can follow up. If you find an article that will interest a contact, drop a quick "thinking of you" note with the link. If you notice printed press coverage of someone you've met, clip the article and send it by postal mail with a note of congratulations. People who see you as thinking beyond your own desires will be much warmer when you approach them asking for help.

SHEL SAYS, IF THEY DON'T KNOW YOU...INTRODUCE YOURSELF

A client of Shel's, Barbara Meislin, has a beautiful picture book called *No One Can Ever Steal Your Rainbow*—and she donates the proceeds to a Jewish-Arab peace village in Israel. By identifying groups likely to be interested, finding out whom she should talk to, writing letters that she sends along with a sample book, and even making personal visits, she has opened a number of markets, including several that are nationally known within the peace, human-service, and social-justice communities—through their catalogs, websites, newsletters, physical stores, and other channels. She's also gotten the book accepted into several school systems, specialty retailers, and museum shops. A partial list:

- Fellowship of Reconciliation (including not only a sales channel but a glowing review with full contact information in the organization's national magazine)
- National Hospice
- Southern Poverty Law Center (another national review and a small bulk purchase)
- Breast Cancer Fund of San Francisco
- Marin Cancer Institute
- Spirit Rock Zen Center (Woodacre, CA)
- Philadelphia Liberty Museum
- The Discovery Museum (Sausalito, CA)
- ASTRAEA (an international lesbian action foundation)

- Global AIDS Interfaith Alliance (based in Malawi, Africa)
- Centering Corporation, which distributes books on grief and loss at national conferences
- Neve Shalom/Wahat al Salam, an Israeli–Palestinian peace and education community in Israel (the charity she supports directly through book sales)
- New Israel Fund

She has also arranged for a bilingual Hebrew–Arabic edition to be distributed in Israel, and is in dialogue with a dance company about turning the book into a ballet.

And speaking of networking, she still doesn't have a website of her own, but she's friends with the songwriter Amanda McBroom (author of Bette Midler's smash hit "The Rose")—and McBroom's site has a lovely endorsement of her book.

Among Shel's networking strategies, getting to know and be known by new people is definitely key:

> I subscribe to a whole lot of marketing newsletters online. Often, I write little notes to the editor when an article particularly impresses me; sometimes I even ask permission to republish the article on one of my websites or newsletters. Of course, these notes (which take about two minutes to write) include my full e-mail sig, and many of them check me out. If they didn't know who I was before, they do now! And then later if I ask them to announce a promotion for one of my books in their newsletters, they know who I am, my request goes to the top of the pile, and gets included in the next issue. The cumulative effect is usually about 200,000 extra readers learning about me.

Online Networking: Shy Author Salvation

Back in the day, if you were not very mainstream and you wanted to find like-minded people, you pretty much had to live in a city, find (or organize) a group, and attend—something that might be scary for shy writers.

But the Internet has given shy people a huge gift: online communities. Starting with Usenet newsgroups in the 1970s, continuing through Compuserve Special Interest Groups (SIGs) in the

1980s, drastically expanding through much-improved chatboard software and easy, free discussion hosts such as Yahoogroups in the 1990s, and continuing to expand through the 2000s through "social networking" sites like LinkedIn, Friendster, MySpace, and Ryze, the Internet has turned into the greatest community-builder the world has ever seen. If you want to find other left-handed vegetarian beagle owners, there's probably a group for you.

Now you don't need to leave your house, you don't need to shake strange sweaty hands, and you don't need to worry about fear of crowds. You don't even have to be spontaneous. You can do your networking from the comfort of your own home or your favorite café, just by posting to e-mail lists and websites. You can take your own sweet time, read over your post before you send it, and avoid bloopers or heat-of-the-moment responses that can get you in trouble. And if your posts are cogent and helpful, you can quickly build a reputation as an expert: a go-to person in your field.

Over the years, Shel has been in and out of dozens of discussion groups.

In some of the best ones, I stay active for years and years; as we'll see in Chapter 7, they bring me book sales, consulting clients, and speaking gigs. They also foster a strong sense of community: I have friends all over the world whom I've never met! At the moment, I participate actively in three discussion lists for independent publishers, lurk (read the posts but stay in the background) and occasionally participate on the lists for the local chapter of the National Writers Union and for a local networking association of work-at-home professionals, and enter various reader-participation features for a few e-newsletters in my niche, a few times per year each—which is often enough to keep my name in the public eye.

One strategy that surprisingly few people take advantage of is to network with "power hitters": industry experts who have their own newsletters. This even gets me referrals for my consulting practice, offers to do teleseminars together, and all sorts of other benefits—and probably takes less than three hours per year (not counting the time reading their newsletters, which I would do anyway). In addition to the quick personal notes, I will often make public comments on blog posts or newsletter articles (which also help the search engine standings for my own sites, since I include a link).

Read Chapter 7 to find out how to locate these communities, identify the best groups, and learn the rules of the road.

Tupperware Parties...for Books!

Len Charla <http://www.countinghousepress.com> encourages everyone in his network to put on a Tupperware party–style event: a small group in a private home who gather with the author.

This is a fabulous strategy to reach people who perhaps don't read a lot of books, and are awed by the chance to rub elbows with an actual published author.

The type of event I love best is talking to book-discussion groups; participants have already read the book and they always have interesting, intelligent questions. And unless the club is local, I don't even have to leave home! When a friend in another state got my book on the agenda for her book group in New York, I arranged to talk with the group via speakerphone.

Here's one author who took that strategy and ran with it: John Shors "visits" at least two book-discussion groups by phone every week to promote his novel, *Beneath a Marble Sky* (Penguin/ Putnam), and has done 170 groups so far, according to John Kremer in the May 15, 2006, edition of *Book Marketing Update*.

With both of these techniques, you can expect to create a deep level of fan. The people who attend will feel a sense of ownership and pride in you and your books, and they will go from passive enjoyers to avid advocates, recommending your books to many of their own friends.

Of course, you can also provide some structure to help them spread the news. A simple form can ask them for the names and contact information of people they know who might want to have a similar event, or who work in the schools, etc. Then, of course, when you contact the referral, you can say that so-and-so suggested you be in touch. And if your original contact is willing to make the contact on your behalf, so much the better.

In short, whether you network in person, by phone, over the Internet, or—as we do—all of the above, the effort and time pays off handsomely in book sales, media contacts, and reputation.

Chapter Five

Your Website

- *How to do an inexpensive and effective website*
- *Seven different ways to organize your site*
- *Bringing visitors and getting them to buy*

For the first time in history, independent publishers, self-publishers, and traditionally published authors have two major sales channels that put us on superior footing compared with large corporate publishers: the World Wide Web, covered here, and other Internet marketing, covered in the next chapter. If you learn a little bit about how the web works, you can create a site that gets found by search engines, gets visited, and generates sales—and putting up a website can be so effective and inexpensive that I can't understand why there are still authors out there who don't have one and don't want one.

How might your website generate interest in you and your book? Remember how many books are published each year. If you want to convince your visitor to take that credit card out and actually buy something from you, you need to convince this prospect that you have something to offer, such as:

- Solid information that will help the reader save or earn money, solve a problem, learn a new skill, address a pressing desire (e.g., lose weight, find a mate, de-stress), shed light on historical or current events, etc.
- Excellent entertainment.
- A brush with celebrity.

And the tools that you use to convey the value in your offer are a combination of third-party recognition (testimonials, awards, reviews/press coverage), materials to create a sense of community and personal acquaintance with you (bio, family pictures, interview with you, fan club), and, of course, pages that convince the visitor of the high quality of your product (excerpts, front and back cover, two-page layouts of illustrated books, Table of Contents, index, multimedia presentations such as movie trailers).

How Much Does It Cost?

It's actually possible to establish and maintain a web presence for under a hundred bucks a year, with a single simple site, a low-cost host (*do not* use a free host, however), and do-it-yourself site maintenance/updating using a blog format. But you can have a much more effective site that might cost a few hundred dollars per year. These sites will probably outperform fancy but useless sites that might cost many times as much. Lots of big companies blow $50,000 or more to design a very beautiful site that few people will visit unless they're already looking specifically for that company, and those who do visit find difficult to use. But your site can show up in search engines and draw traffic through other means, so that people interested in *your topic* can find you even if they didn't know about you ahead of time. And once your visitors arrive, you can steer them through an easy-to-navigate path that can create book sales and other benefits.

We small fry have two other key advantages on the web: ability to move fast and implement/test very quickly, and understanding of the personal nature of the web—which leads not only to creating much more effective sites but also to the ability to market the site effectively through one-to-many tools like discussion groups, blogs, and article banks (all discussed in Chapter 7).

That personal nature includes the amazing capacity to interact with your fans, and create new fans. It used to be that to contact a writer, someone had to write a letter via the publisher or agent, wait months for it to be delivered, and hope for an answer. But now, a fan can e-mail you from your own website and get an answer in an hour or a day. And you can easily solicit content from your fans: letters, endorsements, stories of how they're using your book, and more.

The great thing is you can start small. If you set up a simple blog and later grow into a traditional author site, you can still keep your blog as one page of your new site.

Because your well-organized website will bring you book sales, newsletter subscribers, press coverage, and other benefits, setting up your site can offer a very high return on a fairly minimal investment. It's so cheap that you can easily set up multiple sites to attract different audiences.

Getting Started

At its most basic, you can get started with three things: a domain name, a web host, and at least one page of content. I also recommend adding a blog very early on, and a number of other features as you get comfortable running your site.

Domain Name

This is the part of the web address that comes after the "www." and before the first slash. The "top-level domain" (TLD) is the suffix. In most cases, you'll have a .com suffix, but .net and .org are also common. At one point, .net was reserved for groups that were actually involved in maintaining the Internet infrastructure, and .org was for nonprofits, but these days, it's just a question of who gets there first to reserve the domain. At least three TLDs are still restricted: .edu for colleges, .mil for military, and .gov for government.

There are also over a hundred country-specific TLDs, such as .au for Australia, .il for Israel, and .us for the United States.

And then there's a barrage of newer TLDs that haven't really caught on but are useful in certain situations: .info, .biz, .store, .tv, .coop, etc.

Still, in most cases, you want a .com domain. It's what people have heard of, expect, and absentmindedly type. And even these days, it's still pretty easy to find a good name. Think about your book title, your publishing house, your own name, or your subject area. All of these are possible domain names; try for one that contains your best keywords and is easy enough for listeners to remember (and spell) if you're giving it out on the radio. Note that domains are not case-sensitive; <http://www.frugalmarketing.com> and <http://www.FrugalMarketing.com> are the same address.

If your name or book title is common, the most obvious choice is probably gone—but you can play with variations like hyphens or extra words until you find one available in .com form. So, for example, instead of JohnSmith.com, try JohnSmithOfPhilly.com. If TheGreatEscape.com is already taken, play with variations like GreatEscapeSuspenseNovel.com, Great-Escape-Suspense-Novel.com, TheGreatEscapeSuspenseNovel.com, etc.

To check if a domain is available, first type it into your browser's navigation bar. If you get a "can't find host" error message, it's likely that the domain is yours for the taking. Unless you're going with a SiteBuildIt (SBI) site, which includes domain registration (more about that later), the next step is to visit a domain registrar like <http://www.godaddy.com> or <http://www.000domains.com>. If the name is available, registering it is quick, painless, and cheap.

You'll find a much more complete discussion of domain names in my earlier book, *Grassroots Marketing: Getting Noticed in a Noisy World.*

Still stuck? Hire me to find one! In fact, I have set up a site just for this purpose: <http://www.the-domain-finder.com>.

WEB HOSTING

Your site needs a location: space on a server where the world can come and find it. You may find that you can set up a simple website at no extra cost as part of your e-mail hosting package—but only do this if your provider allows you to use your own domain name, does not inflict their own ads on your visitors, and allows you to be listed as the administrative and billing contact with your domain registrar. As far as I know, you can't do that with Geocities, Angelfire, Tripod, or AOL.

But there are hundreds of other hosts out there who will provide basic hosting at very low cost ($50–$100 per year). For instance, my assistant, Michelle Shaeffer, hosts my wife's <http://www.ddinafriedman.com> site at her <http://www.elementalmuse.com> hosting service. My own sites require somewhat greater complexity, and I have them hosted at <http://www.bluehost. com>.

And then there's SiteBuildIt: a full-featured all-in-one package that provides domain registration, hosting, template-based page design with do-it-yourself updating, search-engine optimization, newsletter tool including automatic archiving, advertising tools, link exchange, and quite a bit more, along with about 1000 pages of information on how to set up a website and market success-fully online. For about $300 a year, it's a lot of bang for the buck. I had one of my sites there for the first three years before bring-ing it to BlueHost. If you want to explore this option, please visit <http://snipurl.com/nthd>.

Plan from the Beginning for Growth and Change

It is much easier to set things up from the beginning to accom-modate success. Some basic strategic moves will position you to much more easily adjust your site to future needs.

- Get a decent-sized partition from your webhost—50 megabytes, minimum, and don't get a plan that charges you extra for large amounts of traffic. My two biggest sites are hundreds of megabytes each.

- Design your site either using Cascading Style Sheets, where the page pulls information from a common header, footer, and page background, or an easily modified template such as SiteBuildIt that affects the whole site. *In plain English*, this means that if you change the design of your site, all you have to do is edit and reload the stylesheet or template, which is a whole lot more pleasant than pouring 1000 pages into a new design and uploading them one at a time.

- Assume that people won't return to the site even if they have the best intentions; any who do return are gravy. Thus, you want a way to capture visitors' e-mail addresses (and an incentive for them to give them to you).

- Focus on *the visitor's needs* in order to get the desired action (a sale, a newsletter signup, etc.). This means that page navigation has to make sense from the visitor's perspective, has to make it easy for that visitor to find what s/he's looking for, and therefore must be clearly and accurately labeled.

- If you're selling from the site, make sure the shopping cart makes sense and doesn't create extra work for your visitors—also, that you can easily add more products in the future.
- Assume that not all of your visitors will be from your own country, and therefore don't put barriers in front of them like the need for a U.S. zip code or state choice.
- If you're selling or giving away electronic products such as e-books, audios, and special reports, set them up from the beginning to automatically download once you've verified payment—but expect to provide some troubleshooting and an occasional resend via e-mail.
- Set up your newsletter subscription and contact forms to automatically pour the data into a database or spreadsheet.

Site Models

For authors and publishers, certain ways to structure a website make particular sense. Let's explore seven different models: Resource sites, author sites, publisher or series sites, buy-my-book sites, blog sites, salesletter sites—and one additional model (ask-me sites) that actually helps you create new products.

COMMON ELEMENTS

The first four of these will have at least some of these common elements (different combinations will be appropriate for different sites, depending on your needs and audience):

- A navigation mechanism to get to the most important parts of the site (usually a bar of choices along one edge of the screen, though there are other ways to do it).
- Pages that create interest in your book(s) and/or you as the author, such as testimonials, reviews, excerpts, author biography, audio and video clips (even up to full-fledged movie-style "trailers," if you have the budget), table of contents, index, and so on.

- Pages that market the author to the media and to meeting planners, schools, bookstores, and libraries looking for speakers/authors—including an easily accessible "Press Room" or "Media Center" that contains press releases, interview questions, high-resolution copies of an author headshot photo, book covers, and possibly an action shot photo. My press pages also have a list of media that have covered me.

- Pages that market your book to resellers: an affiliate program, bulk sales discount schedule, list of wholesalers or distributors, information on using your book as an association fundraiser.

- Materials that others can freely use on their own websites or in their e-newsletters and print publications as long as they include your blurb and web link (thus spreading you to new audiences and improving your search engine positioning).

- A blog that you can update on your own, at any time (many entire sites are nothing but a blog; see the fifth model).

- Schedule of appearances (if you can keep it current—personally, I find it easier to do this in my newsletters).

- Archive of past newsletters.

- Some way of keeping in touch with visitors who, even if they intend to come back, may never visit your site again—usually through an address-capture mechanism such as a guestbook (I'm not a big fan of those), a subscription form for a newsletter (which I strongly recommend), or a drawing/contest (challenging to administer and fraught with legal issues, but with potentially huge payoff)—also alternative methods for those who don't like to give their e-address, such as RSS feeds (a method of subscribing to information without providing an e-mail address; your reader gets notification that the site is updated and views it within an RSS reader or web browser. The term seems to have existed before it was defined, and there are many variations, among them Real Simple Syndication and Rich Site Summary).

- Feedback mechanisms: contact information and forms, order forms, comment pages, etc. (*Warning:* Never put your e-mail address as a text link on your website; the spam robots will collect it and you'll be sorry! I recommend web-based contact forms, which also enables you to create rules that filter on your specified subject lines to flag the message as high-priority in your in-box).
- Links to other *relevant* websites (very important for search-engine placement, as it will encourage others to link to you, and that's one of the key things the search-engine spiders look for).
- A site-wide search tool (Google has a particularly nice one, and it's free).

RESOURCE SITES

When people search on the web, they're typically looking for specific information about a topic. If they find your site while they're searching, you hope the high-quality information you provide will convince them to buy—or at least sign up for your newsletter so you can sell to them later.

To set up this type of site, create a few dozen pages on your topic. You don't have to write them all; dozens of article sites supply content for websites and newsletters at no charge. Resources sites are fun to do and they easily gain traffic, but they can get out of hand pretty quickly, because there's so much good stuff out there. Note: I'm not talking about portal sites here, which send traffic through their "portal" to other sites, but about keeping content on your own site.

You can see examples at <http://www.frugalfun.com> (my site on having fun cheaply, with arts and travel magazines and frugality resources—which gets at least 55,000 visits every month these days) and <http://www.frugalmarketing.com> (my general business site). Both of these sites actively promote my books but also attract a lot of traffic that will never buy, because they just want the specific information they came for. That's okay too—they create a very nice passive revenue stream via Google AdSense: Google licenses the right to display ads on my pages, and pays me a few cents every time someone clicks on one of those ads.

AUTHOR SITES

A site that promotes your "brand" as an author. It should let readers get a sense that they know you personally, as well as, of course, introduce them to your various books. It may or may not have a direct-selling component. This kind of site is also an ideal place to set up a fan club.

My wife's site at <http://www.ddinafriedman.com> is one of these. She has not put in a newsletter, because with her full-time teaching job, she wants to spend her limited free time writing more books, but she has created a site that makes her feel very approachable while highlighting her books.

PUBLISHER OR SERIES SITES

Similar to the author site, but what's being branded is the book series or entire publisher line. Typically, these present a catalog page, with tiny book covers and brief descriptions—but when you click on the cover or description, you get not only a larger cover image but also much deeper information about the book, including all the goodies we talked about earlier–kind of like<http://www.frugalmarketing.com/shop.html>.

BUY-MY-BOOK SITES

All or most of the content is designed to move a sale forward, but there are still several pages to choose from. And I advise, even in this type of site, that you provide resources for free. For instance, my <http://www.principledprofit.com> site not only includes many preview pages and information about bulk sales and affiliate partnerships, but also has a page of ethics articles, a blog, and the complete archives of my free monthly business ethics newsletter. All of this is "search-engine food" —but when I get a visitor, I want that person to buy a book.

My frugalfun site started as a buy-my-book site back in 1996, but once I decided (a year later) to start the arts and travel magazines (the first of the five webzines I currently publish), it rapidly turned into a resource site—and began to birng in a whole lot more visitors.

BLOG SITES

Blogs have a number of advantages over traditional static websites. First of all, they're incredibly easy to use. You can literally be blogging in three minutes—and not just with text but pictures, sound, and video. Search engines love frequently updated blogs and "spider" them (and web pages they link to) much more quickly than typical static web pages. If you're more disciplined than I am and able to keep your posts tightly focused, you can very quickly become a "destination" site in your niche. Posts can be categorized, converted to RSS, and/or e-mailed to subscribers. Visitors can easily comment on them, and link to their own blogs or web pages (don't worry, you can either approve posts before they go live or remove inappropriate ones). And you can visit other people's blogs and link back to your site (in ways that are relevant to the conversation). They can spur big increases in traffic.

Other than the time it takes to maintain them, I can't think of a reason not to have one. And that time doesn't need to be very much. If you do brief posts several times a week, it should only take an hour or so, total. (This is a better idea than longer posts once a week). You can also "share the burden" by having several people post to the same blog on the same theme. And, of course, a blog humanizes your company in ways not possible in a stiff corporate website. (Note: if you let other people post to your blog, be sure they understand about libel, obscenity, and respecting your corporate culture.)

Because they're so easy to set up and run, many people have been doing their whole site as a blog lately. Search engines love these sites, and the blog format makes it possible to keep the site active without involving an outside webmaster or knowing anything about HTML. If you can send an e-mail, you can not only post to a blog but add pictures, audio, and video.

However, think about things from a user's point of view. It's really hard to find specific information on a blog. Categorization is usually weak or nonexistent, and often the titles of the posts have little to do with the content. So I also recommend a set of traditional pages, plus a blog; this way you have the advantages of both formats.

SALESLETTER SITES

This type, often called a "mini-site," is a totally different animal. Instead of a menu of many pages, you get a salesletter—the sort of thing that might show up in postal direct mail—with only one option: to click on the order page. (That option may be presented several times in the salesletter.) Products hawked may range from a giveaway newsletter or teleseminar to trainings costing several thousands of dollars; many salesletters sell e-books.

Sometimes, before you get to the salesletter, you face a "name squeeze page" that captures your e-mail address for a newsletter (especially common if what they're "selling" is a free telephone seminar). You can see a particularly good example at <http://promotingtips.com>. This name-squeeze page is designed to get subscribers to a newsletter; when someone signs up, the e-mail address is entered into an autoresponder sequence that provides several information-only newsletters to build trust, and then around the 10th contact, starts to sell. Craig Sanford, an associate of site owner Matt Bacak, told me that this technique generated $1.6 million in the preceding 12 months![3]

The salesletter may run many pages if you print it out, but there's nowhere else to go except to the bottom of the page, or to the order form. You buy (or subscribe to a newsletter or sign up for a teleseminar)—or you leave.

These sites don't tend to pull a lot of search-engine traffic, since they don't offer much usable content. Therefore, those who use these sites drive traffic through their own and others' e-mail newsletters as well as buying pay-per-click ads.

This is the model that most Internet millionaires use, and they claim it works. Not that any one site will necessarily sell enormous amounts of product, but if they put up several dozen sites, each generating a few hundred to a few thousand dollars every month, the overall effect creates the fabled "multiple streams of passive income"—and a very nice lifestyle.

Personally, I usually find these sites irritating because they tend to be very hard-sell and hype-filled (and because I've seen hundreds of them). But a lot of people with significant real-world experience swear by them. I've just started testing a softer version at <http://www.the-domain-finder.com>.

Ask-Me Websites: A Fabulous Research Tool for Product Development

One last model that's been popular lately: what I call the "ask-me" website. The site is a very simple form offering you the chance to ask an expert one question. Often, this is used in advance of a teleseminar; the host and expert guest use the responses to structure a teleseminar that will address the most popular questions, and to construct a salesletter based on them as well.

From there, of course, it's a simple matter to construct audio CDs or even books that address these same common questions. *Voila*, a product that you know fills a niche in the marketplace. Wow—what a great way to do market research!

Both Fred Gleeck and Alex Mandossian offer special software to set up these campaigns and extract the results into a database (see Resources). If you don't expect a huge number of responses, you can also track the results manually, as I did in structuring this book (I used e-mail, rather than a website, or through Survey Monkey, HostedWare, etc.). I even offered a discount on the final product to people who asked a question in the research phase—and a free e-book copy to anyone who contributed a marketing success story that I used.

Building Traffic

If you build it, they won't necessarily come. Whole books have been written on how to get traffic to your site; here's a brief overview.

Most traffic will arrive at your site through one of four channels: natural search, nonsearch links, off-line promotion, or paid advertising.

Natural Search

Search-engine robots will crawl your site. The more relevant content, the more relevant links to and especially from other sites, and the more often you update, the more frequently the "bots" will "spider" or "crawl" your site.

While it's not generally worth the effort to spend huge amounts of time figuring out what they're looking for—it changes constantly anyhow—some basic principles apply. The term "tag" or "metatag" refers to a little snippet of code that tells the search bot what to do with the information. If you're creating your own site, any decent book or online primer will explain them. When working with a web designer, just make sure your expert is incorporating tags properly, especially on your home page.

- Use search-engine-friendly navigation: verbally describe every image with an "alt" tag, so that the search engines can index the content. Start every page with good, strong, keyword-laden text, and avoid unethical optimization techniques like showing one page to the search-engine "bots" and a different one to human visitors.
- For each page, pick a few keywords that start near the beginning of the page and get repeated several times (but write for human beings, not for bots).
- If you can, incorporate that keyword into the page title and the file name as well as the keyword and description meta tags.
- Write your "meta description" tag carefully; in many cases, that's the text the search engines will display if they return your page.
- Get other relevant sites to link to you.

NONSEARCH LINKS

Links from other sites not only help you with the search engines, they also provide a direct path for visitors from those sites. You can get these links by submitting articles in exchange for a block of resource and contact information, by cross-linking your own multiple sites, by providing great content that people want to link to, and just by asking—but not with those idiotic autogenerated form letters, please! Instead, visit sites you genuinely like and politely suggest to the webmaster that a particular page of your site might be useful to that site's visitors. You may or may not want to offer to reciprocate, depending on circumstances.

OFFLINE PROMOTION

Your website URL should be on everything you ever send out—and not just the address, but a reason to visit. Put it on press releases, business cards, postcards, and bookmarks with the cover of your book, any apparel or other promotional items you create, and so on.

What kind of reason to visit? The same kinds of things you might suggest when you give out the URL (I hope it's an easy one to spell and remember) on a radio interview: get a free newsletter about (your topic), learn the truth about (topic), take a survey and see how you compare, to name a few possibilities.

These are some actual reasons I've given out:

Visit frugalfun.com to find out how to have a $300 wedding. Visit frugalmarketing.com to find dozens of ways you can slash the cost of marketing and boost its effectiveness. Visit business-ethics-pledge.ORG (I emphasize ".org" because people expect ".com") to create a society-wide tipping point toward ethical business.

PAID ADVERTISING

You can buy traffic. Lots of people will sell it to you. I'd suggest that if this interests you, you sign up for Google AdWords—and do some serious research first. It's very easy to drop a big wad of money if you don't know what you're doing. Study the reports from Perry Marshall and others who've been down this road. Figure out very carefully constructed search terms that are specific enough to get people who are seriously interested in what you want, and affordable enough that you can make a profit if even one person in 100 who clicks to your site turns into a buyer. For example, don't buy clicks for "bicycles"; instead, buy "recumbent bicycle racing." And when people click, they should arrive at a landing page that's specific to what they clicked on—*not* to a generic home page. And finally, keep your eyes on your budget, and on your results. Carefully track how much you spend to bring in what number of visitors, how many of them buy anything, and how much they spend.

Convert Your Visitors

When you finally get that precious visitor to your site, you need to know what you want that person to do—especially if you've paid to bring that person there. This is what SBI's Ken Evoy calls the "most wanted response." Usually, that's buying something. But sometimes it might be signing up for a newsletter, or something else entirely; if the prospect isn't ready to buy, the newsletter subscription is the next most wanted response—because it allows you to go back in front of that prospect, with permission, every day or week or month, until that person is finally ready to buy.

And most websites convert pitifully.

Why is that? Because most people who set up a website don't think about what their visitors are looking for, and don't try to make it happen for them. Websites need to be usable, easy to navigate, fast to load, and with multiple paths through the site— many of which guide the visitor toward the response you want.

Read Jakob Neilson and Jared Spool on usability. Study Ken Evoy or Bryan and Jeffrey Eisenberg on conversion. Most importantly, sit down in front of your site and watch someone who has never seen it before. Can she figure out how to find what she needs? Does what he finds meet his expectations as he searched? And does it make her want to buy your book?

My Web Strategy

At the moment, I'm operating one site each for each of my four most recent books. Two of them set up primarily as resource sites: <http://www.frugalmarketing.com> and <http://www. frugalfun.com>. Two are specifically to generate book sales— the buy-my-book site at <http://www.principledprofit. com> and a modified salesletter site [it's actually several salesletters for people with different interests] at <http://www. grassrootsmarketingforauthors.com>), my wife's site to promote her two novels at <http://www.ddinafriedman.com>—a warm and fuzzy site with pictures of our family and such), a rudimentary site under my company name, focused on services <http://www. accuratewriting.com>, a straight-up salesletter for the domain-finding service <http://www.the-domain-finder.com>, a site just for my Business Ethics Pledge campaign <http://www.business-ethics-pledge.org>, and an umbrella site under my own name that currently serves to direct people to my various other sites. This last I set up just in case people look for me by typing my name in their navigation bar, and also as insurance against the possibility that one of the other Shel Horowitzes out there (yes, there are a few others) might buy it. I plan to eventually change it over to focus on speaking. And then there are various domain names I've purchased and haven't developed.

My two most fully developed sites total over 1000 separate web pages and get over 75,000 visits a month (55,000 or more at <http://www.frugalfun.com> and 20,000 or more to <http://www.frugalmarketing.com>). The remaining sites add maybe another 100–150 pages. But when I started in 1996, it was with a single site of about 40 pages, mostly focused on my two then-current books. It morphed fairly quickly into a resource site because I was following my own passions, and eventually I decided to split off the business-oriented material into its own site.

All of this activity together costs me only a few hundred dollars per year to register and host. Because there are so many sites to maintain, I've used an outside webmaster to keep them current, starting around 2000; before that, I handled the whole thing on my own.

Three Final Reasons to Develop a Website

1. In almost any other promotional medium—a classified or display ad, a flier, even a full article or book chapter—your space is limited to somewhere between a few lines and a couple of thousand words. But on a website, you can offer your visitor the chance to go as deep as s/he needs in order to convince that visitor to buy your book, and yet keep things in small enough chunks that you don't scare off the people who need considerably less convincing. In fact, I strongly recommend using every other promotional activity to bring traffic to your site, where you can deliver the right information to the right prospects.

2. Your website is out there selling for you 24 hours a day, 365 days a year. It doesn't sleep, it doesn't take holidays off—

and it pulls in visitors around the world who are already interested in your topic.

3. A website is perfect to promote even a reclusive, stay-at-home author who doesn't like to travel, doesn't like talking to the media, and just wants to stay home and write.

Chapter Six

Google

- *Many services beyond basic search*
- *Google AdWords and AdSense*

L ike Amazon, Google is another powerhouse player on the World Wide Web that can help grow your business, and deserves special attention.

Coming out of nowhere, Google quickly overcame the established search players and became the number one search engine, growing almost entirely by word of mouth/word of mouse. Google was still in beta testing until September 1999; a year later, the company already dominated the search industry.

Why? Because it delivered a substantially better user experience than Yahoo, AltaVista, Excite, or other first-generation search tools. Google's interface is clean, its search results frequently bring exactly what the user is looking for, its database is the most comprehensive, and it's amazingly fast.

Any marketer can learn a lot by watching Google. Even more than Hotmail, the company is the unchallenged master of buzz marketing: spreading your user base by getting other people to talk about you and show you off to their friends. Once a web user has tried Google, that person becomes a convert. Google waited a while to monetize its enormous traffic, but when it did release its ad program, it was, once again, better than anything else out there, and almost immediately started filling boatloads of money.

Personally, I use Google for about 90 percent of my web searches, even when I know the site that will hold my answer (for example, a news story in a major newspaper). About 5 percent goes through Clusty, which sorts responses into categories by definition—and often, I only go to Clusty if I can't find what I want in the first two screens of a Google search—and most of the other 5 percent is searching the specific domain I happen to be visiting at that moment.

The company continues to add features, with a mission of organizing the world's information. Some of these are vital for research, some bring money directly to you, and some simply make your life easier.

Let's look at some of the ways Google can help you as a writer and publisher.

Google Print

Like Amazon's Search Inside the Book, Google indexes the entire text of participating books. The same factors as Amazon's program apply in deciding whether your book is a good choice for this program. There has been talk about Google starting to sell access to the complete books cited via Google Print and sharing revenue with publishers; keep your eye on that!

Google News Alerts

Set up key phrases that you want to monitor, and Google will send an e-mail when each phrase is cited in news stories. (Tip: put your phrase in quotes so you get exact matches only). Set up alerts for your name, your book titles, and key subject areas you want to track. For instance, I have alerts for my name, "principled profit," "business ethics," and "corporate scandal," among others. I used to have one for "grassroots marketing" but the phrase is too common.

I've used these alerts as the basis for letters to the editor, blog entries, story pitches to reporters, leads on speaking gigs, contacting organizations that might be interested in my book or my pledge movement, and in one case, an op-ed article published in the *Orange County Register*, one of the largest newspapers in the Greater Los Angeles area (3000 miles from my home).

Arlene Evans, <h>, a school nurse who writes about colorblindness, uses Google News Alerts very effectively:

> I wrote and self-published *Seeing Color: It's My Rainbow, Too* for children, and *Color Is in the Eye of the Beholder* for teens and adults. I have a novel, *Dinner for Two*, a romantic comedy, coming out from Echelon Press next month...the hero...is colorblind.
>
> From google.com, I get a daily bulletin (mainly newspaper articles) on any story that contains the word "colorblind." Most of the articles are about race relations, but occasionally I do find something pertinent.

How does she use this information to promote her book? Here's one example:

> I received one Google News Alert that was about a fellow in Oregon who was working on a bicycle map for people who are colorblind...I wrote to the reporter who published my letter as a letter to the editor, which was good promotion.

That editor connected her with an expert on making colorblind-friendly maps, with whom she was able to partner.

Google Advanced Search

Using the advanced settings, it's possible to design a very specific query in a single screen (you can actually do this from the home screen also, by using quote marks, plus and minus signs, etc., but it's much easier from the advanced search page). The exact phrase match and ability to screen out certain words are excellent for eliminating irrelevant responses and locating exactly the ones you want. My only issue is that the date field is balky and often returns useless results, because any modification even of the site design will return as a recent change.

Froogle

Froogle is Google's shopping agent that compares prices for particular items. A good place to try when you're buying your next piece of computer or audiovisual equipment for your business.

And since there's no charge to list, anything you sell ought to be listed in Froogle, so that when people search for the subject of your book, for instance, they find you.

AdWords

Google's advertisers purchase mini-classifieds called AdWords: just a couple of lines and a URL. This is a powerful tool to locate people who are looking for exactly what you offer, paying a certain number of cents per click. Typically, advertisers who are succeeding with AdWords bid on (and carefully track) dozens or even hundreds of search phrases, paying anywhere from a few cents to several dollars per click, bringing visitors to a custom landing page that highlights the exact term mentioned in the ad, and often using the one-page salesletter model (we discussed this in Chapter 5) to convert visitors into buyers. Google keeps millions of ads in inventory and offers advertisers a lot of control over the number of clicks, so you can test on a small scale before you commit to pouring a lot of money into the program.

Interestingly, unlike most other pay-per-click advertising companies (and there are hundreds), Google doesn't necessarily give the best position to the highest bidder. Rather, it figures ad placement through a complex and constantly adjusted algorithm that factors in the ad's success: how many times it gets clicked. This means you can't fool Google by designing a "branding" ad that you don't really want people to click on—because if people don't click, your ad will stop being displayed. However, if branding is what you want, Google does offer some pay-to-display advertising in a different program, according to Cathy Stucker <http://www.idealady.com>.

The other big revolution in Google's pay-per-click program compared to older ones is that Google's amazing processing engine uses its own search technology to display ads that are (usually) directly and closely relevant to the content of the page being displayed, and to do it in nanoseconds. Because of this, a much higher percentage of Google ads actually get clicked, and advertisers have a very good chance of converting those visitors to customers—especially if the click brings your visitor to a custom landing page using the exact words in the ad. Once again, the company has put itself directly in front of the right user at the right moment.

AdSense

While Google displays ads on its own search results pages, it also displays ads on hundreds of thousands of other websites; Google shares revenue with its web publisher hosts on a percentage basis, so rather than paying for display space, the company pays per click. It takes only a few minute to set up a site for this program, and then the site owner or publisher has to do nothing more except deposit the checks.

I joined this program in September 2003. The next month I was featured on MSN's home page and had a massive spike in traffic; my first check from Google was for over $600! In 2004, I generated some $3300 from the program; in 2005, $4131.67. Your numbers will vary depending on how much traffic you have and how targeted that traffic is. There are people who make $10,000 or more every month, and others who make almost nothing. But for me, in the last two full years, I've brought in over $7400 that I didn't have to work for.

Put that in the context of my other activities: $7400 for totally passive income—zero work—versus $8500 advance (after subtracting agent commission) from Simon & Schuster or $4000 (unagented) from Chelsea Green to spend six months writing a book.

Or compare it to book sales. I would have to sell 870 copies of my $8.50 e-book or 422 full-price copies of my $17.50 paperback to bring in the same revenue, and in the case of the paperback, I have to subtract my costs of printing and design.

To put it another way, Google has made it worth my while to continue spending time developing the rich vein of otherwise unmonetized resources I have created at frugalfun.com and frugalmarketing.com. And Google has also given me a reason to turn down lowball offers to buy the sites.

Images, Catalogs, Music, and Other Goodies

Looking for an illustration for your next book cover? I've found Google Images a lot easier to search than the search engines of many stock photo houses. And if you have images on your website that might attract viewers, listing them under the appropriate keywords would potentially bring in more traffic.

Google is also happy to index your complete catalog and return it in search results.

And then there are the separate databases of music, maps, movies, news headlines, videos, reverse-number lookups, currency conversions...The list is constantly growing.

Site Search

I replaced the site-specific search engines on my sites with Google's much faster and friendlier version, which is free and installs easily. Goodbye to manually reindexing my site each month and having the index up to a month out of date! The only annoyance is that we haven't found a way to let Google index all my sites with a single click. If you're searching across more than one of my websites, you'll have to enter the search term and click on the appropriate website each time.

I am guessing that letting Google constantly index my site for the sitewide search tool also gets new pages into Google's main database faster—and that's significant, as many new sites are quarantined by Google for a few months before they start showing up in results. So if I open a new site and link it from my existing subhome pages, Google will probably start showing the results much earlier.

Groups and Blogs

Google bought the old DejaNews search engine for Usenet newsgroups and searches posts under the category of Google Groups. It also hosts discussion groups of its own. Google also bought Blogger, the easiest blog tool to set up and use—and posts to Blogger blogs go right into the main index.

Localized Search

This is a boon to travel-guidebook publishers, among others: Google can classify your pages based on geographic content. So if you publish regional books of any kind, you want to be listed, for example, under Massachusetts Bed & Breakfast.

Useful Google URLs

Google Advanced Search: <http://www.google.com/advanced_ search?hl=en>

Froogle:<http://froogle.google.com/frghp?hl=en&tab=wf&q=>

AdWords:<https://adwords.google.com/select/main?cmd=Login &sourceid=AWO&subid=US-HA-CMBNINE2/aw>

AdSense: <https://www.google.com/adsense/?sourceid=ASO& subid=US-HA-CMBNINE2/as>

Free Site Search <http://www.google.com/searchcode.html>

Other Google Services: <http://www.google.com/intl/en/ options/>, <http://www.google.com/help/features.html>,

<http://labs.google.com/>

(All URLs were checked on March 26, 2006)

Chapter Seven

Attract Attention Elsewhere Online

- *Introduction to Internet marketing culture*
- *Discussion groups, newsletters, and articles*
- *Blogs, wikis, chats, podcasts, and more*
- *Major websites*
- *Joint ventures*

What was the "magic secret" that transformed my business from a low-paying concern serving mostly local people to a much better-paying operation serving clients throughout North America, Europe, and as far away as Japan and Cyprus?

It wasn't my website, although that was a factor. It wasn't my blog. It wasn't all the press releases and news interviews. And it wasn't my speeches.

All but two of my international clients found me or were referred to me through my participation in various Internet discussion groups, as have the vast majority of my American clients. My first-ever international book sale (to a man in Poland) came from a member of a discussion group. Between 10 and 20 percent of my ongoing book sales originate through discussion groups, and most of my speaking gigs have been initiated out of my participation, as well.

This chapter will cover discussion groups and some of the many other Internet strategies that go well beyond putting up a website (this is not intended to be a comprehensive list). Some of these I discuss in far greater detail in the original *Grassroots Marketing: Getting Noticed in a Noisy World*, which has an entire chapter just on developing e-mail signatures (or "sigs"), for example, as well as a big section on discussion groups and another chunk on one-to-one e-mail, which I'm not even covering here.

Using these tactics in conjunction with your own website and blog can vastly extend your reach, plaster your name all over cyberspace, and give people the impression that you're "everywhere."

Much of this is possible because of the extremely segmented and community-oriented nature of many online groups. Because they appeal to narrow and very specific communities, they are highly targeted; it's easy to reach not only your prime prospects, but often industry leaders and movers and shakers, who can become important allies to you if you approach them properly. This is true, of course, for instructional and motivational nonfiction—but also for biography, niche fiction, and other creative writing that can be marketed along its topics and themes. It's less true for purely literary works without a topic to tie into.

Overall Guidelines for Internet Marketing

Your success in Internet marketing is much more likely if you take the time to understand the medium. Recognizing that every community within cyberspace is a little bit different, it still makes sense to follow some overall principles.

LISTEN BEFORE YOU LEAP

When joining any new community online, start by reading all the posts for one to two weeks, to get a flavor of the group and understand its culture. Pay particular attention if certain posters are consistently ridiculed; these are people who have stepped over the line of good taste as that particular group defines it, and recognizing that boundary will help you maintain others' respect by not crossing that line. This waiting period will also show you if the group is even right for you. (However, if it doesn't seem useful, you might give it a couple of extra weeks, in case you happened to show up during an "off" period.) The best groups are those that allow you to subtly show off your expertise but also provide information and insights that you can use.

Once you're feeling pretty confident that you understand the group and that it will be useful, very carefully craft your new-member introduction. This is the one time that you can talk directly and explicitly about what you can offer, how you can help; after this, it has to be worked into the dialog, in context.

Often, I wait to post my introduction until immediately after I make my first response to another member's post. By responding first, I show that I expect to be a productive member who contributes to the collective wisdom—and by following up immediately with my intro, I let people know who I am and that my responses didn't just come out of nowhere (and I generally mention that I've been reading the posts for a while).

Here's one I wrote in 2003 (which explains the lower figure for books published annually). Note that in e-mail, you need to make sure you've **turned off** all the nonstandard characters such as curly quotes and long dashes—and when you post to a discussion list, you also need to turn off HTML: no bold, italic, colors, etc. Use tet characters to create emphasis. The <g> is cyber-shorthand for "grin"; "sig" refers to the business-card-like "signature" at the end of the post:

To: publishingandpromoting@yahoogroups.com
From: Shel Horowitz <shel@frugalfun.com>
Subject: new member intro

Now that I've de-lurked, I'd better introduce myself.

"I make the world *insist* on knowing why *you're* special," as noted in my sig. What does that mean?

I'm a marketing copywriter who looks for "the story behind the story"--so that when I create a press release, sell sheet, the copy for a web page, people want to stick around and find out more.

Here's a specific example: I was hired to write a press release by the author/publisher of a book on electronic privacy. If you follow the formulas in most PR how-to books, you'd end up with a headline like

--> Electronic Privacy Expert Releases New Book

But that's boring, and it's not news. 130,000 new books are published every year, just in the U.S.

My headline was
--> It's 10 O'Clock--Do You Know where Your Credit History Is?
The book wasn't mentioned until the third paragraph<g>.

I'm also an author of several marketing books. My two most recent are

* Principled Profit: Marketing That Puts People First (self-published)
* Grassroots Marketing: Getting Noticed in a Noisy World (Chelsea Green)

PP came out this summer, and I'm just gearing up the marketing. But already, I've gotten reviews in PW, ForeWord, Midwest Book Review, and others; pre-pub endorsements from 55 people including Jack Canfield and Jay Levinson...currently I'm trying to reach 200,000 people (through other people's e-zines and newsletters) with a message asking them to buy the book from Amazon on September 15 and make it a best-seller. I figure if 100 buy that day, that ought to put me in the top 100. Oh, yes, and I contracted with a special sales person who sold 1000 copies to Southwest Airlines.

With this new book, I'm positioning myself as "the anti-Enron. I polish people's souls--and transform marketing from expense to income"

And as a newly-minted expert on ethical marketing, I hope to do a lot more (and better paying) public speaking--one of the ways of getting paid to do one's own marketing, of which I'm a big fan.

Enough for now. Happy to be here.

--

Shel Horowitz - copywriter, marketing consultant, author, speaker
Affordable, effective marketing materials and strategies
"I make the world*insist* on knowing why *you're* special"
mailto:shel@frugalfun.com * 800-683-WORD/413-586-2388
http://www.frugalmarketing.com / http://www.principledprofit.com
Books: Grassroots Marketing, Principled Profit, others

Tell, Don't Sell

Internet discussion groups date long before the commercial Internet; the structure goes back to the late 1970s, when the Net was the province of scientists and academics who do not like to be blatantly sold to. And even though the vast majority of today's groups were created much later, they still don't like the blatant sales pitch.

Instead, you have to convey information about (and generate interest in) your offer or the content of your books very subtly, in the context of an ongoing discussion. So if, say, your book is about golf and you participate in a golf discussion group, the approach is more like "Bob, in answer to your question about <topic>, here's what I found when I was researching my book, *Golf Greatness*: <fact or experience nugget>."

But if you go in with both barrels blazing and tell people, "Buy my book, *Golf Greatness*, it's only $14.95 and it tells you everything you need to improve your golf game," you won't get a good reception. In fact, you'll get "flamed"—verbally attacked—and some of the list's most important members will cut you off with a "bozo filter" that sends your messages straight to the trash, unread.

The subtle pitch is not as hard as it seems. I've been doing it for years and have built my business on it. Here's an example of one of my posts that promotes a book.

To: self-publishing@yahoogroups.com
From: Shel Horowitz <shel@frugalfun.com>
Subject: Re: Struggling to write press release
Cc: <the person who posted the original request (whom I
quote in the first few lines)>
Bcc:

> If I found a good book with viable examples of
> press releases written to promote the release
> of non-fiction books, I could probably figure
> this out. However, none of the books I've read
> offered such examples.

As John pointed out, I have an entire chapter in Grassroots
Marketing: Getting Noticed in a Noisy World that tells, step
by step, how to write press releases. Just for the heck of it,
I counted the examples (some are full releases, some are
headline and lead):
* 8 nonfiction book releases
* 2 author appearances (one for a poetry reading and one for
a hypothetical appearance by Charles Dickens)
* 7 from outside the book industry: fine art, nonprofit/
government, activist, chiropractic, etc.

The majority of these were real life examples that I had been
hired to create (or, in one case, was about one of my own
books)

Oddly enough, I didn't use any fiction examples, although
one of the NF was a cat trivia puzzle book, whose slant is
more like fiction.

Just one of 39 chapters, BTW, 6 of which focus on getting
media coverage.
--

Shel Horowitz, shel@frugalfun.com, 800-683-WORD/413-586-2388

News releases, web copy, brochures, newsletters, ad copy, resumes, etc.
Award-winning books on marketing, ethics, and entrepreneurship
http://www.frugalmarketing.com / http://www.principledprofit. com

---

LEARN AND ACT FROM OTHERS' POSTS

The best groups not only give you a marketing platform but also expert advice and opportunities. In the August 2006 *PMA Independent*, Maggie Anton Parkhurst, <http://pma-online.org/scripts/shownews.cfm?id=1368> describes how following up on two different discussion list posts got coverage in two different issues of *Library Journal* for her self-published debut novel *Rashi's Daughters: Book One-Joheved*, <http://www.rashisdaughters.com>, and how that led to a big feature story in *U.S. News and Word Report*-and a very nice sales spike.

CREATE IRRESISTIBLE SIGS

Notice the "sigs" (signature blocks) in the posts above. That's the place where you're allowed to put in a *brief* commercial message. Usually just a line or two in the midst of your contact information.

Your e-mail software should be able to place a sig—the good programs even let you choose among several variations—at the bottom of every message, automatically. I recommend that the sig give readers a reason to visit your website, or at least your URL, address, phone, and some statement of how you can help.

CONSIDER A LEADERSHIP ROLE

All of these e-mail and web-based communities need someone (or a group of someones) to administer them. If you have more time than money, operating one of these communities in your niche is a terrific way to get known, branded, and bought from. My cyber-friend John Audette was able to grow and sell two successive Internet businesses for several million dollars each, largely on the strength of the reputation he established as moderator of the now-defunct Internet Sales Discussion List. And it's much easier to establish a powerful reputation as the co-leader or re-placement leader of an existing group than to start from scratch.

UNDERSTAND DELIVERY AND OPEN FAILURES

Even a few years ago, it was pretty much a given that when you e-mailed someone, that person would receive your message. In the rare cases where an e-mail didn't go through, you'd get a failure notice.

But a lot has changed with e-mail, and you can no longer be certain. You can only be absolutely sure your mail was seen if you receive either an answer or a return receipt (if you requested one, that is). E-mail delivery is uncertain because you may have set off a spamfilter (either installed by the user or the Internet provider), you might have been caught in a spammer blacklist (which could block the entire range of IP addresses assigned to your ISP), the recipient is using a challenge-response spamblocker where your message is only delivered if you click on a website, or the recipient is simply so overwhelmed with e-mail that your message got to the inbox but wasn't noticed. (I receive hundreds of e-mails every day, and that happens to me all-too-frequently.)

So if you send something that needs a response, and you don't get one, a polite phone call may be in order. Often, you'll find that either your message didn't get through, you didn't receive the answer, or it's waiting unread and unnoticed.

There are things you can do to increase delivery rate. Please visit <http://www.frugalmarketing.com/m9-10.shtml> for an article I've written on how to improve your chances

Finding Discussion Groups

Perhaps the most powerful marketing tool on the Internet other than hyperlinking is the ability to identify and participate in com-munities of interest in narrow niches—reaching anywhere from a handful of people to tens of thousands every time you post. There are groups for every imaginable interest group.

There is, unfortunately, no such thing as a complete directory of discussion lists or e-zines/newsletters.

Probably the easiest way to get involved is to visit Yahoogroups <http://www.yahoogroups.com>

Because they're easy to set up and cost nothing to run (if you tolerate Yahoo's ads), hundreds of thousands of e-mail discussion groups and announce-only newsletters have been set up on Yahoogroups (and the two predecessor companies it absorbed, Onelist and Egroups). As we've already discussed, discussion lists and newsletters are extremely powerful marketing mechanisms. Yahoogroups is the easiest place to locate appropriate groups.

Yahoogroups has the largest number, but it has many competitors: Topica.com, which has similar feature sets but fewer groups (and which has shifted heavily toward paid newsletters and away from discussion groups); old-style Internet discussion lists dating back before the dotcom days (these groups tend to have a very short fuse when people post commercial messages; you can often spot them by a name that ends in -L, such as Copyeditor-L); discussions run by the major online services like AOL/Compuserve; newsgroups; wikis (collectively-written websites—more on these later); dozens of commercial services such as Constant Contact or Get Response, (which I use for most of my newsletters); and thousands of private servers that include mass mailing hosting and/or web-based forum capabilities as part of the web-hosting package.

Rather than spending a gazillion hours trying to locate the right groups, I'd suggest joining a few Yahoogroups and then after you become known, posting a question about whether there are other similar groups you should know about.

Look for groups that have at least a few hundred members and at least a dozen posts per week, that allow you to post your sig, and that have a high signal-to-noise ratio.

Your Own E-Newsletter

As mentioned in the website chapter, you can't assume that people will seek your website out again even if they intend to. By getting their permission to send them your newsletter, you are able to get a subtle marketing message to them every time you publish. Plus there are other advantages:

Fresh content for your site when you archive each issue.
- New prospects if your newsletter is so good that others pass it along.
- A built-in focus group for feedback on such things as book titles, cover designs, website usability, etc.
- An audience for special offers such as discounts on damaged or prerelease books, holiday specials, joint-venture promotions, etc.
- Direct revenue streams through product sales (some people are phenomenally successful at this) and ad sales.
- Something to trade when you propose (or are approached for) joint ventures: the ability to be featured in your newsletter and reach your audience.

I even hired my wonderful assistant, who has been working with me for years, by announcing the position and pay rate in my newsletters; I received 17 responses and made an excellent choice.

I find that my three monthly newsletters combined take five or six hours a month: writing the articles (one in each of my Frugal Tips, two for Positive Power of Principled Profit), adding the list of new articles on my sites, adding any special announcements or ads slated for that issue, setting up the table of contents, and running the whole thing through a spamchecker (and adjusting the content to bring the score down). This doesn't count the time I spend with a book I'm reviewing in Positive Power, but does include the time I spend writing the review. The actual writing goes fast for me; it's rare that I spend more than two hours writing my four short articles. It's the other stuff that slows it down.

I use the previous issue to set up the new issue, so I don't have to recreate the format or retype the administrative information. Still, I will freely confess that though they've sold quite a few books over the years, my newsletters are not a cash cow. Those who make buckets of money from their newsletters seem to have a constant stream of new products and joint ventures, and a list that's "wired to buy."

Articles and Excerpts, Including Wikis

As a book author, you have an easy time generating shorter content: you can repackage some of your book as articles, excerpts, tips lists, etc. Sometimes, you won't even have to rewrite, and sometimes you'll need to spend a bit of time tweaking. But either way, you're poised to take advantage of the web's hunger for content. Offer your articles and excerpts to websites that reach your target audience, and place them in some of the article syndication sites that exist only to distribute content to web and print publishers in need of fresh material. You get "paid" through a resource box at the bottom that provides your contact information and reasons to visit your website.

Note that if you publish traditionally, your contract may not allow you to place excerpts—but there's certainly not going to be a prohibition on creating and placing original articles.

Dorothy Thompson <http://www.dorothythompson.net> notes that you can also easily syndicate by contacting appropriate venues directly.

> The most successful grassroots approach I've taken to sell my book, *Romancing the Soul*, was to become an expert in my field by writing articles on my field of expertise. As the book is geared toward relationships, I started writing as many articles on the soulmate experience that I could. Once I had a few under my belt, I started querying as many relationship magazines, online dating sites that offer relationship articles, and whenever an opportunity would come up that my articles would fit into, as I possibly could.

She located publications via Google, concentrating on markets that would syndicate her articles to other sites and publications.

As author of an article, you benefit not only from exposure to the site or newsletter's readers, but also from links—including, of course, the link from the high-traffic site that's offering your article around. And sometimes, as Ed Smith, author of *Sixty Seconds to Success* <http://www.brightmoment.com>, delightedly found out, you can actually get "discovered" through these articles:

> I am in the US and post articles on various free article-posting sites. One of my articles was picked up by a daily newspaper

in Africa and resulted in additional requests for articles from Africa. This in turn resulted in inquiries about my book and this in turn resulted in selling foreign rights to my book in Africa. So we never know where an article posting will lead and the benefits that will come of it.

Wikis

Wikis are a special case. Wiki is a technology that lets anyone post an article, and anyone else modify it. I've always been nervous about trying it, because of others' ability to change my work. But I find more and more often that when I'm doing a web search, I end up on a wiki, usually Wikipedia, which has collected a tremendous amount of information on a vast array of subjects. And the information has *usually* appeared to be accurate, as best as I can determine. If you cite a wiki in research, it's a good idea to look for some independent verification.

Certainly if you're a how-to author, wikis would be worth investigating, especially since if you contribute, you've created a link back from a site with very high traffic. But monitor it regularly to make sure no one's distorting your words.

Chats, Teleseminars, Webinars, and Podcasts

Audio and video online have been touted as The Next Big Thing for a while now, and they do seem to be coming into their own. Find someone to interview you either about a topic covered in your book, your life as a writer, or perhaps the back story of how you wrote your book, invite people to listen either for a fee or at no cost over a free conference line, record the call and publish it as a podcast, listing it in as many directories as possible, including iTunes. You can also sell or give away the MP3 of the recording, either on CD/DVD or as a downloadable file.

Or do a "virtual book tour," where you appear as a guest on other people's websites, blogs, chats, or conference calls, in a concentrated period. You get to reach new audiences, the site owner gets hot content, and the site's audience gets to rub virtual shoulders with you, the celebrity of the moment.

Scrapbooker Angie Pederson of <http://www.scrapyourstories. com> had good luck with this: "I did a two-week, 15-site Virtual Book Tour this spring, which resulted in 5000+ message board views, and reached visitors in the US, the UK, and New Zealand."

You can set up your own virtual book tour by approaching appropriate website owners and bloggers, or hire a specialty publicist such as Steve O'Keefe's Patron Saint Productions <http://www.patronsaintpr.com> or Penny Sansevieri's Author Marketing Experts <http://www.amarketingexpert.com/>.

Other People's Blogs

Many blogs allow comments, including some from major news organizations. Your comment must be a real comment on a blog entry, discussing the post and not simply putting out a promotional message. But of course you can close it with your sig, including a link back to your site. I've been doing this a lot with my ethics campaign.

Yahoo, MSN Hotmail, AOL, Mac.com

These colossuses of the Internet world allow plenty of promotional possibilities.

Yahoo: Yahoo started as a directory of other websites—the first web search tool that really caught on. And plenty of people still search on Yahoo, though Google has far outstripped it. Yahoo has evolved into a kind of concierge of the web, allowing the user to create a MyYahoo page: a highly individualized experience that makes it easy to set up personalized news feeds, events listings, and favorite games that reflect your personal interests. MSN Hotmail and AOL/Compuserve have added similar features.

Hotmail: Every marketing textbook writer's favorite example of viral marketing, Hotmail was the first to offer free e-mail on a massive scale. Meanwhile, Microsoft attempted to capitalize on the popularity of AOL by setting up its own competing service, MSN (Microsoft Network). After Microsoft bought Hotmail, the two services were combined.

AOL: Long before the Internet was opened up to the general public, there were online utilities, which provided access to cyberspace but did not connect among each other or to the wider Internet. In the early 1980s, Compuserve was the largest of these. Then came AOL with its much easier interface and intuitive screen names (Compuserve addresses had been a long series of numbers), not to mention free starter disks distributed in huge numbers. Once AOL added the ability to connect with the existing Internet, its growth was phenomenal. Some years later, the company bought Compuserve, and later merged with Time-Warner.

A Yahoo or Hotmail free e-mail account or an AOL basic account (three hours of use per month) gives you an alternative address, useful in some situations. And each of these has numerous members-only discussion groups, as well as classified ad boards, chats, Instant Messaging, and so forth—all of which you can used in the same ways that you'd use other discussion groups. Many of these communities also have volunteer slots, which allow high visibility (in exchange for a substantial investment of time) and in some cases have expanded into paying jobs. For Mac users, Apple's mac.com community is another option.

All these services also allow user profiles, which might attract some attention for your book. Just don't put an e-mail address in any publicly accessible place on Yahoo or its competitors; it will be spammed without mercy.

Major and Niche Websites as News Media

Believe it or not, it's possible to get news or feature coverage on major websites. My Frugal Fun book, *The Penny-Pinching Hedonist*, is "sexy" in the Internet world. It's been featured at various times on the home pages of MSN Hotmail, AOL, and Paypal (the eBay-owned payment gateway), among other places. Paypal actually solicited my book to feature when I set up my account; the others mostly found me through my own sites or a link from a news story. The Hotmail placement sold 60 e-books (and generated a massive spike in Google ad revenues) the first time it ran, and usually results in a dozen or two more sales whenever they repeat it.

So don't hesitate to send announcements to these sites, especially if you're a member. You never know what will happen.

Beyond the biggest sites, you'll likely find dozens if not hundreds of niche sites that can promote your book to a very targeted audience. Here's how David A. Hall of Mapletree Publishing <http://www.mapletreepublishing.com> used this technique:

> One book on our list is a story about a Boy Scout troop that had its troop American flag go up on the last Challenger mission (*Threads of Honor*). It got a great review by *Boys' Life*, so I did a search on the Internet of Boy Scout-related web sites and e-mailed all of them, telling them about the review and urging them to list the book. A number of them took me up on it. Some of them linked to Amazon because they were affiliates. One of them later wrote an unsolicited review on Amazon and put it on his Listmania list, and we saw increased online sales... Those web sites still list the book to this day...We also had a similar response with *Homeschooling: Take a Deep Breath—You Can Do This!*...One of these web site contacts garnered us a favorable review in *Homeschooling Horizons* magazine in Canada, which led to bookstore orders from Canada besides increased Internet sales.

Similar strategies can work well in the "blogosphere," as Pam Schwagerl of Tsaba House <http://www.tsabahouse.com> discovered. She solicited reviews from 45 blogs that she located on various blog search engines.

> About 40 of them agreed to do so and felt quite honored. All of the reviews have been fabulous and the added exposure has created more sales.

Other Mega-Sites

I've heard from many publishers that it's possible to sell books on eBay, half.com, and similar sites. My only attempt, to sell full cases of a now-obsolete book, met with no bidders.

About.com is a marvelous information portal that combines an encyclopedia and a virtual community for each subject; their "guides" (community leaders) are often very open to letting you share your expertise.

The Well, founded in 1985, was one of the largest of the old Internet communities that predate the dotcom era: a "virtual water cooler" for thousands of people in the San Francisco Bay / Silicon Valley area. It still exists at <http://www.well.com>

Also founded in San Francisco, Craig's List <http://www.craigslist.com> offers local searches in various major cities. While it's commonly used to find house sitters or rides to share, there's no reason it couldn't be used to organize book-discussion groups, for instance.

Joint-Venture E-Mails

In a joint venture, you each bring something to the table. As an example of a common JV, someone contacts you about a new product they're marketing, and you decide it's something you can promote. So you send an announcement to your newsletter subscribers, using an affiliate link, and the product marketer pays you a percentage of the sales you generate (often as much as 50 percent).

Another common scenario: Someone is doing a best-seller campaign (see the Amazon chapter) and asks you not only to drive sales, but also to contribute an electronic download as one of the bonus incentives. You've now put your name and site in front of all the readers of all the newsletters involved in the campaign, and stand to gain newsletter subscriptions and/or product sales.

And Beyond...

Again, this is not intended to be a comprehensive list. Internet strategies change every day, as new technologies come online, and new tools that harness them become popular. But this list should certainly get you started!

Chapter Eight

Hook In the Traditional Media

- *Why you want publicity*
- *The changing media landscape*
- *What the media needs*

Publicity is getting the word out about your product, service, and/or ideas. It brings visibility, credibility, opportunity, and sales.

Publicity provides the seal of approval of a trusted outside source: a journalist. Like testimonials and awards, this third-party validation helps the buyer choose your book in the crowded marketplace. It also means that a lot more people hear about your book. And sometimes, publicity leads to more contacts that advance your career: a meeting planner contacts you to see about doing a speech, a different journalist sees the story and wants to cover you as well, a company president sees the article and decides you're the perfect consultant to get that company out of a rut.

The Changing Media Landscape

Until recently, publicity usually meant mass media: magazines, newspapers, large-audience radio and TV stations—plus maybe a few print newsletters, college radio stations, and local cable TV shows. These days, all those choices are still there (and getting coverage is a challenge because everyone wants it).

But the universe is now much broader: Creative authors and publishers can get valuable publicity in small newsletters, e-zines, blogs, websites, e-mail and Internet discussion groups or forums, teleseminars, podcasts, low-power FM radio shows, satellite radio, Internet radio, niche and trade magazines, regional media... and to top it off, it's so easy these days to make your own media. Production quality that used to require hundreds of thousands of dollars can now be done for little or nothing (or, in the case of video, a few hundred dollars).

And you as an author ought to be participating in these democratized media as well as creating your own media in at least a few of these channels.

For myself, as of this writing, here's what I do:

- Publish three monthly e-zines with combined circulation of over 9,000
- Host a radio show twice a month on a local low-power FM station (my goal is to take it national within a year or so, and the meantime, I intend to start podcasting some of the archives)
- Blog about one to three times per week
- Participate actively on three e-mail discussion lists
- Several times a month, contribute to someone else's newsletter or blog, submit an article to some of the free-content sites, and/or am a featured guest on a teleseminar
- Host my own teleseminars (at no cost) a couple of times per year
- Own and oversee the operation of nine websites, three of which use a voluntary audio clip on the home page

And I also seek publicity in the traditional media, which means that I:

- Respond to over a dozen (usually more like 20) reporter requests for people they can interview every month
- Write and distribute several press releases per year
- Do anywhere from two to ten radio interviews in a typical month
- Write several letters to the editor per year (I've even had a few published in *The New York Times*)
- Make myself available to journalists who contact me through my websites, books, articles, etc.

This may sound like a full-time publicity blitz, but it's only a fraction of what's possible. And all of this together usually takes under 20 hours per month—or an average of one hour per business day devoted solely to promoting myself.

Can you handle an hour a day? It's worth it! I just went to Google (July 12, 2006) and searched for "shel horowitz" (in quotation marks, which means exact match). There are 61,500 hits! Anyone who wants to find me will not have any trouble.

What the Media Needs

If you want to get media publicity, you need to supply three things:

1.   A strong news angle
2.   The ability to use the story easily
3.   Evidence of your relevant credentials—formal or informal

Let's look at these one at a time.

NEWS ANGLE

The media do not care about you, and do not care about your book. The media care about generating sufficient ad revenue to be profitable, and their content—news/entertainment—is their vehicle for achieving those profits. So their goal is to keep their audience coming back for more so they can deliver this audience to their advertisers. And that means they look for stories that entertain, inform, and/or scare. For radio and TV, they also seek a mediagenic personality: someone who sounds—and, for TV, as well as for radio stations that also use visuals on their websites, also looks—comfortable on the air.

This usually means someone who can speak in sound bites: little quick hits that make a point in a way that's interesting. If you're the kind of interviewee who gives long, complicated, hard-to-follow answers, get some media training to be able to boil your message down to its essence and keep things brief and upbeat (I can help you with that—see the Appendix).

Topical "hooks" are also good. If you can tie your pitch to a current, active story, your chances of getting press are much better. Look for ways to be the local angle on a national story, to examine trends, or to establish a celebrity connection. But if the tie is too tenuous, you'll be laughed away.

EASE OF USE

Journalists are some of the most overworked people around. Every day, each reporter and editor at a major daily newspaper is trying to function under a deluge of probably 300–500 press releases. And they have to get out a certain number of stories, most of which are already assigned. If a journalist is researching and writing four articles in a day and has to spend at least a couple of hours going through e-mail and faxes and mailed envelopes, the *only* ones that get any attention are the ones that make things as easy as possible. This is no-brainer stuff, but you'd be amazed at how many people don't cover the basics. So I'll repeat them here:

First of all, include your phone number(s) and e-mail address or contact link in every media contact and on your website. Check your messages frequently and respond quickly if you've got an inquiry from a journalist. Many publicists recommend including your cell phone; however, mine is rarely on and the voice-mail can take hours or days to register, so I generally don't give that number out unless I'm planning a road trip.

Include the pertinent facts in your media piece: the "5Ws" sacred to journalists (Who, What, Where, When, Why, and sometimes How), the news angle, web links that back up your claim, availability of photos or other illustrative material (called, generically, "art" by print journalists) as well as bio, backgrounders, and so forth, maybe a quotation or two that they can lift. You could even make audio or video clips available.

And finally, write clearly and with interest. If your press release is real news rather than feature-oriented, learn and use AP style. If it's a feature, hook the reader in immediately with a compelling story. Your press release or pitch letter literally has only a few seconds in front of the journalist to make him or her read further (and in many cases, all you have is a 50-character headline in a long sequence of e-mails). Every journalist is going to be looking for reasons to hit the delete button or toss your release into the recycle bin.

CREDENTIALS

Journalists want to know that you're someone who can be trusted to know what you're talking about. Fortunately, there are many ways to establish yourself as a valid source—some of them obvious, and some less so. Here's an incomplete list.

- *Academic or Professional Expert.* If it's a medical issue, a relevant degree is almost essential, unless you have, for example, a dramatic story of self-healing through unorthodox methods. However, for most other news stories, you can establish credibility in other ways.

- *Work Authority.* A company owner or C-level executive always carries weight. Depending on the story, a lower-level manager might also have credibility. For stories such as whistleblowing on shoddy construction practices, even a line employee may be the perfect media source.

- *Eyewitness.* If you've survived a fire, a hostage-taking, or a train wreck (or other gruesome event), or were near enough to describe the event, you're golden.

- *Inventor/Trend-Spotter.* When a new trend starts and you can show you had a lot to do with it, the media will want to talk to you. And you don't have to be the actual inventor if you're positioned as if you are. Bill Gates gets tons of media coverage, even though Gates not only purchased most of Microsoft's products already developed but also completely dismissed the potential of the Internet for several years.

- *Self-Proclaimed Expert.* Think about the guy who prepares the annual Worst-Dressed Celebrities list. He's an expert on fashion because he says he is. You, as the author of a book, have already indirectly declared yourself an expert on the subject of your book. Maybe it's time to be more direct about it. On the basis of my books and articles, I've claimed expertise over the years on business ethics, frugal fun, frugal marketing, environmental sustainability, and other topics. And I've gotten a ton of national, local, and even international press!

- *Activist.* Whenever you take on a larger issue, your group needs a spokesperson. This is an excellent way to gain publicity while making the world better—if it's an issue you're serious about anyway. When I started a local campaign to block a particularly nasty housing development that would have ruined a state park, I was quoted in something like 50 news stories over the next year. Of course, I also gave a year of my life to the campaign!

- *Candidate*. Running for office is newsworthy. The larger the office, the more newsworthy you'll be—but only if the media takes your campaign seriously. Just ask Dennis Kucinich, the Ohio Congressman who ran a serious, issue-focused campaign for president in 2004, and was basically ignored by the mainstream media. However, even if you're a nobody, and even if you're running for an obscure position like sewer commissioner, you can get local press if you understand how to work the media.

- *Celebrity*. Shallow though it is, celebrity attracts media. I know one woman who got a story in the paper because she had been Madonna's massage therapist. If there's any connection to the famous, let the media know. Of course, if you *are* a celebrity or can position yourself as one, that's much easier. And if you're a celebrity who writes a book— there's a long list of them, including many past presidents, rock stars, movie stars, and so forth—your book gets taken a lot more seriously than the same book by an unknown author would be.

But some of the above list has nothing to do with promoting my book, you say. On the surface, that's true. But actually, a book is not only a great aid to getting coverage for these types of activities, but, as you get known, these activities can also promote your book. Give some thought to how you can approach things holistically and create synergy around your book and your other goals. It's not all that hard.

Four Tools to Attract Journalists' Attention

There are many ways to get journalists interested in your story. Here are four of my favorites.

PRESS RELEASES

A press release typically goes out to many journalists (though you may benefit by customizing certain aspects—if, for instance, there's a local angle such as "Former Atlanta resident").

Remember—"I've published a book" is not news. It happens roughly 200,000 times a year in the United States alone—that means 548 new books vying for publicity every single day. Thus, for books, most of the time, you won't try to pitch the book as news, but as a feature aimed at the lifestyle departments. For these, you look for "the story behind the story": the entertaining, shocking, titillating, knowledge-expanding, or fear-inducing tidbit that makes the reporter sit up and take notice.

Also note that for each piece of marketing copywriting, you need to know exactly whom you're aiming at. Of course, you want to present differently to audiences that are obviously different, like *The New Yorker* and the *National Enquirer*—but are you aware that you should slant your material differently even within a category? If you think the same pitch will work for all women's magazines, and you send the same press release to *Woman's Day* (frugal homemakers), *House Beautiful* (upscale high-earning women in well-established households) and *Cosmopolitan* (upscale and single), your stuff will be discarded by all of them. That's why the first question I ask my clients is "Who is your audience?" The more carefully you segment your press release, the better it will work.

This e-mailed press release (with a few variations for audience tweaking) about a promotion I did in 2003 for one of my own books went to only twelve media outlets, and got coverage in seven of them, including three extended feature stories. Every media outlet was a trade magazine in the publishing industry.

International Virtual Booksigning Generates In-Store Excitement Levels...in Cyberspace

Hadley, MA: Everyone loves it when an author comes to town. Bookstores sell plenty of books, authors meet their fans, and buyers get signed first editions. But what if you don't happen to live near the right bookstore?

For his sixth book, Principled Profit: Marketing That Puts People First, Shel Horowitz wanted to involve people around the world. "This book is creating such excitement that people are literally buying it right out of my hands. I wanted to generate the same kind of excitement internationally, online." The 46-year-old author and marketing consultant created a day-long "virtual booksigning" at Amazon.com.

What's exciting people about the book? A few of the key ideas:
Businesses can succeed by combining honesty, integrity and quality--surpassing customers' expectations--and building real relationships with people

Consumers can influence companies to be ethical and support their values

Marketing doesn't have to be a cost center; businesses can actually get paid to do their own marketing

In the abundance paradigm, there's enough to share--and that means that competitors--even such warriors as Apple and IBM or FedEx and the U.S. Postal Service--actually expand the entire market by working together

While some authors have signed bookmarks or bookplates, Horowitz wanted to add value to the book itself. Participants--who flocked in from France, Austria, India, Britain, Canada, Malaysia, Hong Kong, and the United States--received a complimentary e-book version directly from the author, with all 92 URLs hotlinked.

Horowitz built more excitement by asking readers to "make marketing history" and help him break the Top 100, just for one day--a probable first for a self-published business book competing on its own merits (as opposed to offering a bunch of bonuses). The book rocketed from an Amazon. com overall rank of 1,558,475—all the way to #83 (and #12 for business books). "I got fan letters and good wishes from around the world. It really felt like bringing the bookstore community into Cyberspace." (After the event, the book settled in the high four figures.)

By asking newsletter publishers such as David Frey of Marketing Best Practices and Eva Rosenberg of Tax Mama to spread the word, Horowitz estimates he reached at least 200,000 people.
The book has received other acclaim. A major airline made a significant purchase for distribution by the company president. And Horowitz collected 55 prepublication endorsements, including Jack Canfield and other best-selling authors, successful entrepreneurs, consumer advocates, national speakers--even a former U.S. Cabinet member.

While the book's Top 100 ranking was fleeting, the event "created a buzz. I'm still seeing residual sales after the event is over--and I got 200,000 people talking about this important new book. It was better 'attended' than any flesh-and-blood bookstore appearance I've ever done," Horowitz said.

More information about Principled Profit, including a full press kit, is available at <http://www.principledprofit. com>. Journalists: Horowitz is available for interviews; review copies are available on request.
Contact: Shel Horowitz, shel@principledprofit.com, 413-586-2388 (U.S. Eastern Time)

Principled Profit: Marketing That Puts People First, ISBN 0961466669, $17.50. Distributed to the trade by Beagle Bay Books and available through Ingram, Baker & Taylor

Screenshots of the book's progress to the best-seller list on Amazon during the alternative virtual book signing are available at <http://www.principledprofits.com/amazon-pics.html>.

These are some actual press releases I've written for author and publisher clients. Let's start with my favorite press release of all time. (On that one, because of the client's concern for privacy, I have disguised the names, title and contact data.) Note that this release was written long before identity theft became a well-known problem. If I were writing today, I'd definitely tilt it toward that issue.

For Release: On Receipt
Contact: Karen Kelly (phone and e-mail contacts)

It's 10 O'clock—Do You Know Where Your Credit History Is?

ST. PAUL, MN: It's 10 o'clock—Do you know where your credit history is? How about your employment records? Your confidential medical information?

How would you feel if you found out this sensitive and should-be-private material is "vacationing" in computer databanks around the world—accessible to corporate interests who can afford to track down and purchase it, but not necessarily open to your own inspection?

According to electronic privacy journalist and technology consultant Mortimer Gaines, this scenario is all-too-common. In a groundbreaking but highly readable new book, *Information Attack: Privacy at Risk,* Gaines explores the twin issues of privacy in an ever-more-wired world, and citizen access to crucial information that governments or corporate conglomerates might prefer to keep hidden.

Gaines, author of over 20 previous books including the acclaimed *Internet Guide* series (Windows Press, 1993–94), is not a rabid privacy nut. He recognizes that consumers often gain value by sharing personal information, in order to take advantage of express car rentals or frequent flier programs, for instance. But Gaines suggests the transaction should be voluntary, freely given in exchange for a clear benefit.

When, for example, America Online mines data from its customer records and combines it with outside market research to create—and sell—precise demographics with specific identifying information (p. 143), Gaines feels the transaction exploits the consumer, who sacrifices privacy and gets nothing in return. Gaines is equally cogent on issues of citizen access to government and corporate records.

Information Attack: Privacy at Risk, ISBN 0-00000-00-X, includes detailed references to specific websites, a comprehensive index, and a six-page bibliography. The 336-page 6"x9" trade paperback is available directly from the publisher for $25 plus shipping at (phone), <http://www.domain.com>, or at your favorite bookstore.

Journalists: to obtain a review copy and/or interview the author, please contact Karen Kelly (phone and e-mail contacts).

###

This is for a novelist who had hired a PR firm, so we put the publicist as the contact for extra credibility.

For Release: On Receipt
Contact: Cate Cummings (phone and e-mail contacts)

Kidnapping...Terrorists...A Foreign Land: Carinci's Latest Suspense Thriller Chases Danger across the Emerald Isle

Will Frank and Joey Luanturco survive their first big
assignment in their new private investigation business—a
deadly kidnapping search-and-rescue that brings them deep
into the Irish terrorist underground?

Frank Luanturco started the brothers' new business after
Frank's near-death experience. They haven't been in
business very long before they're hired to track down a
father and daughter kidnapped in Ireland. Leaving loving
family members behind, they head across the ocean and
into a world of intrigue, suspense, and danger.

> Quickly, I hid behind a large metal tank, trying to blend
> into the room but knowing I had reached the end of my
> rope. I could hear the gunman in pursuit, not fast but
> deliberate. After all, he had the gun—I was in the room
> with only one way out...My back stung, but the pain was
> not intense. So I was sure that the bullet had only grazed
> my back. I stayed focused, knowing I would only get
> one shot at escaping with my life. Just a split second of
> opportunity.
>
> (From *A Second Chance* by John Paul Carinci)

A Second Chance is John Paul Carinci's second published
suspense novel; he has several more forthcoming. When
he's not writing, he runs an insurance agency in New
York City (which he drew on in the setting for his earlier
book, *Better Off Dead*—a story of the Mafia taking out life
insurance on the victims of its hit men).

Journalists: To interview Carinci, or to get a review copy
of either of his books, please contact Cate Cummings, Cate
Cummings Publicity & Promotion Group (phone and e-mail
contacts)

Title: *A Second Chance*
Author: John Paul Carinici

Publisher: Writers Advantage
ISBN: 0-595-23524-7
Price: $14.95
Genre: Suspense/Thriller

Here's an example of a seasonal tie-in for a book with several clearly defined audiences: Vietnam veterans, Vietnam protestors, historians studying the 1960s, and people with an interest in photography. This version targeted veterans and their families.

For Immediate Release
Contact: David Chananie (phone and e-mail contacts)

For Veteran's Day: A Powerful Tribute to the Men and Women Who Were Touched by Vietnam

WASHINGTON, DC: On Veterans' Day, we honor those who served. And a startling new photo collection covering the Vietnam War sheds new light on that experience.

Not Yet at Ease: Photographs of America's Continuing Engagement with the Vietnam War tells the story of all sides of the conflict. Over 150 photographs show the agony of war wounds, the triumph over an enemy, the weight of the world on the shoulders of a G.I. after completing a mission, the grim determination of Vietnamese soldiers... the whirlwind of sorrows and pride running fingers across a name on the Wall...and the struggle of Vietnam veterans to keep the memories alive, through such events as the Rolling Thunder gathering.

The shots include not only photos from the battlefields (including rare footage of Viet Cong soldiers), but many other facets of the war: peace activists and family members, for example. In addition to Chananie's evocative photos, the book includes many rare shots that have lain unseen for decades in the vaults of the National Archives. Now, for the first time, these critical historic photos can be seen by a mass audience. Everyone who was touched by the Vietnam War will find something moving, something powerful in this book.

For Chananie, the war is still a very raw memory. "I can't remember anything that so divided our country—that forced all Americans to come to grips with their own definition of patriotism." Like many of his generation, Chananie deeply questions the role of government in the war—and at the same time is amazed by the heroism of the men and women who served. His book makes a fitting tribute to those who served our country either in battle or on the picket lines.

Not Yet at Ease, ISBN 0971138559, $59.95,, scheduled for official release on August 7, 2002—the 38th anniversary of the Senate's passage of the Gulf of Tonkin Resolution— should be available beginning in May. Journalists: to obtain a review copy or to interview Dr. Chananie, please contact CaptureLife Press, 202-904-4804 (phone and e-mail contacts).

This one promotes a children's picture book by an unknown, first-time, self-publishing author.

For Release: On Receipt
Contact: Ted Lish (phone and e-mail contact)

A Children's Picture Book Where the Good Guys Don't Win? Yes, Really!

VICTORVILLE, CA: In a universe of fairy tale endings where everything ALWAYS comes out right—children's picture books—Ted Lish stands apart. His three protagonists go scratching into the sunset after their encounters with the enemy: a giant flea.

Lish's first published book, **The Three Little Puppies and the Big Bad Flea**, is a lighthearted spoof on the old story of the Three Little Pigs. The flea even mutters, "I'm not going down the chimney and get cooked in a pot like that dumb old wolf did."

Beautifully illustrated by popular children's artist Charles Jordan (whose many book credits include *The Whale Comedian, A Pile of Pigs,* and *The Twiddle Twins' Music Box Mystery,* among others), this zany retelling features houses made of feathers, leaves, and old shoes. Perhaps Lish's whimsy is best illustrated by this Afterword: "We're very sorry, but sometimes the Munchweiler elves like to hide in the pictures. Just ignore them."

For Lish, a second grade teacher in Victorville, California, children can learn several lessons from the puppies' failure:
- There will always be adversity
- Listen to your coaches and mentors
- The good guys DON'T always win, but they can learn from their losses
- Sometimes you have to move on

The Three Little Puppies and the Big Bad Flea, ISBN 0-7940-0000-2, $15.95, is available at your favorite bookstore (via Ingram, Baker & Taylor, Quality Books, and Brodart) or directly from the publisher at (toll-free, regular, and fax numbers, e-mail contact, website).

#

This next one demonstrates an author's success in getting significant awards. I have done quite a few releases for this publisher (who happens to be that author's wife). One of the others, for a different author's martial arts book that she was promoting to her local area, brought this comment: "We had several requests for review copies, and also got an appearance for the author on the Sunday morning show on a Baltimore TV station."

For Release: On Receipt
Contact: Sheila Ruth (phone and e-mail contacts)

Still More Honors for Debut Novel, "The Dark Dreamweaver"—Named an iParenting Media "Greatest Product of 2005"

BALTIMORE, MD: Right alongside products from such companies as Scholastic, Fisher Price, Discovery, and Disney, **The Dark Dreamweaver**—the first children's book published by tiny Imaginator Press of Baltimore and its author's debut novel—was named one of the "Greatest Products of 2005" by iParenting Media.

The prestigious competition draws thousands of entries a year, with many of the winners drawn from the ranks of America's top children's product companies: Lego, Hasbro, Baby Einstein, and Nickelodeon , to name a few more examples.
Said publisher Sheila Ruth, "It's very gratifying after taking a chance on an unknown author to see that the book continues to be recognized for quality. I think the sequel is even better, and I look forward to the new book earning accolades as well."

The award is the latest honor for a book that has already been...
- Named an American Booksellers Association Book Sense Children's Pick
- A Finalist for the prestigious Benjamin Franklin Award
- Praised in major review outlets including *Heartland Review*, *Midwest Book Review*, and *Independent Publisher*

In **The Dark Dreamweaver**, David, a boy from our own world, visits Remin, the world of dreams...does battle with the evil sorcerer Thane...and is aided by an imprisoned wizard battling the dream thief and living repeatedly through the lifecycle of a monarch butterfly. Author Nick Ruth and his illustrator, Sue Concannon, have just released Book 2 in the series, **The Breezes of Inspire**, also published by Imaginator.

Journalists: Ruth, Ruth and Concannon are available for interviews and the books are available for review.
The Dark Dreamweaver, ISBN 0974560316
Author: Nick Ruth
Illustrator: Sue Concannon
Clothbound, 224 pages, 5-1/2x8-1/2
Publisher: Imaginator Press
Distributor/Wholesalers: Greenleaf Book Group, Ingram, Baker & Taylor

###

One of the large subsidy publishers, 1stBooks (now known as AuthorHouse), was a client of mine for several years; I did the newsletter and wrote some pages for its old website. When the company snagged a well-credentialed novelist, I was asked to do the press releases because my contact at the company wanted something better than he'd expect from the in-house publicist. Thus, this release talks not only about the book but also the publisher.

For Immediate Release

Contact: Patrick M. East, Director of Author Promotions (contact information)

Murder in the '68 Chicago Riots Rediscovered

BLOOMINGTON, INDIANA: A maverick rabble-rousing City Councilor with ambitions for higher office. The shady owner of Chicago's most discrete sex club, and his even shadier Iranian financier. The professor who moonlights as host of a tell-all TV talk show—and his no-longer-happily-married wife who finds and releases evidence in secret. A successful singer trying to give something back to the ghetto community he came out of…and the young detective and TV reporter who follow clues even across state lines—all tangled in the murder that the city's mayor claimed never happened: a murder during the riots at the 1968 Democratic Convention.

This only scratches the surface of the complex plot turns in Elliott Baker's tenth book, **When the Flowers Died**. Originally written as a teleplay for CBS (which paid $250,000 for the script and never produced it), it is now in book form for the first time, through 1stBooks Library. Featuring several memorable characters and an ending that will surprise even the most dedicated fan of the genre, **Flowers** will be an important work for mystery and police novel fans, students of politics now and then, and anyone who just enjoys a good read.

Baker's work has been praised by novelist Norman Mailer, the New York Times Book Review, Publisher's Weekly, and many others; the actors and directors who've starred in his film and TV scripts read like a who's who of modern cinema (see enclosed biography).

1stBooks Library, founded in 1997, will offer **Flowers** and several other Elliott Baker titles in both electronic download and trade paperback formats. The company, profitable in its first year, has published over 6000 authors in a new model that eliminates inventory management and maintains author control over all rights. **Flowers** can be previewed and ordered at http://www.1stbooks.com/bookview/5649.

Journalists: to interview Baker or obtain a review copy, please contact Pat East at 1stBooks.

#

You'll find quite a number of other book-industry examples in my earlier book *Grassroots Marketing: Getting Noticed in a Noisy World*; only the electronic privacy release is in both.

Press Release Formatting and Distribution: E-mail vs. Postal Mail vs. an Online Post

All of the above examples except my Amazon release are formatted to be mailed postally or faxed (use fax only if the journalist requests it; very few prefer that format anymore). You can also use that format for posting on your own website or through some of the gazillion places to post a press release online (see the section on "Distributing Press Releases," later in this chapter).

When posting online, prepare a list of keywords and a brief summary; many sites request them and you'll want them for the keyword and description metatags on your own site. Some places not only host your press release on their website, but also do an e-mail drop for you. E-mailed press releases have a few extra guidelines:

For starters, I don't waste that precious first screen with the contact information. I put it at the end, instead. Second, while a printed press release may have a really long headline and subhead, in e-mail I have to get my attention-getting message into the first 50 characters of the subject line. I'll write them longer, but I assume that at least some e-mail programs cut them off if they go more than that length. Third, I work really hard to get a clean rating on the spamfilters (for example, <http://www.lyris.com/resources/contentchecker/> and <http://www.ezinecheck.com/check.html>), which means there are a lot of words I censor out of my writing; for books on topics like weight loss, real estate, and sex, I often advise the client not to even bother with e-mail distribution because it's very difficult to write about these and stay away from the forbidden words. And fourth, I make sure that there are straight quotes and apostrophes instead of curly ones, double-hyphens instead of em-dashes, three periods instead of ellipses, and that I use asterisks or other ASCII characters for emphasis instead of bold or italic. Also, I avoid capitalizing whole words.

Here's an example of the same release packaged for postal and e-mail distribution. It does have two words that flagged the spamfilter—"never" and "wife"—but I decided that the spam score of 1.67 was low enough that I didn't have to weaken the content by avoiding those two words. Surprisingly, the word "income" was not flagged. Note that I removed the italic and bold, using asterisks instead.

Print Version:

> For Release: On Receipt
> Contact: David Ambrose (phone, e-mail, and fax contacts)
>
> ### At 54, He Moved Across the World—Because It's Never Too Late For Dreams
>
> CALGARY, ALBERTA: Just as he turned 54, David Ambrose and his wife Melanie left behind their native South Africa to follow a life-long wish and move to Canada.
>
> It's part of Ambrose's deeply held philosophy that happiness is achievable by anyone, at any age. Even after five decades, even watching a rebuilt South Africa rise from the ashes of apartheid, the couple finally made their Canadian dream a reality.
>
> "There is no happiness gene, but everyone deserves and can achieve it," says Ambrose, author of the forthcoming book, **Your Life Manual: Practical Steps to Genuine Happiness** (Revolution Mind Publishing, 2006). "It does not arise out of any outside influence; income, beauty, and fame have nothing to do with achieving happiness."
>
> Ambrose's 240-page book, which includes a full bibliography, index, and list of resources, is divided into four easily accessible parts:
> - A look at the components of a philosophy of happiness, including the Xhosa concept of *ubuntu* (humanness in relation to others).
> - 16 principles to build a happy life, from personal integrity

to the self-help benefits of forgiveness to the tantalizing idea of "good selfishness."

- 15 transformative steps each of us can take to incorporate happiness into our own lives—to become the happy people we are all meant to be.
- Looking at the big picture, the realms of chaos theory, magic, prayer, and even social conventions around the role of women and appropriate response to crime.

David Ambrose harnessed his diverse background in business, information systems, healing arts, and philosophy to create a system of living emphasizing both personal joy and improving the world. A popular speaker and media guest, he has operated websites on self-actualization for over a decade, and draws visitors from around the world.

Journalists: David Ambrose welcomes interview requests; review copies of *Your Life Manual* are available to qualified journalists. See contact information at top of release.

Summary:
Title: *Your Life Manual: Practical Steps to Genuine Happiness*
Author: David Ambrose, **Publisher:** Revolution Mind Publishing, Calgary, Alberta
Websites: <http://www.RevolutionMind.com>, <http://www.LovePeace.com>
Publication Date: March, 2006
ISBN/ Price: 0973936207, $14.95 US/$20.95 Canada

###

E-mail Version:
Subject:
At 54, He Crossed the World--Never Too Late For Dreams (news release)
Body:

Calgary, Alberta: Just as he turned 54, David Ambrose and his wife Melanie left behind their native South Africa to follow a life-long wish and move to Canada.

It's part of Ambrose's deeply held philosophy that
happiness is achievable by anyone, at any age. Even after
five decades, even watching a rebuilt South Africa rise
from the ashes of apartheid, the couple finally made their
Canadian dream a reality.

"There is no happiness gene, but everyone deserves and can
achieve it," says Ambrose, author of the forthcoming book,
"Your Life Manual: Practical Steps to Genuine Happiness"
(Revolution Mind Publishing, 2006). "It does not arise out
of any outside influence; income, beauty, and fame have
nothing to do with achieving happiness."

Ambrose's 240-page book, which includes a full
bibliography, index, and list of resources, is divided into
four easily accessible parts:
1., A look at the components of a philosophy of happiness,
including the Xhosa concept of *ubuntu* (humanness in
relation to others).
2., 16 principles to build a happy life, from personal
integrity to the self-help benefits of forgiveness to the
tantalizing idea of "good selfishness."
3., 15 transformative steps each of us can take to
incorporate happiness into our own lives--to become the
happy people we are all meant to be.
4., Looking at the big picture, the realms of chaos theory,
magic, prayer, and even social conventions around the role
of women and appropriate response to crime.
David Ambrose harnessed his diverse background in
business, information systems, healing arts, and philosophy
to create a system of living emphasizing both personal
satisfaction and improving the world. A popular speaker
and media guest, he has operated websites on self-
actualization for over a decade, and draws visitors from
around the world.

Journalists: David Ambrose welcomes interview requests; review copies of Your Life Manual are available to qualified journalists. See contact information below.

Summary:
Title: Your Life Manual: Practical Steps to Genuine Happiness
Author: David Ambrose
Publisher: Revolution Mind Publishing, Calgary, Alberta
Websites: <http://www.RevolutionMind.com>, <http://www.LovePeace.com>
Publication Date: March, 2006
ISBN: 0973936207
Price: $14.95 US/$20.95 Canada
Contact: David Ambrose, (phone, e-mail, and fax contacts)

A Negative Example: What Not to Do

Remember that I accused the subsidy houses of using generic press releases? This is the first paragraph of an actual two-paragraph press release e-mailed to me on Sunday, May 14, 2006, by a PR agency working for one of the subsidy houses. The names have been changed to protect the guilty, but I left the actual Subject and From lines.

From: "Booksellers Marketing Group" <noreply@hotmail.com>
Subject: Press Release - New Book

[Publisher's City] – 05/13/06-- [Publisher] is proud to announce that it has acquired the rights to publish [Title] by [Author's City] author [Author]. Executive Director [Official's Name] expressed confidence today that [Author]'s book will quickly resonate with audiences: "[Title] is an eloquent work of contemporary fiction that is well-tailored to our characteristic style. [Publisher] champions books by, for, or about those who surmount profound obstacles by turning stumbling blocks into stepping stones. We believe that [Author] is a promising talent of this genre."

The second paragraph was a standard blurb about the publishing company, ending with a generic PR address (without the code to make it clickable) and the clickable link to the publisher's home page.

So what's wrong with that press release?

- This could be about absolutely any novel. Once we've stripped out the identifiers, there's no clue about why this book—or this author—is different and special.
- The subject line doesn't acknowledge that publishing a book is not in itself newsworthy.
- The release has no contact phone number and a useless return address: noreply@hotmail.com. A reporter who wanted to follow up has to notice that reply won't work (or send a reply that bounces), copy the unclickable generic address at the bottom of the message, and paste it into a new e-mail—or go to the website and hunt for the particular title, then track down a contact.
- It was sent on a Sunday, when most lifestyle journalists aren't working—and there would probably be 200 e-mails on top of it by the time the journalist checked on Monday morning.
- Oh, yes, and lacking in content as it was, it still managed to trigger my spam filter. Maybe a better question would be, What's right with it? While this is a particularly poor example, it is, unfortunately, not much worse than the publicity "help" that many subsidy-house authors receive from their publishers.

BY CONTRAST—A PHENOMENAL SUCCESS

Much more positively, my last example, from Ruth Houston, is more successful than any I've written.

The results? Despite a malfunctioning e-mail contact...

- Coverage in 63 national and international newspapers and other news outlets, including *The Wall Street Journal*, *Chicago Tribune*, UPI, Reuters, the news services of Google, Yahoo, and Netscape, and news media in eight foreign countries
- Seven radio interviews, including one with BBC (England)

- Taping of a CNN interview at their New York studio (which got bumped in favor of a special about Vice-President Cheney's hunting accident—a common occurrence if you have the bad luck to be scheduled when a major story has just broken)
- Stories in several blogs
- Foreign-rights inquiry from a French publisher
- Invitations to appear on Ireland's "Late Late Show" and to do a Valentine's Day Infidelity presentation at a local party
- A foreign-rights agent who wants to represent her book at the London Book Fair
- 20 percent increase in website sales
- 30+ percent increase in amazon.com sales, resulting in a full-case order (60 books) versus the typical five to seven copies

While she had the benefit of both a salacious topic and a timely holiday hook, she's also been out in the trenches hustling media for this book over several years. And this campaign was no exception. She writes (in February 2006), "After putting in many 10 and 12 hour days since January on this project, I'm practically brain dead now (but happy with the results)." This time, the Publicity Gods smiled on her.

Her releases are in my opinion very over-formatted and somewhat hard to read, but perhaps for her celebrity-driven audience, that's what they want (also, she sent them by fax, where it's good to create visual interest—but some of the type is awfully tiny for faxing).

Something she did particularly well: the description of each topic is not only different and timely, but is packaged so that any TV or radio producer can read it, verbatim, as a "coming up next" teaser. Also, she squeezes in an offer of two ready-to-go articles that print or Internet publications can just lift, and broadcast media can offer their audiences as an extra.

Here's her release, in two versions:

3 non-traditional Valentine's Day Story ideas

For release before February 14   CONTACT:, Ruth Houston – 718 592-6039

VALENTINE'S DAY, , ,   InfidelityExpert@gmail.com
                                          www.Is-He-Cheating-On-You.com

The Other Side of Valentine's Day

Valentine's Day is the most romantic day of the year. But what if the romance is between your partner and someone else.

"Infidelity doesn't take a back seat on Valentine's Day" says Ruth Houston, infidelity expert, author of *Is He Cheating on You? – 829 Telltale Signs* and founder of *Infidelity Advice.com* . "In fact, it's the, one day when infidelity and extramarital affairs are at their peak., Nationwide, millions of cheaters are buying Valentine's gifts for, or receiving them from a secret lover."

An estimated 50% to 70% of your readers are victims of infidelity.

Tell them about the OTHER SIDE of Valentine's Day.

Interview infidelity expert Ruth Houston on one or (all 3) non-traditional Valentine's Day story ideas below:

- **Valentine's Day is the best time to Catch a Cheating Mate**, If you suspect infidelity, this is the ideal day of the year to "get the goods" on a cheating mate., Let Infidelity expert Ruth Houston explain why., She'll also tell your readers where and how to find tangible proof of an extramarital affair on Valentine's Day.

- **How Valentine's Day Gifts Can Expose a Cheating Husband**
  ** "Cheating husbands can be exposed by the Valentine's Day gifts they give," says Ruth Houston, infidelity expert and author of *Is He Cheating on You?*, Houston tells wives about, 6 gift-related telltale signs.

- **Is Your Valentine the Cheating Kind?****, "Some men are more likely to cheat than others", says infidelity expert Ruth Houston, author of *Is He Cheating on You?* "You can tell by his background, his history, and certain character traits.", Houston's 7-question quiz lets your readers rate their mate's cheating potential to see if their Valentine is the "cheating kind."

**Available as a complete article. To receive, either article, e-mail InfidelityExpert@gmail. com, with "Gifts" or "Cheating Kind" in the subject line., Please include your name, title, and the name and location of your publication.,

To interview, Ruth Houston:
Call 718 592-6039 or e-mail InfidelityExpert@gmail.com

About Ruth Houston

Infidelity expert Ruth Houston is the author of *Is He Cheating on You? – 829 Telltale Signs*, which documents practically every known sign of infidelity. Ruth has been quoted in the New York Times, the New York Post, the Toronto Sun, Cosmopolitan, the Houston Chronicle, MSN Lifestyle,, iVillage and numerous others., Ruth has been a guest on The Today Show, Good Day New York, Telemundo,, BBC, CBC, 1010WINS, TalkAmerica and over 200 radio and TV talk shows in the United States, Canada, Europe, South America, New Zealand, and the Caribbean., For Ruth's complete bio, a book description, or more information on infidelity, visit the PRESS ROOM at www.InfidelityAdvice.com.

# # #

For Immediate Release   CONTACT:, Ruth Houston – 718 592-6039
VALENTINE'S DAY   InfidelityExpert@gmail.com
                         www.InfidelityAdvice.com

Valentine's Day - the Ideal Time to Catch a Cheating Mate

Infidelity expert Ruth Houston can tell you why.

Valentine's Day conjures up images of love and romance. But what if you suspect there's a romance going on between your partner and someone else?, "Valentine's Day is the best time of the year to 'get the goods' on a cheating mate," says infidelity expert Ruth Houston, author of *Is He Cheating on You? – 829 Telltale Signs* and founder of www.InfidelityAdvice.com .,

Interview Ruth Houston to find out:

- What 2 facts about Valentine's Day make it the ideal time to catch a cheating mate
- How these 2 facts can be used to expose a cheating mate
- Tips a wife can use on Valentine's Day to expose her husband's extramarital affair
- Signs that alert a man that, he's being two-timed by the lady in his life
- Signs to look for on Valentine's Day if you suspect a workplace affair
- How Valentine's Day phone calls can give the cheater away
- Why Valentine's Day is the best day of the year to hire a private investigator to follow your cheating mate
- The #1 excuse men use to get away to spend time with their lover on Valentine's Day
- The #1 excuse women use to get away to spend time with their lover Valentine's Day
- The extremes cheaters will go to to see their lovers on Valentine's Day

- How to find the incriminating paper trail for the purchase of Valentine's Day gifts
- Telltale signs that appear shortly AFTER Valentine's Day

To interview, Ruth Houston:
Call 718 592-6039 or e-mail InfidelityExpert@gmail.com

About Ruth Houston:
Infidelity expert Ruth Houston is the author of *Is He Cheating on You? – 829 Telltale Signs*, which documents practically every known sign of infidelity. Ruth has been quoted in the **New York Times**, the **New York Post**, the **Toronto Sun**, **Cosmopolitan**, the **Houston Chronicle**, **MSN Lifestyle**,, **iVillage** and numerous others., Ruth has been a guest on **The Today Show**, **Good Day New York**, **Telemundo**,, **BBC**, **CBC**, **1010WINS**, **TalkAmerica** and over **200 radio and TV talk shows** in the United States, Canada, Europe, South America, New Zealand, and the Caribbean., For Ruth's complete bio, a book description, or more information on infidelity, visit the **PRESS ROOM** at www.InfidelityAdvice.com.

# # #

DISTRIBUTING PRESS RELEASES

There are literally hundreds of places to distribute a press release—where do you start? For most press releases, I recommend combining several methods. Among them:

- Your own website
- free press release sites, such as erleases.com, 247pr.com fastpitchnetworking.com, and prfree.com (there are many others). In general, you will get better results if you make a small donation.
- E-mails to your own reporter contacts whose previous communications with you and/or regular beat have been relevant to the particular story (do not scatter-shoot!)—either including the whole release, formatted for e-mail, in the body of the message, or giving a quick teaser and a link to the posted press release
- Targeted e-mail delivery to journalists outside your own database, using <http://www.DirectContactPR.com>, which allows you to select the categories of media you want to reach and e-mail to them very inexpensively

- Submitting your press release directly to individual media (newspapers, magazines, newsletters, blogs, radio and TV stations, web-only media) through the contact mechanisms on their own websites—a slow and sometimes frustrating process, but worth doing for a handful of key media that are perfect for a particular release

PITCH LETTERS

If you're pitching "cold"—approaching a reporter out of the blue, without previous contact, Ned Barnett, in his Barnett on Book Promotion blog on February 6, 2005 <http://barnettonpublishing. blogspot.com/2005/02/marketing-and-promoting-books-reprint.html>, suggests giving journalists a choice of how to best use you:

> Try to go for one or two things that are easy to say yes to, such as an interview or a column. Your pitch might say, "I can write a column that boils one of the pitfalls down to 750 words, OR, I'm available for interviews. Do either of these options interest you? If not, is there some other way we might work together?"

Personally, I do almost no cold pitching. My favorite pitch letter strategy is to pitch reporters on the stories for which they're actively seeking sources. There's a wonderful service called Profnet that matches journalist queries with authors who can answer them. Aimed at PR professionals, it's quite expensive. However, a much more affordable version of the service, aimed at authors and entreprenuers, gives you the exact same queries for (as of February, 2006) $99 per month; you can learn about it at <http://snipurl.com/nv6p>. This is how I've gotten most of my "big name" clips, among them *The Wall Street Journal*, *The New York Times* (twice) *Entrepreneur* (seven times), *Woman's Day* (three times), the *Los Angeles Times*, even the Associated Press—as well as numerous lesser-known markets.

During 2005 alone, out of 311 responses that I sent (which typically took between 5 and 15 minutes to write, once in a while up to half an hour), at least 65 different journalists responded favorably to my pitch letters in response to their queries—some of them on more than one story over the course of the year. (This doesn't count those who called rather than e-mailed.) I don't have a way to tell for sure, but I am guessing that at least 40 of them resulted in an interview and/or a quote lifted directly from my pitch, and at least 30 actually got into print.

You'll have the best luck if you:
- Respond as quickly as possible (ideally, within an hour of when the query is posted),
- Use a subject line that clearly demonstrates that you're responding to the query, and
- Give a few bullet points of substance

Here are some actual pitch letters that have gotten me coverage (all of which also included an e-mail "sig" with my contact info and a few credentials). I'll start with one that got me into *The New York Times* on February 27, 2005—a bit longer than most, but it did the trick. Note that she states a geographic preference (but not a requirement) that I don't meet, and without lying, I'm able to establish a connection.

At 2:23 PM -0500 1/27/05, ProfNetSearch@prnewswire.com wrote:
**4. BUSINESS: Impact of Volunteerism -- The New York Times (US)
I'm doing a story on how volunteer work and a history of volunteerism may give one job candidate a leg up on another or may make them more attractive when all other factors are equal. I'd like to talk to hiring mangers or supervisors who decided that the volunteer service was something that affected their decision. I'm also looking for experts on the topic of hiring and volunteerism, and for employees who feel they were hired over others because of their volunteer work. The story also focuses on those switching careers who use volunteer work as a way to gain valuable experience and ease the transition from one area to another. New York metropolitan area sources are preferable. No phone calls, please. I'm a freelancer.
Monitored by eWatch

Need leads by: 12:00 PM US/Eastern JAN 31
>>> Eilene Zimmerman (e-mail) URL: http://www.nytimes.com
Hi, Eilene,

In the 27 years that I've been writing resumes professionally, I almost always ask about volunteer activities. Sometimes I structure the entire resume around them, especially if the client is changing careers and the pro bono work is more relevant. While their volunteer work has been a factor for many of clients as they get hired, I can think of one particularly great case history: a housewife returning to the workforce after ten years as a stay-at-home mom. But she was extremely active in the community--and fairly quickly landed a job as executive director of a local human service agency, based almost entirely on her volunteer credentials. She stayed in that job for many years, retiring quite recently. Back in the days when I was actively job hunting, I found my substantial volunteer experience was almost always a point of conversation in interviews.

And even though I haven't been job hunting for a long time, I find the pro bono work I do consistently helps me get marketing consulting and copywriting clients. Examples range from serving on a committee of the local Chamber of Commerce, which has referred several clients to me, to speaking pro bono at various national conferences, which bring me both clients and referrals (including many from well-respected industry professionals). Of course, it also helps make the world better.

These days, much of my volunteer effort is going into spearheading a campaign to change the business climate toward ethics and cooperation; the vehicle is a pledge campaign with a goal of 25000 signatures. <http://www.principledprofit.com/25000influencers.html>

I'm an NYC native (grew up reading the Times) and still have family there, though I've moved about three hours away.

Often, I reply with a few quick bullet points, as in this example:

Subject: Profnet: Getting Customers to Buy Now, Not Later

At 2:31 PM -0400 4/12/05, ProfNetSearch@prnewswire.com wrote:

**27. RETAIL: Getting Customers to Buy Now, Not Later -- Country Business Magazine (US)

I'm seeking experts who can address an audience of small, specialty retailers on the topic of 'changing customers' minds about sales--in terms of getting customers to buy now, rather than later. I'm looking for good strategies that a small (1-2 locations, 5-10 employees) retailer of specialty goods can use in their own operations to help customers make faster decisions about their purchases. Country Business is a monthly trade magazine for the country gift-store owner. No phone calls, please. I'm a freelancer.
Need leads by: 03:00 PM US/Eastern APR 18
>>> Bridget McCrea (e-mail)

Hi, Bridget. I think small retailers can use a few different strategies
* Informational aids, e.g., signs that explain a bit about what makes the item unique, where it's made, etc.
* Extremely knowledgeable and friendly salespeople who can gain a reputation quickly in a small community for the quality of their information and its delivery
* In-store computer with a hard-drive copy of the store's website, so customers can research in depth on any of the products
* Use of testimonials, maybe even accompanied with photos
* Value-packing of multiple products for in-store specials
* Value-adds by cooperating with other retailers

I discuss some of these strategies in my award-winning books, Principled Profit: Marketing That Puts People First (marketing partnerships, adding value) and Grassroots Marketing: Getting Noticed in a Noisy World (informational signage, value pricing, testimonials)

This one got me written up in Colombia's equivalent of Newsweek:

> **8. POLITICS: Valerie Plame Affair -- Semana (Colombia)
> I'm looking for experts to discuss the political implications
> of the Valerie Plame affair. No phone calls, please.
> Need leads by: 10:00 PM US/Central OCT 21
> >>> Camilo Amaya (e-mail) URL: <http://www.semana.
> com/>

Buenos Dias, Camilo,

I am an author and ethics expert who has blogged about
this:
<http://principledprofit.blogspot.com/2005/07/
vengeance-vs-ethics-rove-and-plame.html>, and whose blog
frequently covers the intersection of politics, journalism,
ethics, and business.

My latest book is all about ethics: the award-wining
Principled Profit: Marketing That Puts People First
(which should be out soon in a Spanish-language edition,
incidentally).

If I can help with the story, I'm happy to oblige.

Gracias,

Sometimes, responding to a journalist's query yields an invitation to write an article. That's what happened with this one, which led to a 300-word sidebar in *PR News* (major trade magazine for the PR industry) with a photo, a byline, and a nice credit listing my book title as well as the ethics pledge campaign I started, and with the URL for the campaign.

I didn't get paid for the story, but it took under an hour to write and put me in front of several thousand key players in one of my primary audiences. My intent in writing was that the reporter would write the sidebar (brief accompanying article) and quote me—a tactic I often use when my response to the query is just a bit off from the reporter's requirements. However, I was happy to write the article myself.

Note that this reporter had used me as a source a few times earlier, so I was able to get away with a pretty sparse query. (CSR stands for Corporate Social Responsibility, a key concept in the business ethics arena.)

> **5. BUSINESS: CSR Trends -- PR News (US)
> For a special report on CSR in the March 2 issue of PR
> News, I'm writing about the latest trends in the space
> with real kick-the-tires examples of solid CSR campaigns.
> We keep hearing about how CSR's impact is ascending,
> as investors are now taking a look at CSR efforts equal
> to profitability and financials. Is that so, though? The
> Economist ran a piece recently that stated that much of
> CSR is misguided and that's another element to consider,
> encouraging corporate examples here with corporate
> sources (but welcome agencies, too, of course that specialize
> in this area). PR News is a weekly newsletter for the
> corporate and agency PR professional.
> Need leads by: 12:00 PM US/Central FEB 23
> >>> Matthew Schwartz (e-mail and phone) URL: http://
> www.prnewsonline.com

Hi again, Matthew,

Perhaps you'd be interested in a sidebar or quote about why CSR and ethics in general actually can make a company more profitable, and how businesses can use the Business Ethics Pledge <http://www.business-ethics-pledge.org>

to boost their standing among key stakeholders, including prospects.

I'm happy to help, if you want to go that route.

PITCHING A "THIN" MATCH

The next query shows how I was able to parley a fairly tenuous connection—a query about smoking and the hospitality indus-try—into coverage, leveraging my personal experience as an activist into something that plugged my latest book. Unfortunately, I didn't quote back his original query for some reason, so I don't have it here. But it did get me a nice two-paragraph write-up that included my book title, as part of a much larger story.

From: "Shel Horowitz, ethical marketing expert"
<shel@principledprofit.com>
Subject: Profnet: Nonsmoking Policies as a Marketing
Strategy

Hi, Jon, I approach this from two relevant angles:
As a marketing consultant and author of four books, and
as a nonsmokers' rights activist who changed a smoking-
oriented culture within our local hospitality industry.

I live just outside a big restaurant destination
(Northampton, MA--and for 17 years, I lived right
downtown). Around 1984, I called my city counselor and
suggested that Northampton needed a nonsmokers' rights
ordinance. I argued that the restaurant industry--which
opposed this--would benefit, because many antismokers
would start dining out.
The law passed, setting aside 25% of every restaurant
for nonsmokers. And it turned out that my argument
was correct. In fact, within a few years, the majority of
restaurants in town had gone 100% smoke-free. Later, they
had to by law, but by the time the new law was passed,
about 3/4 of the restaurants were already smoke-free--
because the owners realized, once they separated them out,
that the nonsmoking sections were in far more demand.

The entire industry sector has continued to grow, and every year, several new restaurants open (I believe there are about 70 now, compared to maybe 40 at the time--and this with a population of only 30,000). I think bars have now gone nonsmoking, too.

As a hotel customer, I request nonsmoking rooms, and if they're not available, I usually choose a different hotel. Thus, hoteliers who don't offer this option generally lose my business.

Yes, businesses that don't stress the availability of nonsmoking are definitely missing out on a marketing edge. There's a huge market of health-conscious consumers who don't want to breathe smoke, and who are active spenders living active lifestyles. Another segment has health issues, and may not be as profitable because they may require extra services.

In my award-winning sixth book, Principled Profit: Marketing That Puts People First, I discuss in some detail the idea of niching one's business to a particular demographic. The nonsmoker/antismoker demographic is a very strong one--and businesses that cater to this market can present themselves as caring, customer-focused, health-conscious...and focused, health-conscious...and ethical. The marketing benefits of that approach are vast.

I'm happy to discuss any of this in more detail, and/or to send you a PDF of the book.

Other savvy publicity hounds also know how to get press from a somewhat tenuous connection. Fern Reiss is about the most successful person I know at this; she is constantly in major media, often on a topic that has little to do with her areas of established expertise.

Another master is Jill Lublin, co-author of *Guerrilla Publicity* and *Networking Magic:*

> It is important to look at everything that is unique about you. Use your ethnicity, religion, obstacles, challenges, and anything in the media that you can comment on. I keep my mind open to possibilities. I ask myself – could this be an opportunity for additional publicity? For example, using my best selling book, *Networking Magic*, I took a holiday like Valentine's Day and became an expert in networking for romance. This got me on NBC TV. When I drove an electric car, I used that fact as an opportunity to draw attention to rising gas prices and environmental concerns. This got me on ABC TV, USA Today, NPR, and more.
>
> I volunteered with an 85-year-old woman for five years as a senior companion and got a story in Woman's Day's issue on Acts of Kindness.
>
> I also recommend to clients, say yes to every offer. I was recently asked to do an interview on a Christian radio station about Super Bowl advertising. There were three problems with this: I am not Christian, I know nothing about the Super Bowl, and I am not an advertising expert (I am a publicity expert)—but I did my research and took advantage of getting myself in front of 45,000 listeners. Go for it and keep aware of trends and issues happening in the news. Use everything you've got to reach your sales and publicity goals.

Oh, and one of Jill's coauthors, Rick Frishman of Planned Television Arts (a major New York PR firm), actually got on Oprah because he pitched a client for a segment on bald men, and when the client found out the other half of the show was about short men, he pitched Rick, who's around 5'2".

Of course, sometimes you pitch "cold"—when the journalist isn't looking. The pitch can either be to have a reporter cover you, or to write the story yourself. As you would with a press release, you grab the journalist's attention, show that you understand the particular market and how your story fits into it, and concisely show how the story could be explored.

Alex Carroll is a master at booking and selling on radio. This is the pitch sheet (a flier, not a letter) he uses to book over 100 interviews a year—about 70 percent of the shows he pitches—and to sell $150,000 worth of product in these interviews. (Note: first he calls the producer and gets an agreement to see his stuff. Then he mails this full-color flier. Please see the Appendix for more on his training materials on booking radio gigs and using them to move product.)

It breaks a lot of the rules, not least of which is that broadcast journalists are not readers and don't want a lot of small-print copy—but the power of his subject matter and the way he's crafted his pitch show that resistance to dense copy can melt under the right circumstances. It doesn't hurt that he's already gotten the producers to request it, either.

Available for Interview: **Contact Alex:**
                                            877-733-3888

Ex-Courier Driver Beats 8 of 10 Tickets ...

Author of "Beat The Cops" tells your audience:

- How he beat 6 out of 7 radar tickets
- How it's possible to speed legally
- About an organization that pays speeding ticket fines
- How to beat tickets without going to court
- How to schedule your trial during the cop's vacation
- How to beat camera tickets
- Two things to never do when pulled over
- How to beat air-patrol tickets
- How to beat out-of-state tickets
- Cop's favorite hiding places
- How to beat visually estimated speeding tickets
- If cops still have quotas
- What to do if you don't have time to fight your ticket

... And much more

- **100,000 tickets issued daily nationwide**

Approximately 30 million tickets annually. The vast majority of them are undeserved. Whether victims of speed traps, improper speed limits, faulty radar equipment, quotas or bad police judgement, the effect is the same. They don't deserve the inflated fines and certainly not the outrageous insurance surcharges that follow. Burglars usually get off easier.

- **Average ticket fine: $125**

Municipalities across the country rake in more than $3 Billion each year in ticket fines. Many speed trap towns generate more than 75% of their operating budgets just from speeding tickets. Sadly, law enforcement officers are being used as nothing more than armed tax collector's in many areas.

- **Average insurance surcharge: $1,000 (over 3 year period)**

Insurance companies are the real winners in the ticket business. The figures tell the story: 30 million tickets times $333 (average annual surcharge increase per ticket) equals a yearly windfall of nearly $10 Billion. No wonder the insurance companies were the only ones fighting the repeal of the 55 MPH speed limit in 1996.

- **75% of prepared ticket challengers win**

While 90% of ticket recipients are obediently mailing in their fines, the

majority of the 10% who actually challenge their tickets are winning, and saving themselves a bundle in the process. Why do the ticketed usually roll over ... even though they're often not guilty? Many don't realize how much it'll really cost them, and the rest are intimidated by cops and courts and don't believe they have a chance.

After **former courier driver** Alex Carroll beat 8 of 10 tickets, he realized that fellow motorists just needed a little help and instruction ... and in plain English, not legalese.

Since writing "Beat The Cops, The Guide To Fighting Your Traffic Ticket & Winning," Carroll has become a motorist's advocate and has appeared as a guest on hundreds of radio and TV shows across North America.

He went on to head the California Chapter of the National Motorist's Association and was a leading spokesperson in the organization's successful drive to repeal the national 55 MPH Speed Limit.

His book has sold well over 100,000 copies nationwid

"Beat The Cops" is available for $14.95 by calling 1-800-3-CAN-WIN
Or visit: www.CleanDrivingRecord.com

ADVERTISING TO JOURNALISTS

A number of "show prep services" exist to market interviewees to journalists, and especially radio talk-show hosts and producers. The best known is Radio TV Interview Report (RTIR). Effective, if not cheap, and you get the benefit of free copywriting by people who understand what the media looks for. In my experience, I typically get around 10 radio interviews per ad. You have to decide if the number of sales you'll get from 10 shows is worth the investment, and to make that decision intelligently, you should do some shows first that you arrange through your own blood, sweat, and tears. If you're a radio phenomenon and you sell 50 books per appearance, then RTIR makes a lot of sense. If, as is more typical, you sell five, then paying to advertise probably won't be worth it unless you have other reasons to do so.

If your subject is light-hearted, you can try Toms Lake Humor Company, which is only $90 as of February 2006. When I used the service for my frugal fun book, I got about a dozen shows.

There are also several vendors who sell relatively inexpensive contact lists of radio-show producers. Three I know about (though haven't used) in alphabetical order: Alex Carroll, William Gordon, Joe Sabah. Contacts for all of these are in the Appendix.

GETTING PRESS THROUGH YOUR OWN WEBSITE

If you've got a focused, content-rich website that uses good traffic-building strategies and has a well-stocked pressroom, journalists may search for story ideas and find you. I've been contacted from my websites by the BBC and ABC TV networks, among others. Journalists might find you through Google, follow links from articles you've written, or catch a link that someone else has put up to you. You and your website should both be prepared to handle this very exciting possibility. You can see my pressrooms (each a little bit different) at

- <http://www.principledprofit.com/press-room.html>
- <http://www.frugalmarketing.com/pressroom.shtml>
- <http://www.frugalfun.com/pressroom.html>

Become a Columnist or an Editor

Multimillionaire self-publisher Jeffrey Lant used to send floppy disks around to magazine publishers—especially those aimed at people who had started or were running a home-based business. Each disk contained a year's worth of columns that the publisher could use, in any order, in exchange for printing Lant's full resource box.

Needless to say, the repeated exposure he got as a trusted and valued source in these markets fueled a lot of book sales, consulting gigs, speaking opportunities, and so forth. These days, of course, he can just make the content available on his website, and/or place the articles on various free-content sites.

Janice Campbell, of <http://www.everyday-education.com>, started growing her platform by editing a local organization's newsletter as a volunteer, then moved up to editing the regional publication.

> Next, the state organization hired me to work on their long newsletter, and ultimately, turn it into a glossy 24-page magazine. Shortly after this, I was invited to speak at the statewide convention. I needed something to sell, so I wrote my first book. It caught on, and I began receiving orders for it from people who had heard of it by word of mouth...
>
> One major benefit of working on the magazine was receiving local and regional newsletters, as well as most state newsletters and several national publications. This helped me learn not only a lot about my field, but also about the second and third tier of influential people in the field.
>
> I edited the magazine for only about 3 years, but the experience was tremendously valuable...Once people recognized my name, attended a workshop, or used my book, they told others about me, which in turn created more speaking invitations, more book sales, and more referrals. I have learned to keep my name out there by speaking whenever possible (industry conferences are critical to gaining credibility), writing letters to the editor, teaching a noncredit class at the local community college on

nontraditional college, volunteering to cover events related to my field for the state organization, commenting on relevant blogs, starting my own blog, and maintaining a personal touch in customer service.

Letters-to-the-Editor, Op-Eds, and Other Reader Features

Two departments in most newspapers and many magazines actually invite and encourage reader submissions: the letters and "Op-Ed" pages. And those with a well-developed electronic presence also may offer the chance to comment on stories or blog entries.

I go into extensive detail on both letters and op-eds in *Grassroots Marketing: Getting Noticed in a Noisy World* so I'm not going to say much here—but I will share with you one author's blatantly self-promotional letter (included in the original *Grassroots)* that got published in the *New York Times*:

> I was astonished that your obituary article on I. B. Singer gave short shrift to his vegetarianism. Mr. Singer contributed interviews and recipes to two of my books, *The New Vegetarians* and *Famous Vegetarians and Their Favorite Recipes.* I can assure you vegetarianism was essential to his vision as an artist.
>
> When I asked him how it was that vegetarian leitmotifs and themes appeared in his novels long before he formally became vegetarian, he said:
>
> ". . . [T]hese things came out through my pen almost automatically. Yes, I always thought about eating meat. These things bothered me all the time."
>
> After giving me two of his favorite recipes . . . for *Famous Vegetarians,* he said I could have them if I also included the following quotation:
>
> "I think that everything connected with vegetarianism is of the highest importance because there will never be any peace in the world so long as we eat animals. This also applies to fish. I do not eat any fish. I had felt guilty and ashamed about the fact

that I had eaten the flesh of an animal. I think that animals are as much God's creatures as men are. And we have to respect and love them, not slaughter them."

This makes a fitting epitaph for a man who was a vegetarian—not because he loved kasha, potatoes and rice pudding (for which he had an inordinate craving)—but because he loved humanity.

Rynn Berry
Brooklyn

The author commented to me that the letter's publication "sparked a good deal of interest in my books. Bookstores that hadn't been aware of my books hitherto, suddenly started carrying them. Moreover, I'm still receiving inquiries more than two months after publication."

Some publications have other reader-generated features. California's *Orange County Register* offers a column with five tips from various experts. It was my turn on March 28, 2005:

How to increase profitability by doing the right thing

Shel Horowitz, author of *Principled Profit: Marketing That Puts People First*, consultant and founder of the Business Ethic Pledge (http://www.principledprofit.com), offers five tips on how to increase profitability by doing the right thing.

1. **Base your business in the "Magic Triangle."** Honesty, integrity and quality make up the three sides. Create the kind of firm that stands for something more than the bottom line, and your bottom line will increase.

2. **Stop worrying about market share.** The world has more than enough customers. Put energy into growth-enhancing activities instead of chopping down competitors.

3. **Partner with your competitors.** Competing and complementary businesses can become your best sales agents. For example, Toyota and General Motors have product partnerships, and FedEx and the U.S. Postal Service cooperate to deliver Express Mail.

4. **Understand the true brand experience.** It's not your advertising and marketing, it's customer service. How helpful and courteous are your staff, both in-store and on the phone? How friendly and useful is your Web site?

5. **Turn customers into sales agents.** At least one third of your business should be repeat customers or their referrals. If you're still struggling to pull in business, you either need a better system to harness these profitable customers or to address the deeper reasons why they don't return.

Other People's Books as Media

Here's one a whole lot of authors never think of: get cited as an expert in someone else's book. Educational publisher Stacey Kannenberg, whose first-in-a-series *Let's Get Ready for Kindergarten!* is a multiple award-winner, trolls the "stories wanted" section of Dan Poynter's free e-mail newsletter, "Publishing Poynters" <http://www.parapublishing.com>:

> E-mail other authors looking for stories or information wanted and help them out. Not only will your story be in another book, for free, you might be making some amazing relationships. I have contributed to 15 books since June on all subjects: weight loss book looking for ladies to review—I lost 16 pounds and my name and title and review [are] on the back cover of her book.

She has also written "reviews for two parenting tip books, a book on successful partnerships, several mommy companies' books, several entrepreneur books and [has been] chosen to be in 'Best of Us' about 50 amazing people that are changing the world! Who knew!"

I'm a big believer in this method and have been cited or quoted in a long list of books, which you can see at <http://frugalmarketing.com/mediainterviews.shtml#books>. Some of them bring me a slew of book orders and consulting inquiries, and some bring nothing except one more credential to cite.

Press Releases as Direct Public Contact

Joan Stewart <http://www.publicityhound.com> constantly reminds her readers that press releases are no longer written just for journalists. When posted on your website or to any of the press release sites, anyone can find them through natural search.

This means you'll want to write at least some of your press releases with that much larger audience in mind: optimize the content for search engines, tell more of the story, include more self-promotional language, etc. She offers an 89-day course (free as of this writing) that gives tons of examples: <http://www.publicityhound.com/pressreleasetips/art.htm>

Chapter Nine

How to Give Great Interviews

- *Why journalists need you*
- *Differences between print and broadcast media*
- *Different types of interviews*

Media publicity provides third-party credibility: You're important enough to be on TV or in the newspaper. It also provides exposure: a way for a whole lot more people to learn about your book—which can (though doesn't always) translate into sales.

And it costs nothing to be featured in the press.

As an author, some of the publicity you get will be on the strength of your book itself. Reviews, for example, are usually written without any contact with the author.

But it's hard to get on the book-review page, and there are so many more opportunities for publicity beyond reviews!

I try to do 30 to 50 interviews a year. While there's usually not an enormous direct sales benefit, the credibility and visibility are well worth pursuing—and occasionally, an interview does actually sell a pile of books.

This chapter will focus on how to be the kind of interviewee whom journalists love, so that they come back to you for future stories, and even pass your name on to other journalists.

Why Should Journalists Talk to You?

Why? Because journalists need a constant flow of story ideas to fill the "news hole" or "editorial window." (In this context, "editorial" means the news and features, as opposed to the advertising; in other contexts, it refers specifically to the opinion pieces on the editorial and op-ed pages.) This is enough of a challenge that a huge percentage of "news" is planted by publicists and marketing people.

The most important thing is to understand how journalists think. Journalists don't care about your book and, in most cases, won't have read it before the interview. They care about providing content that educates and entertains their readers, listeners, and viewers.

Which means the content you deliver has to educate and entertain while keeping interest levels high.

For some authors, this is kind of scary. Maybe you're one of those writers who'd rather sit in your garret, slump over your word processor, and write all day—but getting your message out into the world helps create the economic reality—book sales—that allows you to keep on writing.

If talking to reporters scares you, or even if you're not scared but you feel you could be better at it, I've got one piece of advice for you: **Go and get some media training**. Plenty of people out there can help you get comfortable talking to reporters, become more dynamic and entertaining, and learn to concentrate on your key message points (I'm one of them, and can coach you over the phone for radio and print).

Tip: For radio and TV, arrange ahead of time to get a copy of the segment, so that if you're terrific, you have it as a demo to show major-league producers. And if you're less-than-terrific, you can study the segment and see how you could do better the next time; it's the very best media training you can do.

Sound Bites

For TV and radio especially, but even in print, if you can create "sound bites"—brief quotes that sum up your point in a deeply memorable way—you're ahead of the game.

The best sound bites are memorable because they use familiar metaphors or analogies, draw on pop-culture references, start controversies, and/or incorporate poetic devices such as rhyme, alliteration, and rhythm.

A few examples:

- Spiro Agnew's "nattering nabobs of negativism"
- "Where's the beef?"
- Martin Luther King, Jr.,'s analogy of the check returned for insufficient funds in his "I Have a Dream" speech
- "Go ahead. Make my day."

So...How do you translate this idea of sound bites into promoting something as abstract as a book? By asking the same kinds of "so what" and "what's in it for the listener/viewer" questions that we explored when discussing book titles and press releases—the more outrageous the better, as long as you can document and substantiate the claim. Some ideas:

- Don't be cloned by a criminal! (for a book on identity theft)
- Murderous burgers: you'd be better off starving than eating that fatty patty (for a book on healthy eating—uses rhyme and an outrageous, controversial claim)
- Park your car safely and inexpensively in Manhattan, in any neighborhood, any time of day (something most people think is impossible; I actually know someone who's written a book on that)
- Some I've used in promoting my own books:
- On the Internet, a stay-at-home mom can market more successfully than a Fortune 500 company (for *Grassroots Marketing*)
- Nice guys *don't* finish last—they finish first! (*Principled Profit*)
- How'd you like to plan a fun, memorable wedding—for $300? (*The Penny-Pinching Hedonist*)

For novelists, sound bites can be tied to topical or geographic themes. Even poets can use sound bites—by reading poems that contain vivid images.

Expand beyond Sound Bites

But don't build the whole interview as a string of sound bites. You'll come across as really shallow and superficial unless you build some depth. For fiction and creative nonfiction (such as biography or memoir), listeners will want to get to know you, and your characters. And for instructive nonfiction, use sound bites as jumping-off points for more in-depth discussions. So for my frugal fun book, the sound bite might be, "Even a waitress can afford a great vacation!" And then the follow-up: "My wife and I took a really nice six-night vacation in Greece. Including everything—airfare, food, lodging, admissions, even souvenirs—what do you think we spent?" I pause while the host guesses several thousand dollars and then I give the answer: $400. Then I spend a minute explaining how, and of course mention that there's much more information in the travel chapter of *The Penny-Pinching Hedonist*—and I mention the title by name; I *don't* just say "in my book."

Be Prepared

Nothing makes a worse interview than a flustered source. The more prepared you are, the better your chances of doing well. Some tips, noting the appropriate media where it makes a difference:

- Offer the interviewer a list of questions but if s/he declines, don't worry about it (radio, TV)
- Provide whatever materials the producer requests: a bio, book cover, author photo, copy of your book, etc.; a lot of this stuff can be up on your pressroom page so journalists can instantly download it
- Get a friend to practice with you, asking the questions on your list and other questions you might not have thought of; tape this and play it back—and if you ramble, or mumble, or speak in a monotone, or talk over the audience's head, use it as a tool to improve: Practice again, listen to the tape, and see where you improved and where you still need work (all media, and especially radio and TV)
- Write your three to five most important points in big letters and put this sheet where you can comfortably see it while talking on the phone with the reporter (print, radio)
- Have a sheet at your fingertips with a pithy quote or two from your book, that you can read if it's appropriate (print, radio)

- Research the reporter: Visit the show's or station's website, read other articles the journalist has written, listen to/watch a few segments
- Know your best sound bites inside and out
- Think on your feet—or retreat to some safe verbiage such as "I don't have those numbers in front of me, but I can get back to you with them"—and then follow up as promised!
- *Never* say anything that you wouldn't want splashed across page one in your exact words, or the lead story on a newscast—stay away from irony, sarcasm, and negative examples; they'll be thrown back in your face out of context as if you meant them just the way they sound
- Always remember that journalists and media folk are people too, and for the most part, are trying to do a very difficult job under extreme pressure—very few will be deliberately out to make you look bad, other than the occasional "shock jock"

Styles of Interviews

Because not all media are the same, not all interviews are either.

PRINT MEDIA AND ITS COROLLARIES

For print and most Internet media—newspapers, magazines, newsletters, blogs, webzines, e-zines, etc.—the interview will be conducted either by phone, in person, or by e-mail, and the reporter will take the material and shape it into a story, later. You may or may not be quoted accurately or in context, and the reporter has complete control over your message. At the same time, you don't face pressure to be perfect, as you do in a live on-air interview.

Also, don't be surprised—or angry—if you spend half an hour with a reporter and only one or two lines gets into print; this is common. Think of it as an excuse to write a letter to the editor, thanking the media outlet for including you in the story, respectfully correcting any errors of fact, and offering some new and relevant tidbit to those who liked the article (and *don't* complain about your paltry coverage!).

BROADCAST MEDIA

Radio and TV (and other audiovisual media such as podcasts and teleseminars) rely much more on other aspects besides the words. In radio, the sound of your voice, plus music, is all you have to work with. I am an expressive speaker, and I find that actually liberating: I can create a world with the sound of my voice. I can focus on the message I want to put forth, and in many cases, I'll have a fair amount of time to do that.

TV, however, is a visual medium. You have to pay attention to your visual appearance, make a constant effort not to use mannerisms that look terrible on camera (such as scratching, fidgeting, or drinking water excessively), and your message is most successful when it's not just a "talking head"—when you have additional background footage ("b-roll"), a demonstration, pictures, or other visual components.

While I've been lucky enough never to be afraid of radio or print, I had to work hard to gain some comfort on camera—and I still don't think it's my best medium. Being "natural" on camera is a learned skill, and I'd advise not only getting trained but also starting with small local cable stations where it doesn't matter much if you blow it. Make your mistakes on these little shows with few viewers; you really don't want to be a deer-in-headlights if you're lucky enough to get on "Oprah" or "Good Morning, America."

LIVE VERSUS TAPED

Broadcast media may tape ahead, or may go live. The majority of radio interviews I've done have aired in real time, during the interview—but I've taped some in advance. When I've done network TV, it's always been taped ahead, and sometimes, boo-hoo, it ends up on the cutting-room floor—even if I've spent a whole day with a camera crew (and several hours are not unusual, even for a 5-minute segment). I've done several long-format community access cable shows that were live, however.

Taping does give you the option to stop and start over—but don't over-use this, especially if you're on-camera. If the taping is reasonably smooth, just go with it. Of course, if you make a mistake live, there is no second take, and you just transition as best you can and move on.

CALL-INS

Sometimes in a live show, the station will take callers from the audience, and you're expected to interact with the callers. Radio producers love guests who "light up the phones," so don't be afraid to be controversial—just don't be hostile. If a caller is totally off-base, the host will normally get the caller off the air very quickly.

But still, you have to be prepared for the unexpected. One of my funniest radio moments was doing an hour-long call-in show in Taiwan, on the phone from my home in Massachusetts. The host actually translated the Chinese questions into English for me, and my responses back into Chinese. I was promoting my frugal fun book and was asked about how to get cheap jewelry (something I know basically nothing about). So I retreated into general principles of frugal purchasing for any luxury item, and showed the caller how to extrapolate into jewelry purchases.

SEGMENT LENGTH

TV and radio producers think in terms of segments: the length of time your part of the program will take. A segment could be three minutes, or it could be an hour. On magazine-style commercial TV shows, segments are typically 5 to 7 minutes. Talk format might give you half an hour. And news might use all of 90 seconds. If you're going longer than 15–20 minutes, on either TV or radio, you'll probably be chunked up with commercial breaks in the middle.

Know ahead of time how long your segment will be, how many times you'll take commercial breaks, and so forth.

Never rely on the host to plug you. It's always better if the host does it, but if you sense the segment wrapping up and the host hasn't given out your information, gracefully squeeze in your website with a line like "and your viewers can find out much more about this at frugalmarketing.com." Or even better, "Your listeners can get a free report, '10 Tips to a 20-Year Home Exterior,' at paintyourownhouse.com." Good hosts will make sure to promote

you, but not every host is considerate. Remember: All they're after is the segment, and if that segment doesn't tell people how to
follow up, you've wasted your time.

HUMOR OR INAPPROPRIATE QUESTIONS

A lot of hosts think it's their job to tease their guests. Take it in
good fun. Don't take it personally, and above all, don't act offend-
ed. If you can gently tease back without offending, great. If not,
just roll with it and laugh along. The hosts have loyal audiences,
and if you get mad, you've lost your public.

If the host asks an off-the-wall question, or one that you don't
want to answer, the response will be a bit different if you're live
or if you're taping ahead. If you're on the air right then, or if the
interview will be broadcast in its entirety, transition as quickly as
possible to your main point, but acknowledge the question. For
example, "That's a really interesting question, but the answer is
long and complicated. I believe that..." (and continue to your key
point), or "I'm glad you asked that but I think the real heart of the
matter is..."

If the interview is taped, and it's clearly a format where only
your answers will be played back (such as a news story), you can
simply ignore the question and answer the question you wanted
to be asked. But if the questions will be aired, this will make you
look like an idiot.

Personally, I find media interviews a great deal of fun. I enjoy
joking with the hosts, making outrageous but substantiated state-
ments, reading my name in the paper or magazine...and especially, reaching thousands of people who otherwise would never
have been exposed to my ideas. And of course, it's nice when an
interview actually sells books.

PART III

Get Into—And Out of—
Bookstores and Libraries

Chapter Ten

Understand the Bookstore System
"Bookstores are a lousy place to sell books."
—Dan Poynter, author of *The Self-Publishing Manual*

- *Why the above statement is true for most authors*
- *How return policies, pricing, and title glut make it tough*
- *Real-world numbers*

D o you dream of walking into a bookstore, far from home, and seeing a whole display of your best-selling titles? Sure, it could happen—but even if we have prominent publishers, most of us will be lucky to find one to five copies of our book, shelved spine-out in an obscure section toward the back of the store, right next to two dozen competing titles, some of them much better known than ours.

Unfortunately, it gets worse. Much worse.

Bookselling the traditional way is unique and troublesome in a number of other ways. Most industries would simply laugh at the idea of doing business the way bookstores and their suppliers do. And for most of us, the system puts us at a disadvantage right from the start.

This chapter will explain how the system "works"; I use the quotes because for most of us, it won't work very well. Whether you publish on your own or with a publisher, this understanding is important, although what you do with the information is more relevant to those who wear the publisher's hat. If you publish traditionally and don't want to concern yourself with this, skip down to Chapter 11.

The Returns System

Here's the biggest dirty little secret of the bookstore industry: Bookstores, for the most part, don't actually buy books. They order them, put them on the shelves, and then send them back if they don't sell quickly. In other words, they're really selling on consignment, and taking a discount of 40–45 percent off the cover price. The publisher pays not only all the upfront costs, but also the cost of shipping to distributors, wholesalers, and retailers—and the cost of shipping the books back through the supply chain when the bookstore doesn't want them anymore.

Oh, and remember those old signs in retail stores, "You break it, you buy it"? Not in a bookstore! Expect a substantial portion of your returned merchandise to be dinged, stickered, even coffee-stained. You/your publisher will not be able to sell these as new. (The good news: Many publishers actually make better profits selling their "hurts" at a discount, directly to buyers, than they do selling through the bookstore channels in the first place.)

And the time your book has to prove itself is getting shorter and shorter. Bookstores want to see inventory that turns over rapidly. If the book hasn't sold in as little as 30 days, back it comes. If the bookstore's policies are more generous, you may have as much as three months to sell through. Unless you're a blockbuster author with a big budget, that makes it very tough to coordinate your publicity and marketing with the brief moment your book has to get "traction" in a bookstore.

Returns in Real Numbers

Actual example: A wholesaler ordered 250 copies of one of my titles. Some time later, I received 290 returned copies (the extra 40 were purchased through other channels, but returned to this wholesaler for credit—and I had to take them back). These were in tough enough shape that I couldn't sell them as full-price, new copies: The bookstores' pricing stickers were hard to remove and left a sticky residue, corners were bent, and so forth—nothing critical.

Had these copies sold through in bookstores, I would have received $7.65 per copy (55 percent off the $17 list price), less maybe 20 cents per book for bulk shipping, for a net of $7.45, times 290 books. That's a total of $2160.50. By selling them directly to my own e-zine subscribers as slightly damaged at $10 per copy plus

$3.50 domestic Media Mail shipping, I did much better, even factoring in multiple shipping costs. So each book grossed $13.50, out of which I had to pay to ship the books to my wholesaler and back again ($0.40 for two round-trips in bulk at $0.20), plus approximately $1.75 to ship the book to the buyer, including postage and bubble-mailer, but not the time spent addressing and packing. So I netted $11.35 per book, or a much healthier $3291.50. In other words, for less than 300 books, I cleared an extra $1131, even paying the costs of getting the books back.

Of course, if I'd sold them direct for full price of $17 plus $3.50 shipping, I'd have done far better: subtracting the same $1.75 shipping cost means I'd take in $18.75 per copy (not counting production and marketing costs) for a total of $5437.50 on 290 copies.

If this book had been traditionally published, I might have received 80 cents per book on full-price sales; the publisher would probably not have had the patience to sell them discounted one at a time, and they would have been remaindered or destroyed—so I as the author would have received little or nothing: probably somewhere between zero and $50 for the whole batch of 290.

Competition for Space

Here's another ouch: In 2004, 181,189 new titles were published, just in the United States (well more than double the 86,000 published only as recently as 1996).[4] While most of them sell fewer than 5000 copies in their lifetime, a large percentage are trying to get on the shelves of bookstores that rarely carry more than 50,000 titles, and often much fewer. Those shelves have to accommodate popular backlist titles that sell for years, so the number of slots for new material by unknown authors is not very large. And to make matters worse, if you chose to self-publish or, especially, publish with a subsidy house, you also have to battle to establish the perception that your book is actually worth some time and attention. It's not your fault, but people in the book trade have seen an awful lot of junk from these sources.

Bookstore sales are a primary reason to put up with the shenanigans of a big publisher. The publisher *will* get you into stores. But then *you* have to get the book back out again, through the front door, in customers' hands—or they'll exit through the back door, cases at a time, back to the publisher for a refund.

Don't get me wrong: I've self-published a number of times, and I think it's the best way to go in many situations. And I've recommended subsidy publishing to authors when that made sense for their plans. I am not opposed to these publishing methods. All I'm saying is that they can create a barrier if you're trying to sell within the traditional book industry (bookstores and libraries).

Put yourself in the shoes of a buyer for a chain or independent bookstore. Perhaps you can accommodate 500 new titles this month—but you receive marketing materials about more than 2000, so you have to make choices. If you know that for every five books from a traditional publisher, three of them are likely to be worth the trees—but only one out of every eight or ten self-published books, and perhaps a single book out of every 300 subsidy-published titles, is worth a second glance, which pile of books are you going to pick up?

Now add in some other factors:

- Professional appearance: a brilliant cover, professional typesetting, and content that doesn't have obvious errors jumping out on almost every page. These things sell books. Almost no subsidy-published books have the solid production values needed to succeed in the marketplace, while self-published production quality ranges from award-winning excellence to absolute trash.

- Prominent endorsements: Your Aunt Mary is not a significant endorsement, unless she's a credentialed expert in your field.

- Print run: A book that's running 20,000 copies can support a national marketing campaign; a 2000 copy print run is not even enough to put one in every bookstore in the United States, and to a bookstore, a P-O-D print run in the two or three digits isn't even on the radar.

- Ease of ordering: Major publishers allow bookstores to order through just a handful of distributors and wholesalers, which greatly simplifies their billing and paperwork.

Bookstores are extremely reluctant to open up new vendor accounts with one or two or even five or ten titles apiece. If you can get your book into Ingram or Baker & Taylor, you'll be taken more seriously because this obstacle will go away, but that may or may not be feasible for you.

- Favorable terms: Bookstores want 40–45 percent off the cover price, fully returnable, with payment in 90 to 120 days. Are you prepared to offer those terms? Subsidy publishers typically offer just 20 percent off the cover price, usually nonreturnable, and with a higher-than-market cover price. Is it any wonder that subsidy books are almost exclusively ordered one at a time to fill a customer's order, or in slightly larger quantities to meet anticipated demand at an author event?

- Ease of returns: As noted above, book inventory isn't really sold until the customer walks it to the cash register. Bookstores are reluctant to take a chance on an unknown book that can't be returned, or has to be returned through nonstandard channels.

- Cooperative marketing payments: Big publishers *pay* for high visibility in stores, especially at the national chains. End-cap displays at the end of an aisle, for instance, can cost thousands of dollars a month in the larger chains. More and more bookstores, even independents, won't even schedule an author event without a few hundred dollars in co-op marketing. Most small and self-publishers can't compete.

Even if you've landed a major publisher, the bookstore system may or may not work for you. The big companies put their marketing resources into a few books they've destined, rightly or wrongly, for greatness. "Mid-list" authors, with advances under $50,000 or so, don't get much attention. We're expected to do our own marketing, even if we have a publisher, and while it's certainly easier to get into bookstores if you have a respected publisher, it's not very easy to build enough momentum to be taken seriously in that arena. However, if this is your situation, Chapter 11 will help you shift the odds in your favor.

Dan Poynter's April 13, 2006 newsletter had a very telling note about book sales as tracked through bookstores by Neilsen BookScan: Out of 1,241,423 separate ISBNs tracked in 2004, only 1123 sold more than 50,000 (32 of those sold more than half a million). But 1,150,000 titles sold fewer than 1000 copies in bookstores, and the *average* number of sales per ISBN was 15—which means one successful signing puts you in the top half!

The 2005 figures, according to Neilsen BookScan's own site <http://snipurl.com/p8bk>, are only slightly better: "In the 2005 list, the 500,000-copies-mark occurred at No. 34, versus No. 32 in 2004; and the 200,000-unit-mark cut-off, at No. 148 in 2005, fell at No. 133 in 2004."

Only six books sold more than a million copies in 2005; *Harry Potter and the Half-Blood Prince* was the only one to sell more than two million, cresting the seven million mark—more than twice as well as 2004's best-seller, *The Da Vinci Code*. The other million-sellers: James Frey's *A Million Little Pieces*, with a huge controversy about whether he had lied on "Oprah" (1.8 million units); *The Kite Runner* by Khaled Hosseini (just under 1.6 million copies—a book I loved, incidentally, but had no idea it was a best-seller); *1776*, by David McCullough (1.2 million copies); *The Da Vinci Code* (1.09 million); and Thomas L. Friedman's *The World Is Flat: A Brief History* (1.07 million sold).

Tell me again why bookstores are worth pursuing?

Fortunately, there are plenty of other places where it's much, much easier to sell books. In fact, many successful authors sell little or nothing through bookstores, and still do quite well, thank you very much.

Of course, if you publish with a traditional publisher whose contract prevents you from selling directly, you have no choice. Chapter 11 is especially for you.

Chapter Eleven

Succeed with Bookstores, Libraries and Other Retail Venues

- *How to get noticed by bookstores and libraries*
- *Successful in-store/library events*
- *Co-op advertising*
- *Retail outside of bookstores*

N ow that I've depressed you about the difficulties of selling through bookstores, I'll cheer you up and tell you that it actually can work. I know plenty of authors who do quite well in bookstores: many with major publishers, of course, but also a surprising number who are published by small independent publishers, or self-published. Some of them are super-promoters, like Jack Canfield and Mark Victor Hansen, and some have written books for a well-known brand like the Dummies series, where the brand itself actually does most of the marketing—but a lot more are ordinary authors and publishers who simply make bookstore sales a priority and spend several hours each week fueling that engine through media publicity, in-store appearances, and advertising...and by carefully building relationships with booksellers to build a powerful support base for their books.

So, although the odds are against you, you can actually make a go of the bookstore market—especially if it's not your only channel.

Get Booksellers' Attention

In order to get books into the bookstores, you have to get the booksellers themselves to notice your book. And yes, even though there's a whole lot of competition, you can achieve this if you set your mind to it.

Keep in mind that bookstores are a segmented audience. Every store has its own specialties. You won't have much luck pitching a cookbook event in a science-fiction store, or a local-author mystery novel in a store geared toward celebrity titles.

THE BOOKSELLERS YOU ALREADY KNOW

As an author, you are, I hope, also a reader. You can't expect anyone to buy your books if you yourself don't buy books. If you haven't been buying books and building relationships with a local bookseller (or a few of them), start now. Even if it's only six months before your book will be available, you'll have a much easier time getting their attention if they know you as a supporter and customer.

In the United States, look for independent booksellers who are members of the American Booksellers Association (ABA); they usually display the "BookSense: Independent Bookstores for Independent Minds" logo and slogan in the window or near the cash register. In other countries, seek their analogs; many countries have a professional association for independent bookstores.

There are a few good reasons to seek out the ABA members:

- They're in a position to help you participate in programs that bring you to the attention of independent booksellers around the country (more about that in a moment)
- The owners and staff tend to be book lovers; if you can get them "hand-selling" your book, their recommendations carry a lot of weight with their regular customers
- They're more likely to carry "quirky" books that may be hard to categorize, or to have vast depth in the market sectors where they claim expertise—and also very likely to be open to local authors
- If you're a regular customer, they're much more likely to say yes when you approach them about doing an event together
- When you speak at local conferences and the organizers select your chosen store to run the sales table, you'll already be a known quantity to the booksellers
- These booksellers help to make your community what it is: They donate to local causes, sponsor Little League teams,

host important events that would otherwise have problems finding a venue, provide jobs to local people, and spend their own shopping dollars in local stores

So, first of all, build those relationships. My wife and I personally know (and patronize) independent booksellers in five stores within a ten-mile radius of our house. This doesn't mean we never buy from our local chain superstore or from amazon.com, but it does mean we typically look first to one of these independents.

If there's no independent, use the same principles at your local chain store. You won't get the benefits of the BookSense programs, they probably won't be in a position to influence sales corporate-wide, and it may be harder to find the same people from visit to visit—but they'll still work with you to promote you as a local author, still be open to the possibilities of hosting an event, and in some cases, may be willing to hand-sell.

Once you start to know these people and they start to know you, it's time to tell them about your book and offer to do an event for them, or at least offer to sign the copies they'll order.

Notice that phrasing: you are not begging for an event; you are bringing something to the table as well. Ideally, you'll be bringing a large mailing list, a lot of buzz, and the potential for significant sales.

If you're a teacher, speaker, or frequent media guest, you can also win brownie points when you approach the manager by saying you'd like to direct people to that store to buy what they need for your class or talk.

GET NOTICED OUTSIDE YOUR AREA

To reach bookstores, put yourself where they hang out. Booksellers read *Publishers Weekly* and other trade magazines; if you can get coverage there, fabulous. If not, perhaps a carefully constructed (and cost-controlled) ad or direct-mail campaign may be effective; see Chapter 16.

Niche bookstores read niche publications. If your book is New Age, *NAPRA Review* should be on your press list. If it's a sports book, and you get covered in *Sports Illustrated*, the sports-oriented store owners will notice.

Distributors, at least in theory, sell your book to bookstores with catalogs, fliers, a website presence, and so forth. If you have a distributor, bring that company in as your marketing partner and spend some good planning time working out how you can support each other (expect to spend some serious money if you participate in some of the distributor's marketing programs).

For books with a great deal of bookstore appeal, exhibiting at regional and national book-industry trade shows may be effective; we'll cover that approach in Chapter 14.

Of course, reviews for new books and awards for older ones can help a lot; we've already covered those in detail.

ABA Programs

Members of the publishing trade organizations PMA and SPAN get a discount on the fee to participate in these programs; if you use a recognized ABA Partner distributor, you can get the fee waived. Details can be found at <http://www.bookweb.org/booksense/publisher/3311.html>

BookSense Picks: You designate a certain number of galleys as available to ABA members who request them. Follow up with the booksellers to get feedback, and if they like what they see, ask them to nominate your book as a BookSense Pick; if you're chosen, you can exploit it as you would any other award.

Dan Cullen of the ABA describes the program as follows:[5]

> Several times each month, we email over 1000 independent booksellers with news of galleys, reading copies or finished books that you are offering for review. After receiving a free review copy from you, stores will read and decide whether to carry the title, and hopefully even nominate it for the BookSense List. We make no promises, but the Advance Access program has proven to be a very effective way to get the word out about your titles. Stores will email you directly, and generally, you can expect requests from 25-50 booksellers. The stores do know that it is "first come/first served," but the more booksellers you can provide copies for, the better, of course.
>
> All book descriptions must be sent to Peter Reynolds via email at <mailto:peter@booksense.com> peter@booksense.com,

with title, author, publisher, ISBN, subject category, publication date, the number of free copies you have to offer, a maximum two-sentence description, and an email address to which the booksellers can write to directly request a copy. Please put this all in one paragraph, without actually putting in the words 'Title, Author, etc.', and put the email address to which booksellers are to respond at the end of the paragraph without a period. This is all so the information can be easily cut and pasted into the larger email to the stores. An example follows:

TITLE XYZ by David Smith, (Publisher, ISBN: 0-000-00000-0, $23.95, hardcover, September 2004, Mystery/Thriller). A two-sentence description of the title here. No more than 50 words, please. XX number of galleys available. mailto:yournamehere@ emailaddress.com

ABA Whitebox: You send materials to the ABA for inclusion in a big white box of goodies. These could be covers, blads (marketing pieces consisting of the cover, table of contents, and a couple of excerpts in final-design form), galleys, whole finished books, whatever. Publishers report that they have the best results with finished books (and in general, not terrific results even then), but of course, those also cost the most.

BookSense Database: E-mail your ISBN, title, author, publisher, publication date, binding type, price, and BISAC category code or genre to addabook@booksense.com

Advance Access: The ABA sends a monthly e-mail that lists all the available books. Bookstores contact you to request sample copies and promotional information.

Advertising in ABA's daily and weekly newsletters and in the BEA Show Daily, a newspaper distributed on the floor of Book Expo America.

ABA also rents out its postal mailing list. Direct mail may work for you, but I strongly advise first reading the two chapters on direct mail in *Grassroots Marketing: Getting Noticed in a Noisy World*, as well as Chapter 16 of this book, before moving forward.

Before You Go after In-Store Events—Be Ready

Many first-time authors see the long lines waiting at celebrity book signings, and they think that's the way to market books. The bookstore event definitely has a place in the book-marketing toolkit, but it's a long way from the top of my list—and unless you're already famous, it's *not* going to be successful if all you do is sit at a table and sign. And while a multicity book tour may sound glamorous, it's actually exhausting. Also, it's beyond the budget of almost all publishers, except for their very top authors. In most cases, an author gets precious little marketing help from the publisher, and certainly not an expenses-paid tour.

First of all, plan to create an exciting, buzz-worthy event that truly engages your audience. Do not just sit behind a table and sign books; you won't be signing very many! Plan a talk, a reading, a show-and-tell of some kind. The more active and entertaining you can make it, the more you can actually get your audience involved, the more books you'll sell—and the more likely you'll get invited back.

Yes, it's true—this means yet another set of skills to acquire: the skills of attracting and holding an audience. You want your words to be clear, your volume to be appropriate, your eye contact to be sincere, and your delivery to be entertaining. This means you vary tone, pacing of your delivery, volume, intensity, and direction you're looking. And in most cases, it'll work better if you're not behind a podium. If you need to read some material, stand to the side of the podium so you can still see your notes but you haven't isolated yourself from your audience. It also means you may want some training in public speaking and/or media interviewing. (Please see the Appendix for ways to get started on this path.)

Can you succeed without being a thrilling speaker? Certainly. If you want proof, go to your library and find an audiobook written and read by the late Isaac Bashevis Singer, and another one by Amy Tan. Singer was a dreadful speaker. His stuff is all delivered in a monotone, and hidden behind a very thick, almost incomprehensible accent. I have tried a few times to get through one of his recordings and I never make it past the first few minutes. But Tan is a pleasure to listen to. She is engaging, uses different voices for different moods and characters, and breathes life into the book.

Singer had to build his audience exclusively through the written word. Tan and others are able to use their presentation skills to build audiences and reputation; that option is not open to a truly terrible speaker. It's just much, much easier if you're comfortable and relaxed in front of an audience, yet dynamic enough to keep their attention. You don't have to be mesmerizing—but you do need to hold an audience for the 20 or 30 minutes of your talk or reading, for the question period that follows, and for the fun part when people come up to you afterward, tell you how much they enjoy your work and enjoyed your talk, and ask you to sign the copy of your book they've just bought.

If your presentation includes riveting visual or sensory additions—I'm not talking about dull-as-dishwater text-only PowerPoint slides, but stuff that really makes the audience sit up and take notice—so much the better.

Among the memorable presentations I've seen:

- A talk about Ernest Shackleton's ill-fated Antarctica voyage in the early 20th century that included both historic black-and-white and recent color slides and film footage from a PBS TV special
- Cookbook talks that include preparing foods and passing out samples
- Preview showings excerpting as-yet-unreleased films, some of which had a strong tie-in with a book
- The author (a good performer) and an actor acting out a scene from a novel or play
- A business author's very engaging presentation on the deadly-sounding subject of incremental improvement; his slides included photos, charts, quotes, and more, and his delivery was upbeat (he sold a lot of books that night)
- And of course, plenty of wonderful performances by authors who used no props or pictures, among them novelists Alice Walker and Madeline L'Engle, and nonfiction authors Medea Benjamin and Greg Palast

PUBLICITY HOUND'S FIVE PROMOTION TIPS FOR FICTION WRITERS

Joan Stewart, whose wonderful e-zine, "The Publicity Hound's Tips of the Week" <http://www.publicityhound.com> is full of great resources, had some great advice for novelists, much of which can also work for nonfiction authors:

Authors who write fiction think they face an uphill battle trying to get publicity for their books.

That's because most fiction authors see themselves as storytellers, not experts. Yet many of them do far more research before writing their books than authors of nonfiction.

Here are five ways authors can get publicity for their fiction titles:

Piggyback onto an upcoming major or minor holiday, or a day, week or month of the year. Did you write a romance novel? If so, supply tips on how to be romantic to tie into Valentine's Day, or Sweetest Day in October.

Offer helpful how-to advice that ties into your topic. Bill and Susan Albert have a series of mystery books featuring China Bayles, the main character, who has an herb shop, and they've promoted themselves as experts on the topic of herbal lore. Their e-mail newsletter includes information and recipes about herbs, in addition to news about their latest books.

Sponsor a contest that ties into the topic of your book. The bigger the prize, the better the publicity.

Create your own day, week or month of the year that's associated with the topic, and submit it to Chase's Calendar of Events at <http://www.chases.com>. [Note from Shel: also notify Celebrate Today <http://celebratetoday.com>] Then tie news releases and other promotions to the special day.

In their book *Jump Start Your Book Sales*, Marilyn and Tom Ross suggest that authors can ask their local newspapers to sponsor a "complete the short story" contest. You write the beginning and readers submit their own endings. "This has been done very successfully on the Web by celebrity authors," they note.

Finally—You're Booked in a Bookstore

Okay, you've gotten a bookstore event set up. How do you make the most of it?

First of all, develop a clear understanding of how the bookstore will promote the event. Be clear on the topic of your talk, the format, and what publicity the store will do. The best bookstores excitedly describe you in both print and e-mail newsletters, put the announcement on their website, send out press releases, widely distribute fliers, put posters in the window and around the store, announce your event at all their events in the weeks leading up to your date—and are known in the community as a place to hear great authors. In the days before the event, they put a display of your books on the front counter and maybe even in the window (though that's a lot to ask), along with signage about your event. And in the hour or two before you get started, they regularly announce your appearance over the store's PA system (if it's a big enough store to need one—supply them with two or three different 30-second announcements they can rotate). Oh, yes, and they stock enough copies of your books to meet the demand.

For celebrity authors, the store may even organize a lecture at a nearby college or other larger venue that can accommodate several hundred attendees. As an unknown, you won't get that kind of treatment, but if the store has a good track record with large events, it's likely to be well prepared for smaller ones too.

The worst bookstores do no publicity for you at all. Most are somewhere in the middle. Therefore, get some commitments in writing about what the store will do to promote your event.

BE THE BOOKSTORE'S TREASURED PARTNER

Now, the question is, what will you do for the store? As in any good marketing, a successful book event is a partnership. The bookstore brings an audience, you bring an audience. You provide a great event, and the store tells other store owners. And you both team up to sell a bunch of books.

So think about making it great for all three constituencies: the store, the audience, and yourself. These are some things you can do to make bookstore staff love working with you:

- Use the in-store event as a hook to land advance publicity with local radio stations and newspapers, which drives traffic to the event and builds prestige and visibility both for you and the store (keeping in mind that your press releases must have hooks of their own, much deeper than "I'm showing up to sign books").

- Send e-mail notices to your own newsletter subscribers— and ask them to tell their own contacts in the area.

- Mail postcards with your book cover on the front and the event details on the back.

- Use electronic notification services such as <http://www.evite.com>, send listings to <http://getlocalnews.com>, and post announcements on the various free press-release sites.

- If you are a member of any kind of association that has a local chapter near the signing, send an announcement (well in advance) to the chapter's newsletter.

- Show that you understand the bookstore business and that you have realistic expectations.

- Go the extra mile for them—take a tip from my friend Kare Anderson and offer to do up a handout that not only provides some helpful hints from you, but also recommends a "companion collection" of three to five books. The store can set up a nice display of these ahead of time, along with a display of your books, and as you refer to them in your talk, you will generate enormous good will among the staff—because this creates many multiple-book sales.

- Do a foamboard or poster of your book cover and/or a picture of you that you can bring from event to event. Leave room at the bottom for the specific event information, and then supply a boldly printed copy of the specific information. Suggest to the store manager that it be in the window for one to two weeks prior to your event.

- Ask if the store would like to have a few signed copies on hand before the event, for people who are interested but can't make it.

- If you'll be using a microphone, sound equipment, slides, videos, or computer demonstrations, get there early enough to check the equipment, the sound levels, and anything else. And be totally prepared to go ahead anyway if the power goes out, the equipment breaks, or you brought the wrong set of slides. If using the store's projector, check ahead of time that the store has a working spare bulb.
- Once the event is concluded, ask if the store would like you to sign the remaining copies on hand. This gives you an excuse to linger, strike up conversations, and sell more books. And it helps the store, because autographed copies are extra-special in many customers' eyes. It's usually a myth that signed books cannot be returned, however.
- Take some time to get to know the staff—these are the people who can hand-sell your book long after your event, if they like you.
- Roam around the store with a copy of your book for 10 or 15 minutes before you go on, finishing at least 10 minutes before your event is scheduled. Introduce yourself to people, tell them you're the author of the book, and that you're personally inviting them to be a part of your event (clear this with the event coordinator ahead of time!). Be enthusiastic and friendly, but never pushy or phony.

Here's a particularly great set of tips taken or modified from Larry James, whose "40+ Ways to Make Your Next Book Signing an EVENT!!" is must reading if you're doing bookstore gigs (see Resources).

- Arrange ahead of time for a volunteer to bring a digital camera. Your friend should take a picture of you with each person who is getting a book signed. Announce ahead of time that you can e-mail each person a copy of his or her picture with you, the celebrity. This requires careful recordkeeping, so you know who gets which picture—but it also lets you collect e-mail addresses so you can tell them when you're going to be in the area again. (Another way to get contact information is to do a giveaway drawing of some kind—but not for the book you're signing, as you want people to buy that!)

- Alternatively, bring a Polaroid camera and give the pictures out right then and there, signed and dated by you. (However, this will be a lot slower and more expensive than the digital method.)
- Also get pictures of you with the store manager, with the CSR/event planer, and with the whole staff. Make sure your book cover figures prominently in the picture. Give them copies that they can display permanently around the store.
- Always have a stash of books with you. If the store didn't order enough, you can make up the difference. Be sure to get an invoice signed for the number you're supplying, and sell them to the store at the same discount.
- Check with each person who presents a book for signing: who would you like this book signed to, and how do you spell that? Better yet, have a staffer or volunteer go through the line with a Post-It pad and have that information attached to the book by the time your customer gets to the front of the line.
- Have a few stock phrases you can write that are germane to your book. I used to inscribe copies of my now-out-of-print book on having fun cheaply, "In frugal friendship," and one of my marketing books, "Success, always." These days, I often sign my business ethics book either "In friendship" or "Ethically yours." I know one author, Phillip Dale Smith, who writes a long paragraph. Yes, it takes time, but he says people run around the store with their signed books showing them around, and the line grows longer.

And a few more suggestions from former bookseller Linda Urban's workshop at the 2006 New England Society of Children's Book Writers and Illustrators, which my wife attended:

- Fit your presentation into an existing program at the store—many stores have an educator week, a teen reading group, etc. You'll have a built-in audience, and the store will know how to promote it to that group.
- Write your own descriptions of book and author for the store.

- Bring in cosponsors.
- Partner with other authors, either as part of a panel (where each of you brings in your own fans and they cross-pollinate), or for sequential events such as a series of three writing workshops, where each writer takes turns leading each group on different nights.
- As you're signing books after your talk, take a moment to talk personally with each fan. Go a little beyond asking what name it should be signed to.
- Have someone take a photo of you with every person getting a copy and make those available to the store for a scrapbook.

BENEFIT YOURSELF, TOO

You can also do certain things at book events that build an audience for you, but don't particularly help the bookstore. Have a take-away of some kind, with your titles, ISBNs, website, and reason to visit. Pass around a clipboard and pad to collect e-mail or postal addresses for your mailing list. Collect event evaluation forms that include a box to check for permission to be quoted (great way to get testimonials!) as well as an option to be in touch if they can arrange an appearance. You can also include your newsletter address collection form. Invite local teachers or others who could generate bulk orders, if what they teach is germane to your book.

Hand-Sell to Booksellers and Librarians

Just as booksellers and librarians can get personally involved with a title and recommend it verbally to their customers and patrons, you can create that enthusiasm among these powerful influencers—if you have a book that appeals to a large audience.

My wife, Dina Friedman <http://www.ddinafriedman.com>, always carries her books with her. Whenever she travels and passes a bookstore or library, she goes in to show her two young adult novels, published by two different large New York publishers. She has been repeatedly told, "Oh, yes, this is something we can sell!"

My books are more specialized and have considerably less mainstream appeal; even my traditionally published books didn't meet with great enthusiasm from booksellers, although libraries have been somewhat more receptive.

When you visit a bookseller or librarian to hand-sell your titles, be sure you have a leave-behind with the ordering information. This is an excellent time to use a postcard with the book cover on the front and the ISBN, price, wholesalers, etc. on the back (ideally, along with a nice review quote or important blurb and a statement of key benefits).

Co-op Possibilities

If you didn't publish your own book, always ask your publisher about its co-op arrangements. Just to confuse things you'll find at least three different meanings for the term, "co-op marketing":

ADVERTISING SUBSIDY

"Co-op," as I'm using it here, means that when a store pays to advertise your event, the publisher kicks in some bucks. Obviously, if you can approach a store manager and say that your publisher will cover a percentage of the ad, that store is more likely to advertise your event. The actual deal may be structured differently depending on the size of the ad, the medium running the ad (e.g., the publisher might be more inclined to fund an ad in *The New York Review of Books* than in a small hometown newspaper), and, of course, your clout as an author and how much the publisher wants to see this book break out.

When dealing with large publishers, many bookstores often expect this co-op money. And some are starting to demand payments from small publishers as well. To my mind, it is generally not worth it to a small or self-publisher to pay several hundred dollars in order to put on a book event—especially since the author, who may be a highly paid speaker in other venues, is already showing up for free.

IN-STORE DISPLAYS

Another kind of co-op marketing happens when publishers essentially rent prime in-store display space, such as endcaps (displays at the end of an aisle) or store windows. Barnes and Noble and other large chain booksellers count on these co-op revenues for substantial profits.

Borders has gone even farther, selling off entire categories to large publishers who pay in the neighborhood of $100,000 to control the contents of the shelf. I'm a bit surprised no one (so far) has brought legal action claiming restraint of trade or unfair trade practices.

From the publisher's point of view, this procedure is expensive but often effective—at least on books with a large enough print run to support not only the cost of the promotion, but also the logistical challenge and expense of supplying so many books to each participating store. If a bookstore chain usually orders 3 to 5 copies of most titles for each store but you have an endcap display of 50 copies in each of 10 stores in a regional market, that's 500 copies compared to 30 to 50. A national rollout, obviously, would be far more inventory-intensive than that.

And of course, the publisher has to stay on top of the sales patterns. If the books *are* moving, if the endcap promotion is successful, someone has to make sure bookstores are reordering, getting the product in as quickly as possible, and properly restocking the endcap display.

And then, if the book is moving slowly in spite of the promotion, your publisher has the huge headache of returns for full credit. This can happen even to celebrities; former House Speaker Newt Gingrich's publisher was stuck with hundreds of thousands of unsold copies of his book, and all the endcaps in the world didn't help. Sometimes, these books end up on the remainder table, at maybe 10 to 25 percent of the original list price. (If you want a very insightful perspective from a bookstore owner on the remainder game, read *Rebel Bookseller* by Andy Laties, listed in the Appendix.) If you are your own publisher, or you're working with a small independent publisher who wants to try this, there are, of course, ways to hold your costs down:

- Start small; do a test in a single location, or perhaps a group of stores within one city where you're actively doing publicity

- Mix themed titles on a single endcap—if you have a few books in a series, or even a few on related topics that would appeal to the same buyers, your endcap can mix the different titles
- Share the cost and the display with another publisher who has complementary titles

Still, this method is not for the faint of heart. If you try it, go into it only after you've done your research. Ask for the names of other publishers who've promoted similar books, contact them, and find out if the sales figures justified the investment.

Libraries: Similarities and Differences

Marketing to libraries is in many ways similar to marketing to bookstores. Similarly, they are driven by the needs of their own markets and the places where they've chosen to have strong collections. And similarly, you can propose author events as a foot in the door.

Also, when prominent libraries begin stocking you, that's another credibility-builder you can use in other marketing; as an example, see what I've done at <http://www.frugalmarketing.com/libraries.shtml>

Now, for some of the important differences:

- Far more than bookstores, libraries make purchasing decisions based on reviews in important trade publications, particularly *Library Journal, School Library Journal, Booklist, Choice, Críticas* (for books in Spanish), *Horn Book, ForeWord,* and *Midwest Book Review*
- Once you have a few reviews, excerpt them in all your other library-oriented marketing (e.g., direct-mail, brochures, fliers)
- Patron requests can make a big difference for libraries; if you can get even one or two patrons requesting a specific title, it may be enough to generate an order, at least in smaller libraries
- If you qualify for the official (no-cost) Library of Congress Cataloging in Publication (CIP) data (typically, that means your U.S.-based publishing house has at least three different

authors and you're publishing nonfiction), you may get some library sales just for being listed in the database; third-party CIP data blocks are nice to have for librarians, but not mandatory

- At some libraries, you can even get paid for your appearance at an author event
- Librarians are much more open than booksellers to carrying "important" books that add depth to a collection but may not be strong sellers
- A much higher percentage of librarians than bookstore owners tend to participate in Internet discussion groups—which means that if you can get them talking about your book, they have an easy way to talk to one another (one interesting case was a book by left-wing pundit Michael Moore, whose publisher, apparently bowing to pressure from the Bush administration, was planning to physically destroy his then-latest book; librarians organized to demand that the publisher get behind the title, which became a strong seller. Moore spoke about this at BEA and I took notes. You can read about it at <http://www.frugalmarketing.com/dtb/freeexpression.shtml>)
- Libraries will keep books on the shelves for years, sometimes decades, if they get checked out frequently enough
- Large library systems could potentially buy several copies per branch, if demand is strong enough
- Trade shows for libraries include some that are considerably less vendor-friendly than bookstore shows, with limited time in the exhibit hall and poor layout; know how it's set up before you decide to exhibit
- Not all libraries allow you to sell books after a reading; find out ahead before you commit to the event (if you can't sell at the event, know exactly how this event will be worth your while before you agree)

"FRIENDS OF THE LIBRARY" GROUPS

Many libraries have Friends of the Library groups; this can be a powerful marketing channel for you. Authors can often take full advantage of these organizations as partners for library events.

Offer to donate a couple of bucks per copy sold at the event to the Friends group, and in return, expect that the group will publicize you in its newsletter, put up appropriate signage in the library, talk your appearance up at its meetings—not to mention help convince the library to order your book through its normal sources.

Non-Bookstore Retail

Most books have a specific subject, and chances are good that this topic is served by its own networks of retailers, websites, and catalogs. Outside of the book industry, retailers typically sell products for twice what they pay for them (this is called "keystoning"), and their purchases are usually nonreturnable. From gift stores to gas stations, from party stores to pet shops, there are probably numerous retail outlets that would be thematically appropriate for your book.

Self-publishing guru Dan Poynter got his start doing books for parachutists. He notes that he's far more likely to sell a parachute book in a parachute store than in a bookstore.

The possibilities are endless, and the terms are usually much more favorable, plus these stores will often be willing to work with you directly, and in many cases are actually more likely than a bookstore to reorder if your books sell well, because of the bookstores' tilt toward new releases.

And they may be open to creative marketing approaches, as David Hall of Mapletree Publishing <http://www.mapletreepublishing.com> explains:

> Our new publicist, Wendy Christensen, wrote a little book, *It's the Little Moments That Matter: 26 Simple Steps to Enrich Every Moment of Your Life*. She submitted it to us in 1993 and we turned it down, so she did it on her own. She broke all the publishing rules—had a wire binding, no ISBN, no printed price, no bar code. She did the typesetting herself in MS Word. But she went around to a small specialty bookstore and several gift shops and offered to let them display it on consignment and to let them set their own retail price. She asked for $15 wholesale. And she has sold hundreds of these over a few months' time in

her hometown of Richland, Washington, with that technique. She says that whenever she goes back to the gift shops, they're always sold out.

When Christensen called him to pitch the book again and tell him about her success, Hall was so impressed that he hired her!

Sometimes, a store can take a book because you've combined persistence with serendipity, as Laura Ramirez, author of *Keepers of the Children: Native American Wisdom and Parenting* <http://www.walk-in-peace.com>, discovered:

> One of the challenges in marketing my book has been its unique Native American slant. While I thought this would be a benefit, it has also been a hindrance. Many people falsely believe that Native American philosophy is a religion, but actually it is a way of being present and creating connections to the world around us. It is a spiritual practice that has little to do with religion. As I say in the book, "Religion divides people into separate camps, while spirituality unites us."

> ... I knew that the General Manager of a local Costco was of Native American descent...I met with him and talked about my desire to reshape misperceptions about Native Americans and their culture with the intent to focus on those ideas that lent themselves to a nurturing view of parenting and helped parents become more humane. Since I was speaking directly to this man's heart, he became my ardent supporter and readily agreed to let me do a book signing at his store.

> I laid the groundwork by convincing the paper in the area to do an article on what Native American ideas have to teach us about parenting. (This newspaper was adjacent to the city in which I lived and was initially resistant to the idea of an article because they didn't consider news from my city "local news.") The article appeared the day before the signing.

> On the day of the event, I was pleased to see that people of all ethnicities showed up to buy the book. Some people purchased as many as five copies. Others hung around to talk about their experiences growing up Native and the prejudices they faced.

The managers of Costco received so many exclamations from their shoppers about their positive interactions with me and my husband (I am white, my husband is Native) that they invited us back the following Saturday to do another signing! Believe it or not, some of the same shoppers came back the following week to buy more copies of the book or to tell us how intrigued they were by the ideas in the book. At the Costco signing, we created a network of new supporters and sold 100 books.

Nonretail Co-ops and Co-marketing Deals

Outside the scope of this chapter, but worth mentioning: a co-op can involve any kind of mutual-aid arrangement with another party. Just to name a few possibilities:

- Adding in a flier from another publisher when you mail out books on direct-to-customer orders
- Joining forces to exhibit together at a trade show or book fair
- Creating a partnership with a museum, association, or event
- Sharing the cost of a collective ad that's larger and more impressive than any of you could have afforded on your own (see *Grassroots Marketing: Getting Noticed in a Noisy World* for a fabulous nonbook example).

Chapter Twelve

Amazon.com and Other Online Bookstores

- *Making the most of Amazon's myriad of promotional tools*
- *Bestseller campaigns*
- *Amazon's affiliate program*
- *Other online bookstores*

It's hard to know whether to put Amazon in the Internet marketing section, the bookstore section or the publicity section; it serves all three functions, and a whole lot more. And with its emphasis on "Earth's biggest selection" of books, it's an especially good platform for small publishers and self-publishers, because a book from a one-title publisher can be displayed in just as much depth as a title from Random House or Simon & Schuster.

As long as your book has an ISBN and meets certain rudimentary standards of good taste, it's a pretty safe bet that you can get a page on Amazon's website. In fact, even if your book violates every community standard you can think of, Amazon will likely set up a page, but it might take it down again if there's a tremendous outcry that your book is full of lies or blatant plagiarism, incites hate crimes, etc. (There have been only a handful ever questioned; I'm not sure of the outcome.)

Amazon also provides an amazing and valuable service to people who live in rural areas, who now have access to almost every book in print. No more three-hour drives to discover the book you want isn't available at your "local" store.

Where Amazon has had a negative impact is on the health of independent bookstores around the country and the world. Since I live in an area that has many indies, and since I very much value what indy stores have contributed to the culture, I do most of my shopping at locally owned stores in my area. But even I have been known to shop at Amazon once in a while, usually either to help a friend with a promotion or because a book was not available locally and I needed it in a hurry.

Amazon as Research Tool

In addition to the marketing aspects, Amazon is a powerful research aid, both to create the book and to determine the market. Competitive analysis is much simpler when you can pump in a few keywords and see all the relevant titles, search for specific phrases in those books that Amazon has fully digitized for the Search Inside the Book program, and of course read the reviews and so forth.

You can easily find out:

- How well a book is selling compared to other titles (and, for the top sellers in each category, where it ranks in its category)
- Who's reviewing the book and what they're saying about it
- What formats have been released (e.g., paperback, hardcover, CD)
- What companion books Amazon's computers recommend
- Whether Amazon keeps it in stock ("usually ships within 24 hours"), orders as needed ("ships in 4–6 weeks"), or believes the book is out of print

Basic information such as the authors/editors, publisher, year of publication, and price (with and without any Amazon discount)

Whether third-party sellers are offering the title through Amazon Marketplace, and at what range of prices and conditions

You can also see at least the front cover of most books, and often the back cover, table of contents, and an excerpt or two. And for those books participating in Search Inside, the full text has been digitized, and other excerpts will come up when you put in any string of text found in the book.

I have used these features to identify or compare versions of books I might buy, to determine the market for books I might write, to research articles, and to locate source material for my own webzines and e-zines.

Amazon as Publicity and Marketing Engine

For authors and publishers, Amazon is a powerhouse promotional tool. You can spread awareness of your books to the far corners of the globe, with minimal effort. Amazon provides many ways to promote your book, and yourself as an author. The list, however, is constantly shifting. This chapter is accurate as of March 2006.

Here are some of the many ways to take advantage of this Internet giant (and no, I haven't done all of these—but I've done quite a few):

Make Sure Your Listing Is Complete

Amazon conveniently posts instructions on how to take full advantage of your listing, at <http://www.amazon.com/publishers>.

Have you posted to your page, with Amazon's "I am the author" or "I am the publisher" feature? Have you uploaded your cover?

Are you participating in Search Inside the Book, which lets readers view any section of your book that contains the phrase they searched for? Note that this programs is not right for every book; if readers seek only a small piece of information and you provide it, they have no need to purchase the book. So, for travel guides, cookbooks, and certain kinds of how-to books, you probably don't want your full text available—but for big-picture nonfiction books, fiction, biographies, etc., this can be very helpful. Because I felt it would cannibalize sales, I chose not to have my frugal fun book indexed for this service, but for my book on ethical marketing, I figure it can only help.

Are you posting photos on your book's page?

How about a profile on the About You page?

Have you gotten a few people to post reader reviews? Or at least posted comments from the reviews and testimonials you've received elsewhere?

Are you offering your e-books (or e-versions of your print books) for sale on Amazon? You can find out how by sending an e-mail to edoc-inquiry@amazon.com.

Do you check your listings regularly for accuracy? If you find errors, report them through the online form at <http://www. amazon.com/exec/obidos/tg/browse/-/13685621/ref=br_ bx_c_1_3/104-7346516-0487923>. If your error isn't covered on the form, send e-mail to catalog-typos@amazon.com or book-typos@amazon.com—and be prepared to do this periodically, as sometimes Amazon's maintenance replaces current data with older versions.

My friend Cathy Stucker says that you can suggest more keywords that Amazon can use to categorize your book. And Aaron Shepard <http://www.shepardpub.com>, who's writing a book about marketing through Amazon, says the place to request removal of inaccurate/slanderous reviews is community-help@amazon.com.

LOCATE POPULAR REVIEWERS IN YOUR GENRE

If you write a certain book and you notice that a volunteer reviewer has done five or ten titles in the same field, track that person down and offer a review copy. It may be one of the easiest ways to get decent quotes for a small-press title. You can even locate top reviewers on Amazon's own list and offer them a chance to review your book. Recognize, though, that these people are besieged just as the staff of major review publications are besieged. Some of them will even want to charge you a fee (which I don't recommend you pay).

CREATE QUALITY CONTENT FOR AMAZON

Review Others' Books. When you've read a book that attracts the same audience as yours, write a brief review—and identify yourself in your bio as the author of your book. Of course, you can't include your URL—but savvy shoppers who want to know more will pop your title into Google and find you anyway.

Submit Listmania Lists and So You'd Like To Guides. When you visit Amazon, if you've purchased in the past you'll probably find a link called Listmania, offering lists of books that readers have organized around particular subjects. Visit someone else's list, and you'll be offered the option to create one of your own. I've begun setting up lists, identifying myself as "Author, *Principled Profit*"—and I start my lists with my own book. Both as a reviewer and a list maker, you get to fill in information about yourself, which of course can include your books, areas of expertise, and so forth. You can even upload a photo.

Cathy Stucker notes that you can also provide a So You'd Like To Guide: a how-to article that mentions some products, including yours in the third or lower position, and a link to your article will show up on the pages of those products you mention.

Set Yourself Up with Amazon Connect. In the winter of 2006, Amazon launched a blog-like feature that allows you to reach out directly to your fans; it shows up on your own book pages, and also on the browser pages of people who've bought your book from Amazon. The more content you put up (not too self-promotional), the more likely it is that some future fan will stumble on you.

Post to the Product Wiki and Product Forum. The first time I actually used the AmazonConnect blogging feature, Amazon also invited me to post to a wiki page and a forum page just for my own book. Keeping in mind that a wiki should be encyclopedia-like in tone, while a forum is a personal comment, I threw up these two posts:

Wiki: Principled Profit: Marketing That Puts People First shows business owners and managers how to maximize success by maximizing ethical behavior, an attitude of service, and cooperative marketing strategies that turn not only customers but even competitors into your marketing allies. It has won an Apex Award, is endorsed by over 70 business leaders (among them Jack Canfield of *Chicken Soup for the Soul*), and has been sold to publishers in three other countries.

Forum: It was, of course, the Enron scandal unfolding a few years ago that was a key inspiration to write my book, *Principled Profit: Marketing That Puts People First*—which shows that strong business ethics and fabulous customer service attitudes are far better success drivers than thievery. Now, finally, we're about to get a verdict in the Enron trial.

Recommend "In Addition." For a while, on every book page, there was an option to recommend other books instead of or in addition to the book you were previewing, just by entering the ASIN (Amazon's version of ISBN). I always recommended my own book "in addition to," as I'm generally not in the habit of trashing other people. Amazon seems to have eliminated this feature, but if it shows up again, do a whole bunch of books before it disappears.

Submit Articles through Amazon Shorts. Like any other channel for articles or excerpts, Amazon wants to gain content in exchange for driving traffic to your book pages. First, send a list of the titles and ISBNs you have on Amazon to shorts@amazon.com (use the subject line, Amazon Shorts Verification), and then you're able to post original unpublished content, from 2000 to 10,000 words. Amazon in turn will set up an author profile page including bio, bibliography, and photo.

USE THE TAP PROGRAM TO GET IN FRONT OF BIG PUBLISHERS

Believe it or not, if you self-publish or publish independently, Amazon may help you market to large mainstream publishers that might want to buy you out or serve as your distributor! This new initiative, called the Talent Acquisition Program (TAP), allows Amazon Advantage publishers to authorize Amazon to send their sales and marketing data to the biggies—and there's no cost to the small press. If you are moving substantial numbers of books through Amazon, send for an application at TAP@amazon.com

Amazon Best-Seller Campaigns

Organize a campaign to get a bunch of people to buy your book from Amazon on the same day, and watch your sales rank move up by orders of magnitude. It will settle back down pretty quickly, but probably a good deal ahead of its original position. But this is not as simple as it seems. First of all, to make it work, you'll need to enlist the cooperation of e-zine editors who reach, collectively, a bare minimum of 200,000 readers (some experts say 2,000,000) *in your market niche.*

Usually, the way this works is to enlist their participation by letting them offer a bonus to everyone participating, which in turn includes a subscription incentive to the e-zine. So what the e-zine owner gets out of the deal is exposure to new audiences. And lately, it seems the trend is toward such ridiculously high numbers of bonuses that it almost doesn't matter what book is being sold.

However, I think many segments are getting kind of tired of these campaigns, and their effectiveness is dropping. Even good books don't always reach their ranking goals, and people are also more aware of just how volatile the rankings are. Sometimes a single purchase can change the sales rank by many thousands.

I am very proud that my own Amazon campaign for *Principled Profit* succeeded on the merits of the book; the only bonus I offered was an electronic copy of the same book. As far as I know, it is still the only book that's ever used this technique without any bonuses. My goal was to crack the top 100, and I reached #83. With only slightly more effort, I probably could have reached Top 50 if that had been my goal.

Several consultants (among them Warren Whitlock <http://www.marketingresultscoach.com> and Randy Gilbert & Peggy McColl <http://bestsellermentoring.com> will cheerfully run the campaign for you, for several thousand dollars. But if you have the contacts to reach enough readers, you can do this yourself. If you choose to try this method on your own, a few bits of advice:

- Notify Amazon ahead of time, and make sure they've got a case or two in stock.
- Set up both a web page and an e-mail address to receive the proofs of purchase (typically, the Amazon receipt number) in order to get the download information for the bonuses.
- Test that all bonuses download properly, well before your launch date; you really don't want to spend vast amounts of time on customer support.
- Extremely important: Set up a reminder mailing list, where publishers who send their announcements before your date can send people, and they can sign up to get a

note from you when the promotion starts—immediacy is a very important characteristic, and some of your targeted publishers will only distribute monthly.

- Let the campaign take place over three to five days, rather than on a single day.
- Carefully target both your letter to your marketing partners and your letter to customers; they must have the right tone.
- Encourage marketing partners to give their own affiliate link, so they can collect a commission on the sales they generate; also consider rewarding them if they generate a certain number of sales, and invite them to become your affiliate so that once the promotion is over, they send customers to your own website. You may even want to consider paying your regular full commission, even though the sale won't go directly through you.
- Suggest to the participating newsletter owners that they send a solo mailing on the first day of the promotion, with no other content than the information about your event; point out that this, of course, will vastly increase your partners' affiliate commissions.
- Invite all participants to sign up for your own newsletter, and to post a review of the book once they've read it.
- Promptly thank all your marketing partners and all your new customers.
- Consider doing the campaign at bn.com (Barnes & Noble) rather than Amazon, because it will take fewer sales to reach the bestseller list (and of course, pick one or the other; don't dilute your impact by splitting across two channels).

Options to Get into Amazon

Aaron Shepard points out that if you or your publisher are printing through Lightning Source or (Amazon-owned) BookSurge, you are automatically included in Amazon's database; this includes many of the subsidy publishers. Infinity, which has its own print equipment, can also get your titles into Amazon. If you've chosen a different printer, you need to get into the Amazon system.

Amazon, unlike many other bookstore channels, is willing to deal directly with micropublishers. If you have a proper barcode and your book is available in North America, you can get into Amazon through the Advantage program <http://www.amazon.com/advantage>. You pay a $29.95 annual fee and provide books at a 55 percent discount. I'd happily give 55 percent to a wholesaler, but not a retailer—and in my opinion, this constitutes an unfair trade practice on Amazon's part.

But Amazon will also buy from wholesalers and distributors, at the standard 40 percent bookstore discount. Since I have a distributor, I let Amazon order through my distributor.

And then there's the Marketplace program, which is simply the way Amazon hosts third-party e-commerce on its site. The seller, who is independent of Amazon, takes the order from the buyer over Amazon's secure servers and ships the order directly, paying a commission (and fees) to Amazon. Many publishers have reported that they successfully use Marketplace to get rid of damaged books, offer autographs, or sell used books from their own personal libraries. And of course, they get to collect the customer's address, which is not possible when Amazon transacts the sale directly (unless you've got them registering for a bestseller promotion, of course). To sell through Marketplace, the book must already be in Amazon's database.

Caution: Although they're supposedly prohibited from doing so, reviewers often dump their surplus inventory via Marketplace— but those vigilant publishers who watch and complain do typically get those listings removed. It can be pretty frustrating if galley copies are being sold for just a few dollars and competing with your own full-price copies.

Amazon's Affiliate Program

Let's face it: Not everyone will want to give you their credit card number. So consider becoming an affiliate of Amazon. If someone is not comfortable buying directly from you, s/he can follow your Amazon link, buy the book there, and put at least a few pennies into your pocket. For traditionally published authors who may be prohibited by contract from selling books directly, Amazon's commission is a welcome revenue addition. And if the purchaser buys anything else in the same visit, you can collect commissions on those sales, as well.

Amazon pays more when someone follows a direct link to a specific book than it does if you just send the visitor to a generic Amazon page.

Let's examine one of those specific links: <http://www.amazon.com/exec/obidos/ASIN/0961466669/ref=nosim/globalartstravel>

The string, "exec/obidos/ASIN," is simply the way Amazon structures its links. The ASIN number that follows "ASIN/" is the unique product code for that item—for books, typically the ISBN number. In this case, it represents my book, *Principled Profit: Marketing That Puts People First*. "globalartstravel" is my affiliate code, so Amazon knows whom to pay. And the "nosim" string makes it less likely that Amazon will lower my commission by directing people off to other books, for which I wouldn't get the direct-link commission.

Consider taking your long, unwieldy affiliate URL and running it through SnipURL.com or TinyURL.com (both free services), to get something short and manageable. For one thing, if the address is posted where it can't be clicked, people will be more willing to type it. And for another, it makes it harder for an unscrupulous person to replace your affiliate code with his or her own. Keep a list of your shortened URLs and what they lead to.

Some people claim to have done very well as Amazon affiliates. I've done poorly and offer it primarily as a service to my readers.

To become an affiliate, visit <http://associates.amazon.com/gp/associates/join/002-2487638-5956839>

Other Online Bookstores

Though sometimes it seems that way, Amazon is not the only game in Cybertown. While Amazon's pubic branding and market share obviously dominate, there are tens of thousands of sites selling books, and you may want to investigate many other options.

First of all, there are those who compete with Amazon as general-interest booksellers. This includes bn.com (Barnes & Noble, by far the biggest U.S. bookseller in the physical world), other chains in the United States and elsewhere, such as Borders and Chapters/Indigo, the American Booksellers Association's booksense.com (where I go for gift certificates for people who live far away from me, because I like to promote independent bookstores), physical stores that have developed a major national online presence, such as powells.com, one-location independent bookstores with websites that are designed to bring traffic to the physical store, like my local bookseller's odysseybks.com.

"Sell anything" Internet giants like buy.com and half.com also sell books, as do the websites of non-bookstore retail channels like Costco in the United States and Tesco in Great Britain.

List your books on any sites that offer a free listing, especially if they include a link back to your site. One such directory is <http://www.bookhitch.com>.

Then there are thousands of book and reader sites that are not trying to carry every book; one example is the literary site bookbrowse.com.

Other sites define a narrow niche and offer books, often as affiliates of amazon.com or another online seller, and sometimes as part of the services offered by a professional association. These sites are valued highly in their communities, because they help filter the vast array of choices into something manageable. For an example, visit my client Sheila Ruth's wandsandworlds.com, focusing on young adult fantasy and science fiction.

Don't forget Amazon's international subsidiaries. English-language sites include amazon.ca (Canada) and amazon.co.uk (Britain); non-English sites include at least Germany and Japan.

Finally, of course, almost every publisher has at least one website.

Which of these endless channel choices will be worth your time? If you find niche sites with a fair amount of traffic, those are probably among your strongest bets. The site owners are for the most part not deluged with submissions, and it should be relatively easy to build a personal relationship with the booksellers, who will want to take your book because you've provided great content for their site and of course offer a revenue stream on sales they generate. Often, you may find that because you can offer much higher commission, they will even link back to you rather than channel sales through Amazon.

PART IV

*Advanced
Marketing*

Chapter Thirteen

Speak to Sell

- *Why speak to promote your books?*
- *Become successful from the platform*
- *Whether, when, and how much to charge*

I've always been a big fan of getting paid to do your own marketing, and that's part of why I have a sideline business as a speaker. It's wonderful to be handed a check to deliver content that has people lining up afterward to buy my books, and a few of them thrusting business cards at me and asking for information about my consulting and copywriting or book-packaging services.

This is not the only reason why I speak, of course. I have several others:

- It has always been my goal to improve the world through the power of my ideas; this is why I was drawn to writing. Yet some huge percentage of people never pick up another book after they graduate, and even then, relatively few readers will happen to find and read my books. By speaking, I bring my ideas in front of people who otherwise would not have encountered them.
- As a writer spending hours a day in my own house, with my own computer, I find the public contact exciting.
- Questions from the audience challenge my assumptions and expand my thinking, causing me to refine and test my ideas in the real world—and this is healthy.
- I meet fascinating people and get to hear their stories.
- Often, I speak at conferences, and get to not only attend the rest of the conference for free, but also network with the

other speakers—high-powered industry experts who then treat me as a valued colleague. Some of these conferences would have otherwise cost me upwards of $1500—and the amount of work these other speakers have funneled to me over the years typically adds tens of thousands of dollars to my annual revenues.

When I speak, my offer to provide a handout for attender goodie bags is almost always accepted, and that gives me a way to reach people who skipped my session (often, many sessions run concurrently). I have had some success getting a goodie bag item in at conferences where I'm not speaking, but my turndown rate is much higher.

Oh, yes, and I do enjoy being treated as a celebrity, and getting feedback that my presentations are exciting and useful.

How to Succeed on the Platform

Most occasional speakers and presenters are clueless and dreadful. You've seen them, no doubt, mumbling verbatim from dense PowerPoint slides in a monotone, hiding behind a podium, and avoiding eye contact. Maybe they really are too terrified to make the audience feel valued—and you can stand head and shoulders above the pack with a few simple techniques:

1. Be animated—vary your voice, your body language. Don't be afraid to move your hands. Get out from behind the podium as much as possible (but remember, if you're being recorded, to stay within range of the camera and microphone). Make eye contact. Studies consistently show that we retain much more of the message when it's conveyed not just through words, but through tone and gestures. Be passionate about your topic. If you don't care about it, why should your audience?

2. Just forget about the number of people watching you. Imagine that you have two or three good friends in the audience; speak as if you're talking on the phone with them. You can even pick out a few friendly faces in the crowd to make more than the usual amount of eye contact—and pretend they're your good buddies.

3. Try for personal rapport. Get there early and circulate—

spend a few minutes each with a dozen or so people (long enough to come away with something meaningful), find out why they chose to attend and what they expect to learn, what problems they need to solve—and sprinkle references to them in your talk, e.g., "Mary was telling me that her horse has lost his appetite." In the Q&A period, call on at least a couple of these people by name.

4. Keep it brief (but don't rush). Don't try to cover a book's worth of knowledge. Pick a few areas to concentrate on, and stick to them. If you have an hour, leave at least 20 minutes for questions, but be prepared to keep talking if you have a dead audience. And don't let the questions knock you off your train of thought. Make your points, take questions when *you're* ready, then go back and make your next points. Otherwise, you run the risk of appearing very scattered and disorganized. If you started late and you're running out of time, cut back on your points—don't try to squeeze them all in by talking fast. End on time or slightly early; be the hero in the conference planner's and attenders' minds by getting the conference back on schedule.

5. If there have been other speakers ahead of you on the program, or if you're going more than an hour, lead the audience in a stretch break. Here's one I use a lot: If speaking to business owners, I say, "Reach for higher profits" (stretch arms to ceiling), "expand your markets" (arms out to the sides), "watch the bottom line" (arms to floor), "contract those budgets" (hug yourself). If speaking to community organizers, I change it to "reach for higher objectives," "expand your constituencies," and "down to the grass roots"; I still contract the budgets.

6. Design your talk for this exact audience. Spend some time with the meeting planner ahead of time, and find out what the concerns are—why they want to bring you in. Make the talk specific and relevant to the people who have brought you there.

7. Build in interactive exercises, plenty of time for feedback, and specific steps that attenders and sponsoring

organizations can take to move forward after your talk. One of the most successful talks I've done was on cross-marketing. I asked volunteers to give a sentence or two about their situation, and then asked, "Who could help their own business by helping Jim?" When everyone was in a small group, I let them brainstorm for 10 or 15 minutes, then brought them back into the whole group to report back. This talk could actually lead to long-term business relationships among the attenders—a big value-add for the sponsoring organization, and a reason for that organization to say nice things about me to others. I've seen successful presenters incorporate games, one-to-one discussions, and many other types of genuine interaction.

8. There are only two times you should be reading your lines. One is if you're dong a book-focused event and the audience is there to hear from your forthcoming or just-released novel, story, or poetry—and the other has nothing to do with book marketing, but is for a tightly controlled setting where your speech had to be cleared by lawyers and deviating from the script could be trouble—such as a press conference to refute allegations of corruption. If you're in that situation, you need a book on damage control and not one on book marketing. Otherwise, glance as needed at your one-to-two-page outline of key points, in big print, that you can see as you stand to the side of—rather than behind—the podium.

Fee vs. Free vs. Paid

In the speaking world, some gigs pay in "exposure", some in real money, and some actually want the speaker to pay for attending! Typically, the third category consists largely of for-profit academic and professional conferences, where big universities or corporations pay the freight.

Just as I would never pay to publish an article or book chapter, or to host a radio show, so I will never pay for the dubious "privilege" of speaking to an audience. And you shouldn't either, unless you have a careful and well-thought-out way to monetize it. These conferences are typically held in exotic locales, so that employees pressure their organizations to send them. I've never attended one and so can't speak to their value.

WHEN TO SPEAK FOR FREE

I will speak for free sometimes, however—but only if it dovetails with my personal goals: If it puts me directly in front of a key audience of prospects, if it adds significantly to my prestige and reputation (as, for example, my speech a couple of years ago to the Public Relations Society of America's International Conference), if the conference organizer is willing to buy a book for every attender, if it provides me with a chance to showcase my abilities in front of meeting planners I've been trying to woo, and/or if it's a group and cause that I personally support, I'm likely to consider speaking without a fee—or work with the organization to come up with ways of paying me that don't involve out-of-pocket costs on their end, such as finding corporate sponsors for the event. And if I can drive to the event in under half an hour, I'm also more open to it. Also, if the organizers pay my travel costs and the conference is an expensive and interesting one, I'll consider the request.

Then there's the possibility of barter: If I am promised a DVD of the speech and the rights to sell it, that might make it worth my while, for instance. Or if the meeting planner is willing to do so much advance publicity that I become extremely well branded to its members, that would be a factor. If the organization barters an exhibit booth at its trade show, that could leverage both the speech and the exhibit far more than either one alone. However, I've learned the hard way that the reality doesn't always live up to these promises. At this point, if someone offers me a DVD, I'd have something in my contract providing fallback compensation if the DVD turns out not to be usable.

If I get asked to speak for free to some group that's not a core audience for me and isn't providing me anything useful in return, I say no. At this point in my career, I don't need "exposure" for its own sake, especially if it's not to the right audience.

There is another category of speaking for free: that's the kind of speech deliberately designed to create a "table rush" and make thousands of dollars in product or seminar sales. This is another piece of the marketing millionaire method. The people who do this (and you know many of their names if you've spent any time on Internet-marketer mailing lists) typically offer a range of products from a $20 book to a several-hundred-dollar tape set to a boot camp costing $5000 to $25000. This can be quite profitable. As an example, if the speaker addresses 600 people at a seminar and sells 50 books at $20, 10 tape sets at $395, and two $10K seminar seats, the $24,950 in gross revenue, typically split 50/50 with the seminar organizer, leaves a net revenue of $12,475—not bad for an hour's presentation! Add to that a few hundred new subscribers to the speaker's e-newsletter, who will probably spend many thousands more over the next few years.

These numbers represent a conversion of just over 10 percent, but many "table rush" speakers often convert 25 percent or more to buyers. Other than the famous, not many people achieve those kinds of speaker fees—but lots of people can pull in those numbers at the product table.

You'd think this would be tough to pull off, but I've seen quite a few speakers do this. Of course, it helps that they speak to audiences that are already groomed to spend vast amounts of money on information products. This doesn't work at all, for instance, if you're talking to line employees at nonprofits. But it can bring in boatloads of money in a free-spending audience of entrepreneur wannabees. However, it can also create resentment in an audience that perceives the event as a "pitch-fest." The successful formula is to deliver at least 95 percent solid content; keep the pitch to 5 percent or less, and phrase the pitch as a continuing educational benefit.

SPEAKING FEE PLUS ADVANCE BOOK PURCHASE: MY FAVORITE DEAL

In many cases, educational materials are a different line item in organizational budgets than speaker fees. So you may be able to work out some deals where the organization purchases a copy of your book for every attender, in addition to your fee. Of course, you'll sell the books at a discount, but you still come out ahead, and you don't have to worry about staffing the sales table after-wards (though once you have more than one product, you may still want to).

The organization may buy books for some attenders and not all. I did one speech where the organization took three cases of my book—72 copies—and used them as early registration bonus-es. I brought the books with me when I drove down to give the speech.

Speaking for Pay: What to Charge?

No clear answer here, but some guidelines:

- The more established you are, the more you can charge. If you're just getting started, you may need to accept token fees of $100 to $500.

- The more specialized and useful your information, the more you can charge. Telling engineers how to be in compliance with the next set of ISO standards is going to pay a whole lot more than telling retirees how to travel and dine out on a budget.

- Charge more if you're not allowed to sell your products.

- The more established your target audience, the more you can charge. Corporations usually pay more than nonprofits, and nonprofits typically pay more than individuals. (But not always; remember those multi-thousand-dollar boot camps I discussed earlier.)

- If you can engage people with your material, through participation exercises, inoffensive humor, directly relevant training, etc., you can charge more.

- Meeting planners want to see "ROI" (return on investment)—so offer specific, structured takeaways and action steps.

- The more you speak to audiences that are already conditioned to pay, the more you can charge. This is why there will always be a big market for people who tell others how to get rich. An audience that thinks it can turn your lecture into an extra half-million dollars per year will not balk at paying several thousand dollars.

- The sponsoring organization should pick up your expenses, above and beyond your fee.
- If the organization can't pay your fee, suggest going after grant money or corporate sponsorships.
- If you accept a reduced fee, either extract some barter (such as a series of advertisements in the group's newsletter, an exhibit table, a usable audio or video recording, a letter of recommendation from the president, an introduction to the right person at the organization's national office) or discuss ahead of time which components of your usual program you will not be doing.
- When you travel outside your area, your prices should reflect that you've taken at least two days off other work, plus significant preparation and rehearsal time.
- Bookstores expect that you will speak for free and that they will supply and sell the books (which you will sign).
- Cruise ships also expect free services—but you and a companion get the full cruise experience, so why not?
- Libraries and K-12 schools often provide a small honorarium, far less than you could get paid in the corporate or college market.

A Success Story: Joyce Brooks

Speaking has sold over 2000 books for Joyce Brooks, author of *Around the World in the Middle Seat: How I Saw the World (and Survived!) as a Group Travel Leader* and *Seven Before Seventy: One Women's Quest for the Seven Continents.*

> My sales took off when Collette Vacations (whom I had booked many of my group tours through) invited me to speak to one of their Group Leader meetings a few months after my first book was published in 2002. This started the domino effect. At that meeting was the director of Heritage Clubs (an organization for bank travel directors) and he invited me to speak at their upcoming convention in Nashville in 2003. At that meeting were 360 bank travel leaders, and I invited them to give me their business card if they would like me to speak to their bank club—I received 180 cards. From this, I mapped out a tour

through the Midwest, and spoke to 30 clubs in 30 days all the way from Texas to Minnesota in 2004. Also, at that meeting was a representative of the Clipper Cruise Line who invited me to speak aboard their ship. The next year, other group leaders had heard about my program, and I scheduled 20 bank travel clubs from Texas to Iowa...I sell my books at each venue, plus receive all travel expenses and honorarium—ranging from $100 to $1000.

Chapter Fourteen

Trade Shows and Book Fairs

- *The right expectations*
- *Large national and small local shows*
- *Take a booth or walk the floor?*
- *Contrasts among book tradeshows, events for writers, and events in other industries*

A national or international book-industry trade event feels pretty overwhelming. Tens of thousands of people jam the exhibit halls...animated meetings between customers and vendors take place in back corners of the booths...seminars and special events sprout up everywhere you look...and authors give away signed copies of their books by the hundreds. Lots of glitz, noise, and confusion.

Yet trade-show marketing at the national level opens up many doors that would be otherwise much more difficult to even approach. I am going to focus much of this chapter on Book Expo America <http://www.bookexpoamerica.com>, held every spring; it's the largest book-industry trade event in the United States, and yet even a one-book publisher or author can get a whole lot of value out of attending.

Industry movers and shakers attend and actually make themselves accessible. In the book industry (unlike some others), you might actually find the publisher or a senior vice president staffing a small or midsized publisher's booth. Even at the largest publisher booths, you may meet senior editors. And if you can't meet the right person, you'll be able to find out whom to contact at that publisher (or distributor, etc.), and be able to say that so-and-so (the employee you speak to, and whose card you'll request) suggested that you get in touch. Be sure to send that employee a thank-you note after the show!

Meanwhile, you might bump into Dan Poynter (author of *The Self-Publishing Manual*) or John Kremer (author of *1001 Ways to Market Your Book*) walking the floor, taking notes for their newsletters, or Gene Schwartz, working on his roundup story for *ForeWord* magazine. Jan Nathan, Executive Director of PMA, or her son Terry, can almost always be found at the PMA booth, and are always happy to learn about quality offerings from small presses; ditto for SPAN Executive Director Scott Flora in the years when SPAN takes a booth. In other words, it can be very worth your while to go and network.

One great way to network is to spend some time volunteering. If you exhibit through PMA and attend the show, you're expected to put in an hour (and you get free admission to the show). Catherine Franz of <http://www.abundancecenter.com> actually suggests putting in time at several booths, in return for displaying your book.

The trick with any trade show, large or small, national or local, is to know why you're there and what you expect to get out of it. Your action plan will be significantly different depending on what you hope to achieve. Here are a few possibilities that you might go after at a major show such as Book Expo America (these don't have to be exclusive; you can pursue several at once):

Sell foreign rights? Make appointments ahead of time with appropriate foreign publishers and agents. Have postcards of your book plus a one-page sell sheet with reviews/endorsements/awards, quick summary of the contents and what makes the book different. Walk through the foreign-publisher areas as early on the first day as possible, and make additional appointments with publishers who seem to be a good fit.

Create massive buzz? Take a booth and make it eye-catching. Give away thousands of books. Design a promotion that pretty much forces everyone at the show to stop by. Advertise in the Show Daily. Arrange a reading and a signing for your author, plus a VIP reception. Treat your author as a major celebrity, and let your publicity reflect this. Send out mailings to all the reporters a few weeks ahead of the show, offering some gift for bringing the postcard back to the booth. (Collect these and note on your database that the journalist responded.) Be prepared to spend many thousands of dollars.

At the 2005 BEA, Discoverhelp <http://www.discoverhelp.com> not only handed out innumerable galleys of Ratanjit S. Sondhe's *TEA: The Recipe for Stress-Free Living*, but also provided incentive for people to wear buttons advertising the book. Hired greeters handed out buttons at the show entrance; if two attenders had the same number on their button, each got a $100 prize when they went together to the booth. Normally, you see a few dozen people wearing a button, but it seemed as if half the show was wearing the *TEA* button. The book managed to get some major press, including reviews in *Publishers Weekly* and *ForeWord*.

Jonathan Somich of Discoverhelp noted that this expensive and successful promotion was carefully orchestrated:

> In order to execute the promotion, Discoverhelp worked closely and coordinated the efforts of several professional promotional agencies out of Cleveland, Ohio to very specifically carry out every aspect of this effort, including the hiring and training of the right talent, setup and display of the booth so that it was appealing and in line with the TEA thought process, and an attention-getting and targeted marketing message with graphically appealing designs. Without this attention to detail, proper balance, and the very high overall level of quality, we do not feel that it would have been anywhere near the success that it was.[6]

Become a better publisher, marketer, or bookseller? Attend at least one of the various conferences in the days preceding BEA: PMA has its PMA University, covering every aspect of publishing and marketing. Rick Frishman and Fred Gleeck run a seminar aimed at getting massively wealthy as an information publisher. The Jenkins Group (publishers of *Independent Publisher* webzine and organizer of the Ippy Awards) sometimes does one, as does Chicken Soup co-creator Mark Victor Hansen. And the American Booksellers Association has its own bookseller-oriented educational program that starts ahead of and runs throughout the show. There are others. Go to Google Advanced Search and put in the two dates before the show and the words "publishing seminar" in the "match all" box.

Attend several of the awards events, such as the Ben Franklin, Ippy, *ForeWord* Book of the Year, NAPRA (New Age), and Lambda Literary (gay and lesbian), so you can see what kinds of books win awards. Attend at least a few of the ABA seminars during BEA. If you recognize an industry expert roaming the halls, attending a party, or sitting in a café or bar, start a conversation—and if the expert shows some interest, politely ask if you can show your book. You might get some priceless consulting in the next two minutes. Be sure to say thank you (I also recommend dropping a thank-you note as soon as possible), and don't hog the expert's time.

Choose vendors? Face-to-face meetings can be very valuable in choosing whom you want to do business with. BEA (and particularly PMA University) provides a chance to meet suppliers (printers, distributors, cover designers, etc.), get a feel for the kind of work they do and for their personalities. PMA-U is an especially good place to do this kind of networking, because the exhibit area is much less harried than the BEA show floor, and you'll have much more chance to talk in depth. You also have a much more manageable number of vendors, all in one area.

Get free books? Personally, I'd say save your travel money and go to the bookstore, if that's all you're after—but you *could* spend all your time standing on autograph lines and picking up freebies. I never chase them, but I will usually seek out three or four specific autographings, and just by wandering the floor, I usually end up with about 50 new books or galleys.

Network with others in your niche? Mark the relevant publishers in the show guide and make a point of hitting all their booths.

Actual Results

I've been to ten international Book Expo America (BEA) trade shows and one national American Library Association (ALA) conference, plus many smaller, regional shows, such as New England Booksellers Association (NEBA) and Massachusetts Library Association. I keep going back to BEA because I can do an awful lot of marketing and networking there, plus research for future books, industry trends, and so forth. Nine of those ten years, I've gone with a press pass, and you can see my reports in the Publishing section of my Down to Business webzine <http://www.frugalmarketing.com/dtb/dtb.shtml>.   They're worth reading to get a sense of what goes on at these shows and how the industry is evolving.

What can you get as a first-timer participating in a large trade show? Here's what I got from my very first BEA, in 1997: Four potential foreign-rights republishers, three potential distributors, two possibilities for book authorship or coauthorship, several people interested in my marketing services, a few easy no-work comarketing deals, and a new agent to represent one of my books. And for my wife, the fiction writer, I brought home three agent and six publisher contacts who'd seriously consider her new novel. Plus I was able to attend PMA University (an extremely useful three-day conference, especially for a publisher just starting out) and get priceless feedback from at least three industry experts.

And that was when I was a know-nothing newbie!

That year, what materialized from all that were some of the prospects for my services and some of the comarketing deals. I also implemented several suggestions from those experts—and I got myself booked as a speaker for the following year's (and several subsequent) PMA-U, the premier independent publisher education event in the United States. Speaking repeatedly at PMA-U, I believe, is one of the reasons why I keep getting invited to speak to publishing groups around the country.

The following year, I actually initiated the contact that led to the contract to publish *Grassroots Marketing: Getting Noticed in a Noisy World* with Chelsea Green. And since then, I've made two foreign-rights sales through the show.

Note that I've done this without ever taking a booth. Typically, I exhibit my book at one of the cooperative stands such as PMA's, where my book is displayed along with hundreds of others, for a nominal cost. Even though I work the foreign-publisher area heavily and come away with several contacts, both of my foreign-rights deals occurred when foreign publishers found my book on display in the PMA booth. Some of my own contacts went as far as my sending reading copies, but the two deals that actually happened both came out of the exhibit rather than my own networking efforts.

Trade-Show Etiquette

If you treat people with respect, you'll get a whole lot more out of the show. Some basic pointers:

- Don't interrupt a conversation at a booth. If people are having a meeting, wait until they're done. For the most part, meetings are brief.
- If you initiate a conversation, be prepared either to have the conversation right then or to schedule an appointment later in the show.
- Be respectful of people's time; get to the point quickly and be organized with any leave-behinds you want to give out.
- Don't be pushy, aggressive, or loud.
- Smile sincerely, and master a firm but not bone-crushing handshake.
- Quit smoking far enough ahead of the show that you and your clothes don't prejudice people against you by reeking of nicotine.
- Show up on time if you have an appointment.
- If you see a massive pile of one title, it's safe to assume that you can take a book; if there are fewer than 20 in the pile, ask first (and respect the answer).
- When you take a business card, jot a quick note on the back about why you took the card and what kind of follow-up you need to do. I actually take five or six envelopes so I can categorize and prioritize them at the end of each day.
- Wear comfortable shoes, and duck outside every now and then for a few minutes of sunshine! These two simple things will help your whole attitude.
- Have strong, focused intentions, and let serendipity guide you to fulfill them. Chicken Soup co-creator Jack Canfield often tells the story of how he and Mark Victor Hansen set a goal of selling a million books in a single day, and on a BEA shuttle bus, he "happened" to sit next to someone who could potentially make that goal a reality: an executive at WH Smith, a chain of airport bookstores. Jack is still working on achieving this "impossible" goal,

and he knows this connection could take him several steps closer. He writes, "We did not actually achieve the goal of selling one million books in a single day. The story I tell is more about the law of attraction, which states that when you have a goal and you visualize it and talk about it as if it were a certainty, you will attract all the people you need into your life to help you achieve that goal, which we did."[7]

Exhibiting vs. Walking the Floor at a Major Show

TAKING YOUR OWN BOOTH

Exhibits on the main part of the floor are very expensive, and then there are hidden charges like drayage (having your exhibit components moved by union labor from the loading dock to your exhibit space), electricity, better-than-bare-bones decorating, etc.

And of course, you have to bring, house, and feed enough people to staff the booth at all times, while some of you are out making contacts on the floor.

In all, it will probably cost you several thousand dollars to take an exhibit on the main floor, and you'll have to get noticed amid the nonstop multimedia spectaculars of the large and well-funded vendors. Publishers with many titles may find exhibiting worth the challenge, especially if they can build their display around a compelling theme. But for the rest of us, there are better ways to get known.

If you take a booth anyway, make it memorable, but make the memory relevant to your books. I feel sorry for the publisher who brought in celebrity look-alikes who posed alongside various attenders; I can't even remember what booth it was.

Master marketer Greg Godek, author of *1001 Ways to Be Romantic*, once toured the country in a custom RV, painted with his book title and cover, for several months, promoting all the way. When he exhibited at ABA (BEA's predecessor), he drove his RV right into his two-booth exhibit space. Yes, he got noticed!

If you do exhibit, be sure to set up a contact follow-up system that only attracts genuine prospects. Far too many exhibitors collect random business cards for some sort of giveaway, and then they have no clue which 50 or 100 of those thousands of business cards should be followed up immediately.

ALTERNATIVE EXHIBITION STRATEGIES

At BEA or ALA, one way around the problem of getting lost amid the huge exhibits is to take a booth as part of the PMA complex, where the whole aisle will have modest booths and the people walking through have a demonstrated interest in small press.

Your other alternative as an exhibitor is to take (or better yet, share) a table in the Small Press section, which costs only a few hundred dollars. You'll have fun here among some of the most interesting vendors at BEA, and you'll have lots of time to get to know each other—because the vast majority of attenders will never walk past your booth, unless you consciously drive traffic with expensive promotions like ads, advance postcards, handing out fliers in the lobby, etc. ALA is better, at least the one time that I exhibited. The Small Press tables were right in the middle of the floor and got plenty of traffic.

Finally, consider participating in a cooperative exhibit rather than your own booth: For a very modest fee, your book is exhibited with many others in a large booth. Travel authors/publishers should definitely consider the Travel Publishers Association cooperative exhibit organized every year by Joan Peterson of Ginkgo Press—an extremely well-run stand. PMA's exhibit displays every book face-out and organized by category, and the full-time staff take the time to get to know the books and will steer prospects toward specific titles. Avoid cooperative exhibits that display books spine-out or randomly lump books from different categories together.

Cooperative exhibits, by the way, are also an excellent strategy to get your book in front of audiences at conferences you won't attend. I have used co-op exhibit services (among them PMA's, *ForeWord Magazine*'s, and Bob Erdmann's Columbine

Communications & Publications <http://bob-erdmann.com/> to send my books to the massive Frankfurt Book Fair (the largest in the world, several times the size of BEA). I've also used co-op services like Association Book Exhibit and Combined Book Exhibit to have a presence at shows that would not be worth my while to travel to and attend, such as the Maryland Library Association; these groups specialize in library and academic conferences. Some of these exhibits have generated nibbles for me; some have not (even through the same organizations).

INSTEAD OF EXHIBITING—WALK THE FLOOR

So what about walking the floor? Can you really make good contacts? Absolutely! Set up appointments ahead of time with exhibitors who are on your "must" list. But leave time to go up and down the aisles systematically, looking for the unexpected opportunity. I got the contract for *Grassroots Marketing* when I came across a foamboard advertising a cartoon book on "sustainable hedonism." I went over to the publisher, pointed at the foamboard, pointed at my T-shirt with the cover of my book, *The Penny-Pinching Hedonist,* and said, "We need to talk!" Six months later, we had a signed contract.

Show your book to publishers in your niche—and listen to their feedback. Take the business cards of publishers who might want to buy you out or distribute for you, for whom you can create a winning premium deal, or with whom you can comarket. Talk to distributors and wholesalers and find out how you can make their system work for you (and for them). Let printing companies show you their latest technology. Network with journalists who cover the publishing beat. Pull industry experts aside for some quick advice. Browse the foreign-publisher displays looking for compatible books, talk to the country coordinators for recommendations, ask publishers about other companies that would be a good fit. Meet and get to know the executives from major independent-publishing trade organizations and media. Find a cool premium item that you can use as a sales incentive. Attend the educational conferences and become a much better publisher and promoter.

Should You Do a Signing?

If you do any author signings at the autographing area at major trade shows, you're giving away a huge number of books, donating any unsigned at the end of your slot to charity (something you can avoid by having the signing at your own booth rather than the autographing area), and running the risk of having these books compete with your own new copies on Amazon Marketplace. As fewer booksellers attend these shows, the promotional advantages of free copies are rapidly wearing out. As an alternative strategy, I recommend autographing "blads": samplers of the book, with the real cover modified to indicate publication date, page count, etc.

Consumer-oriented book fairs are a different matter—because there, when you sign a book, the customer is buying it! And you can often arrange a signing without needing to exhibit. If you are exhibiting, use attractive visual merchandising to bring people over and hook them long enough to check you out.

Other International Shows

I've never attended a book trade show outside the U.S., but there are several important ones. Among the most critical:

- Frankfurt, Germany: the largest book-industry event in the world, filling several massive exhibit halls. Frankfurt is structured almost entirely around advance appointments; you will not have much luck just wandering the halls.
- Bologna, Italy: an international children's book fair.
- Tokyo, Japan: the most important show in Asia.
- Guadalajara, Mexico: key to Latin American rights sales.
- London, England: a rights marketplace for the English-language world outside the U.S.

If you'd like to exhibit at any of these shows, I recommend using one of the exhibit cooperatives mentioned above.

Smaller Trade Shows

If there's a good fit, exhibiting may sometimes make more sense at a smaller show. While exhibiting at NEBA as part of the Independent Publishers of New England cooperative exhibit, I discovered that the regional booksellers loved guidebooks covering obscure corners of New England—but had absolutely no use for my business book on ethics. Yet, when I walked the book around to show the other vendors, it generated a lot of excitement.

I've also discovered that certain shows view the exhibits only as a way to subsidize the conference and set things up in a way that's not at all friendly to exhibitors. If there are only five minutes between conference sessions and the only event in the exhibit hall is a book-destroying reception with chocolate-covered strawberries and other gooey stuff, save your money. The few attenders who make their way into the exhibit hall will spend their limited time with the more established vendors.

At the same time, some shows really understand the needs of the exhibitors. I exhibited at a speakers' conference in Los Angeles organized by Susan Levin of <http://www.speakerservices. com>. Not only did she provide plenty of time to walk through the booths, but she also allowed all exhibitors to attend the full conference and repeatedly used her time introducing speakers to highlight particular vendors and the exhibit area in general.

Before committing to exhibit, ask for (and contact) a few references from other small publishers or authors.

Consumer Book Fairs

Big public book events like New York Is Book Country and the Printer's Row Book Festival in Chicago attract vast crowds. The question is—are they the right crowds for you? I exhibited at Printer's Row one year, and watched a friend of mine who publishes books about Chicago get rid of all her damaged and obsolete stock at a discount, as well as a bunch of used books from her personal collection. But this crowd wanted either local books or bargains, and my full-priced book on finding bargains for fun didn't make the cut (I sold four copies and lost one to wind damage). Neither I nor the three other publishers who shared my booth did very well.

Of course, many schools, libraries, museums, church groups, bookstores, even radio stations put on much smaller book fairs, where you can easily be one of a handful of "celebrity" authors for a reading or a talk. These are excellent ways to get your feet wet with public speaking, but probably won't bring many contacts. They may, however, generate a goodly number of sales, and are worth doing if it's a good fit.

Other Types of Shows

Fiction writers should be attending and perhaps speaking at several writers' conferences per year, especially if you work in a genre (SF, fantasy, mystery, romance, children's, etc.). Attending writers' conferences allows tons of networking opportunities, often including chances to rub shoulders with publishing executives, agents, and successful authors (who might perhaps give you a blurb on your next book). There also may be vendors selling books on the craft and business of writing and publishing—a possible exhibit venue if those are the kinds of books you do. But if you're not presenting, don't expect to sell a lot of books to your fellow attenders.

Usually, there will be a speakers' book table, with books by conference presenters—staffed by a local bookstore. If you're speaking, make sure the bookstore has your ordering information.

Religion and spirituality authors, or authors who write about environmental sustainability or social responsibility, could make a full-time career of attending events in those markets.

Self-help and other nonfiction authors should consider relevant professional conferences and niche trade shows; you may get a lot more noticed as one of ten tightly niched authors or publishers among 50 vendors (especially if you also speak and/or do a book signing), rather than trying to compete as one among hundreds at a book-industry event. Also attend as many of the sessions as you can, and seek opportunities to make informative comments and questions during the Q&A (I've had amazingly good results from that).

When I spoke at Public Relations Society of America's International Conference, I approached the organization ahead of time and asked about doing a signing. To my amazement, even though this event had over 100 speakers (many of whom had books), only about 5 had asked about signings. The organization made a big foamboard poster for each of us (mine has my pic-

ture and my two then-current book covers) and placed the posters strategically on easels at the entrance to the exhibit hall. We
were also given prominent placement in the program guide. The
result? I actually had more people at my book signing than at my
talk! And I got to take the poster home; it looks great on my office
wall and attracts attention to my books when clients come to see
me.

Betsy Lampé, of the Florida Publishers Association, has the
brilliant idea to exhibit at journalist conferences, with the idea of
providing story ideas. She mentioned that at a recent conference
she attended, only two publishers had booths, and they were both
promoting books on journalism. Is that an opportunity?

In short, no matter what kind of book you've done, there are
events where it makes sense to promote it. And that promotion
can include speaking (very low-stress if you're a panelist, seat-
ed and doing a short presentation of 10–20 minutes), donating a
handout (with a weblink to a freebie) for the goodie bag, donating a book or two to be raffled off, making contacts by walking
the floor, and so forth.

For more on trade show marketing, please refer to <http://
www.frugalmarketing.com/marketingtips.shtml>, where I have
articles on how to organize a cooperative exhibit and what to
bring while walking the floor. Also, see <http://www.frugalmar-
keting.com/dtb/dtb.shtml> for several trade show articles from
industry experts. And of course, *Grassroots Marketing: Getting
Noticed in a Noisy World* has an entire chapter on trade shows.

Chapter Fifteen

Affiliate and Joint-Venture Marketing

- *Finding affiliates*
- *Components of an affiliate program*
- *Differences in print books and e-books*
- *JVs with your competitors*
- *Other types of joint ventures*

It's an old idea: get someone to sell your stuff, and pay only for results. Industry after industry uses this model—so why not use it for books?

Many publishers have been paying on commission for decades; 21st-century technology—the Internet, affiliate tracking software, and e-books, among others—makes the whole thing much smoother.

No doubt you've at least encountered amazon.com's affiliate program; it may have been the biggest factor in Amazon's early growth, because the program encouraged mom-and-pop websites all over cyberspace to have their own bookstores, administered by Amazon. No inventory to manage, not even any addresses to keep track of—just a click over to Amazon's site and a small commission earned. So thousands and thousands of sites signed up as affiliates.

I'm an Amazon affiliate: If someone is reading a book review or excerpt on my site or in one of my newsletters and is inspired to get the book, it's only a click away. No fumbling with checkbooks and stamps and envelopes, or even with being on hold forever over the phone. But I stay in the program mostly as a convenience for my readers; it earns me very little. I suspect the majority of Amazon's affiliates are in the program to supplement their content, and not to make any real money—though I know there are hundreds if not thousands who do earn good-sized checks.

On the other side of the coin, affiliate tracking technology is available to you. You can develop a network of affiliates or re-sellers who either send you orders to fill or buy books and resell them directly; you can track the orders, issue payments as need-ed, communicate with all affiliates at once, and provide yourself with a healthy revenue stream. It may be challenging to set up and test the system, but once it's in place, all you have to do is write the commission checks.

Build Your Affiliate Network

Like any other type of marketing, finding affiliates involves lo-cating people who have a vested interest in your success. For the most part, these will be people who are in the same niche and offer complementary products or services. In many cases, they'll already know you—they'll be subscribers to your newsletter, website owners whom you've approached to offer articles, asso-ciations where you're active... You can even recruit through a flier inserted into your outbound book packages.

You can also list your program with various affiliate program sites such as <http://www.associateprograms.com> (run by my cyber-friend Allan Gardyne), <http://www.affiliateprograms. com> or <http://www.refer-it.com>. I'd also recommend looking at Dr. Ralph Wilson's list of resources at <http://www. wilsonweb.com/cat/cat.cfm?page=1&subcat=em_Associate>

What You Need to Have in Place (before You Start Recruiting Affiliates)

E-commerce with an affiliate program involves several differ-ent components, and they don't always work together smoothly. Here's what you want:

- A shopping cart to add the customer's product choices, including multiple quantities, and to calculate shipping and tax (you can get away without this if you have a very simple product line, say, five or fewer items).
- A method of tracking how the purchaser was referred to you, crediting the affiliate, and keeping a running total of money owed that gets adjusted when you make the payment.

- At least one way to get paid: a credit-card merchant account, Paypal account, or other method of converting the sale to bankable currency—and either a virtual or physical terminal to submit each transaction to your processor and close the batch at the end of the day.
- A way to process the order and send download instructions for electronic products, or a thank-you/order confirmation for anything you'll be mailing.
- A notification system that tells both you and your affiliate that a sale was made, and tells the buyer that payment was accepted.
- Affordable monthly fees and transaction charges: $20 and 3 percent or less.

Do-it-yourself solutions typically assemble these different components from various sources, and usually require some time getting it all properly integrated. One of the reasons programs like 1ShoppingCart.com (rebranded and resold by many Internet entrepreneurs, among them Fred Gleeck, Tom Antion, and Yanik Silver) or Ken Evoy's e-commerce module for Site Build It are so popular is that by getting all the pieces from a single source, you expect that they'll work together flawlessly.

1ShoppingCart also includes some nice extras like sequential autoresponders, although you still need your own merchant account on top of the shopping cart fees. But these programs cost quite a bit more than you can spend on your own, and you still may not get the functionality you want.

Another, even pricier, option is to go through one of the affiliate clearing houses that offer hundreds or thousands of merchant programs, such as Commission Junction, BeFree, Kagi, and Kolimbo. The best reason to go that way is that you have automatic access to all their affiliates, who are already set up to sell your product. But that's counterbalanced by the "general store" nature of many of their websites, their lack of knowledge about how to market books, and lack of audience that's already there to buy books. The high commissions and fees are another drawback.

My assistant and I spent over two years trying to figure out something that would work for us; the main stumbling block was my desire to have different commission rates for different classes of products. I finally simplified it to just three rates: 50 percent for digital goods (e-books and special reports), 25 percent for printed books and speeches, and 10 percent of the first order for consulting and copywriting.

Before setting up the affiliate program, I had already been using the free shopping cart from Mal's Script Archive <http://www.mals-e.com/> to sell online. What we ended up doing was setting up a second shopping cart with a different commission rate and transferring all the digital products into it. The original shopping cart gives me credit-card information that I punch into a free-standing terminal and process through a credit-card merchant account I've had for years. I bought my reconditioned terminal outright in 1995, then bought a used printer a few years later (before that, I used an old-fashioned hand-imprinter). The two together cost me about $400 and are still working. The terminal is now obsolete and I've just replaced it with one that supports newly required security features. A "virtual terminal," in which it's all handled online, might be cheaper, but since I still have in-person sales, that wouldn't meet my needs.

The e-book cart puts the funds directly into my Paypal account and sends a download link as soon as the charge has been accepted. No muss, no fuss, no bother.

Are you wondering—what about the 10 percent commission on services? That's easy. There are only a few of them, and most don't come through my cart in the first place. Typically, clients either call the credit-card information in or send the number or a check as part of a mailed package. I figure the commissions out manually and pay the referrers. It's easy to track them because the referrers generally send me an e-mail informing me of the referral, and I also ask all my marketing clients how they learned about me.

Oh, and if you'd like to earn an income stream as one of my affiliates, please visit <http://www.frugalmarketing.com/affiliate-program.html>.

E-books or Hard Goods?

There are a few key differences in selling electronic versus physical goods; I recommend doing both.

The most important difference is that purchasers of e-books expect immediate gratification. They want their payments processed in real time and then they expect to be able to download the book. In my experience, of the titles I have in both formats, those who buy the electronic version either want the information immediately or live on another continent and want to avoid high shipping charges.

The other big difference, of course, is that an e-book costs nothing to manufacture or store and never runs out of inventory. For that reason, in my own affiliate program, I pay a 50 percent commission on e-books, but only 25 percent on physical books—because my costs of processing an e-book are close to zero, especially now that we've set up automated downloads. ·

Once or twice a month, I have to provide some minimal support to someone who either lost the download link, wasn't able to download successfully, or simply doesn't understand the instructions—but in a typical month, it's less time than I spend processing two or three orders of physical books. The time I spend on a physical book—retrieving the credit-card information, entering it into my terminal, packing the order, printing out the right flier for the order, generating and attaching the mailing label—is about 5 to 8 minutes per order. If I have 10 orders to do on a particular day, I've spent nearly an hour, sometimes longer. By contrast, an e-book order that doesn't require technical support takes 10 seconds for me to open up the e-mail, glance at it, and transfer it to a different mailbox; 10 orders take less than 2 minutes.

And oddly enough, in some market sectors, there seems to be a whole lot less price resistance on e-books. People don't seem to mind paying $49 for a chintzy little 20-page report. (I keep my own prices far lower, though.)

On the negative side, many people want to buy a book they can take to the beach, read in bed, etc. And it's obviously a whole lot easier to violate copyright on an e-book. Even with digital-rights management safeguards in place (and there are reasons not to bother with that, mostly having to do with high price and additional support time), a determined hacker can almost always unlock and redistribute your file. (Actually, if someone wants to steal and resell your stuff, all the crook really needs is a copy of your actual book, a scanner, and OCR software—but e-books do make theft easier.)

You can protect yourself to a limited degree by setting up Google News Alerts for key phrases buried deep in your work—but a better solution may be to simply embed so many URLs that link back to you that even if your work is stolen, it generates newsletter subscriptions, ad revenue, and yes, book sales.

Speaking of crooks, it's a lot easier to spot phony credit-card orders (typically ordering large quantities of several products at full price) if they come through a manual cart that doesn't automatically process the card. This is a luxury you have with hard goods but not usually with downloadables, and that's one reason why my shopping cart for downloads uses PayPal exclusively.

Turn Your Competitors into Affiliates or Marketing Partners

Conventional business wisdom tells you to fear your competitors and do what you can to impede their progress—but in the real world, that's spectacularly bad advice. If it were true, you would never find strategic partnerships among major competitors like Apple and IBM, General Motors and Toyota, or FedEx and the U.S. Postal Service—and all these pairs have strong operational partnerships.

I see competitors as potential allies with whom I haven't yet struck an alliance; it actually helps your business to go after partner relationships with your own competitors! The trick is to figure out *how it will be to your competitors' advantage to help you reach that market.*

This is particularly easy to do in information marketing, because it's not a rigid win–lose market. If I'm in the market to buy a computer or a car, I'm generally only looking to buy a single unit. So if I choose Apple, it means I didn't choose IBM. But information is an expansive market. Many people buy several, or dozens, or even hundreds of books on the subjects that they're passionate about. You'd have a hard time finding a serious golfer with only one golf book in the house. Most households have quite a number of cookbooks. And my library of books on publishing, marketing, ethics, and entrepreneurship is overcrowded on seven long shelves.

The desire to foster joint ventures is one of three good reasons why I have my competitors' titles in my bibliography; when I refer you to them, I make it more likely that these competitors will want to partner with me. The other two reasons are that I want to provide the most useful book I can, and to create a resource that librarians are more likely to notice and order—they love books with solid bibliographies and resource sections.

So...how can you work together? Among the numerous possibilities:

- Become affiliates for each other. Sell each other's products and earn commissions.
- Enclose fliers in each other's mailings, and as package stuffers in outgoing orders.
- Create a much more attractive and eye-catching display at trade shows by sharing a booth (which also allows each of you to spend time exploring the show and making more connections).
- Put together a cooperative catalog, website, and/or direct-mail package.
- Increase your desirability to bookstores' event managers by featuring not only your book, but a few titles in a "companion library"; three or four books that you'll feature at your event in addition to your own. You dramatically increase the total sales ticket per customer, send your attenders home with a variety of perspectives, and make a lifelong friend of both the bookstore manager and the competing author/publisher.
- Use the other person's freebie products as bonuses to increase the likelihood of purchase—which then helps funnel the customer into both your and your competitor's databases.

- Partner with each other to take advantage of each other's strengths. If you are really good at book design, for instance, and a competitor has a powerful distribution network, contract to use each other's services.

If you come up with an innovative way to co-market with your competitors, please use the contact form at <http://www.frugalmarketing.com/contactform.shtml> to tell me about it. Maybe you'll be featured in the next edition. And if you want to know more, I explore this concept in far greater detail in *Principled Profit: Marketing That Puts People First.*

Other Types of Joint Ventures

In Chapter 7, we discussed one type of JV: letting others send a salesletter for you. In Chapter 12, we explored JVs for bestseller campaigns. Just now, we talked about the wide range of JV possibilities with your competitors, and in Chapter 17, we'll discuss another particular type of JV: sales to special markets. But there are many companies and organizations whose efforts complement yours, in addition to competitors. Enter creative partnerships whenever they make sense.

Carol White of <http://www.roadtripdream.com>, whom you met in Chapter 3, has a great JV story:

> Before my book was published, I ran across MyTripJournal.com, a robust, online journaling/mapping/photo posting website. We traded industry contacts and information, promoted each other's products on our websites, but never really hit upon a comarketing idea until he caught the attention of The Good Sam Club—a major player in the RV industry. They wanted to do a "scavenger hunt" through a website (looking for travel clues) leading up to their big annual Rally, using MyTripJournal.com. Dan needed a robust travel journal to "scavenge" through— and thought of mine!
>
> Not only did we make my travel website everything that Good Sam wanted (with my book prominently displayed on the opening page to thousands of "scavengers"), we decided to continue the idea at the Rally by sharing my real-life example of

how a trip develops into a MyTripJournal.com site...and created many sales for both of us. We have continued to work with each other on additional "win–win" opportunities and cross-promotions.

Another type of JV is a partnership with groups that bring you in to speak and/or buy your book in quantity. You arrange ahead of time to donate a percentage of book sales back to the sponsoring organization; and then the group gives you tons of publicity in its newsletters, catalogs, web pages, etc. Talk about a win–win! You sell more books, the organization raises significant money, and its supporters are eager to buy because they know they're helping their group. This is one way to get significant sales if you're doing an event for a school with children in grades K–12. In this situation, for instance, the school will probably be willing to send advance order forms home with the kids, so parents can order and pay for an autographed copy ahead of your event.

Chapter Sixteen

Advertising and Direct Mail

- *Principles of paying to reach an audience*
- *Ways to hold down cost and boost effectiveness*

Is it possible to make a profit while putting out serious bucks to get your book in front of an audience? The answer is yes, it's possible—but only if you really know what you're doing.

Shel's Opinionated Basic Principles

1. Advertising should serve both a branding and a direct-sales function. You'll see plenty of "image" or "branding" ads that don't actually try to sell; I think that's a huge mistake. Image advertising that brands and doesn't sell is for rich companies with lots of disposable capital—not for you.

2. The more exactly you can match your offer, your ad, the medium you've chosen, the frequency of insertion, and your target market, the better you will do.

3. In most cases, an ad won't be comprehensive enough to make the sale. If you're lucky, it will just generate interest— so the second step has to be something that can make the sale, such as getting the prospect to visit a website, read a sample chapter, or request a direct-mail follow-up for more information.

4. If you're spending money to reach new prospects, become a compulsive tracker and tester. Measure the dollars per ad, the number of responses it gets, how many of the responses convert, how often those people buy from you and how much they spend over the next two years, etc.

Read as much as you can of the research about effects of different variables on direct response.

5. Test only one variable at a time, even something as specific as the word order in your headline or whether to put a word in quotes. Testing more than one variable throws the whole thing off. Remember that different audiences and different offers will pull different results, so use other people's results only as a starting point.

6. With postal direct mail, test at least 500 to get meaningful results; if you mail only 100, you won't know if your single response is 1 percent, half a percent, or a tenth of a percent. But you know that 5 responses in a test of 500 is 1 percent. Many experts actually suggest testing much higher numbers, like 5000—but I think that's better once you've tested and refined the initial offer in small, less expensive batches. (Using Google AdWords and web-based salesletters, you can drastically shorten the testing curve; it's a reasonably safe bet—though definitely not a sure thing—that changing a variable that increases response online will also increase the response in postal mail.)

7. If your customers have high lifetime value (the amount they will order over time) and you have a strong "back end" of other products you can sell, it may be worth bringing in a customer even if you lose money on the first sale. But it's far, far better to make a profit on the initial offer.

8. Run the numbers based on the worst-case scenario. If you're doing direct mail, make it profitable if you convert just one half of 1 percent to paying customers; that way if you do a more typical 1 or 2 percent, you'll make a nice profit, but even if your mailing performs poorly, you're likely to break even. On a website, you should be able to make money on one tenth of 1 percent.

9. Figure all your real costs. Let's look at a hypothetical example in real numbers. If you spend $1 per envelope (a bargain, once you factor in copywriting, postage, printing, list rental, envelopes, and labor) to mail 5000 copies, the mailing costs you $5000. If it sells 1 percent, that's 50 orders. The profit on those 50 orders has to not only cover

the mailing cost, but also the printing and shipping costs of the books (including labor). So let's say you're selling a $20 book, and your net before marketing costs is $15 per book. Thus, if you sell 50 copies, you've brought in $750 in actual dollars. Subtracting the mailing cost puts you $4250 in the hole. Big ouch!

So you try to make this work. You lower the cost 15 cents per envelope by switching from first class to bulk mail, increase the profit margin on the book (say, by pricing it at $25 and also printing more efficiently to lower costs from $5 per unit to $2). You've saved $750 on postage and $150 on production, and added $400 in revenues. For the sake of argument, we'll assume you manage to bring in the same 50 orders (unlikely, since both the higher price and the switch to bulk mail will probably lower response rates). You still lose $3150 on the mailing. See why you need a strong back end?

But say you've tested and refined and gotten your numbers up to 5 percent. Now you've got 250 orders from that same 5000-piece mailing. Using our better numbers, you net $23 on each $25 sale, or $5750. Less your $5000 in mailing costs, you show a profit this time of $750. So then you roll it out to the full list of 100,000 names. If your percentages hold, you actually net a respectable $15,000 (actually a bit more, since you've already amortized the cost of copywriting).

Do this kind of analysis every time you contemplate purchasing an ad or sending postal direct mail. And remember that in most cases, it's going to take several impressions to convert people from unaware to aware to interested to prospect to buyer. Remember, too, that the more your offer matches its audience on relevance and offer quality, the fewer impressions will be required. (If that confuses you, I explain it in detail in *Principled Profit*.)

Now That You're Thoroughly Discouraged— Here's Hope

While I'd be very cautious in spending these kinds of dollars to advertise a single low-priced book to a consumer audience, there are many other situations where paid ads and direct mail can be quite effective. To name a few:

- Use postcards instead of envelopes to cut costs dramatically and eliminate the "I don't open junk mail" problem
- Join forces with others to cooperatively mail sell sheets for three or four books that complement one another (have one publisher coordinate the orders)
- Promote a line of several related books—or offer a catalog with hundreds of items
- Promote a business or specialty title with a much higher price point of anywhere from $75 to several hundred dollars (*if* your target audience spends money easily—buying the right list or placing ads in the right medium will be crucial)
- Mail to your existing list, where response rates could be many times that of a "cold" list
- Instead of going after end-users, go after resellers and/or influencers (such as journalists or acquisitions librarians) who will presumably move considerable quantities for you over time
- Advertise in a publication that has already reviewed your book, and quote the review in the ad; this should outpull other ads
- Promote items that are already well branded and don't need to establish their identity and credibility: If you've got a book about the history and mythology of the magical creatures in Harry Potter (I actually own such a book), you have that kind of branding advantage. You also have it if you get Stephen King or Alice Walker to publish a book with your publishing house or write a forward for one of your titles (good luck!)
- Advertise in a trade show program specifically to draw people to your booth, especially if you were able to get a cheap location off on a side aisle someplace

Translate Advertising and Direct Mail Strategies to the Internet

Online, the cost of ads is often quite reasonable, and in many cases (including Google's AdSense program), you only pay for actual clicks. But those per-click fees of 25 cents to several dollars can add up fast; I advise capping the daily costs unless you're sure a lot of those visitors are becoming buyers.

Pay-per-click is only one among many Internet advertising strategies. Text ads in e-zines can also work well. For the most part, though, I'd stay away from display ads like banners and skyscraper, and certainly never bother with free classified sites that no one visits except spammers harvesting addresses.

You can also exchange e-mail blasts with other publishers and send to each other's lists. However, *never* spam, and that means never using a list from someone you don't trust completely.

For both e-mail direct mail and pay-per-click ads, I recommend the long salesletter webpage model I discuss in the website chapter. And I recommend thoroughly studying what works for the people who are doing this successfully.

Additional Information

My earlier book, *Grassroots Marketing: Getting Noticed in a Noisy World* provides nine chapters on various forms of paid advertising and direct mail. If you're serious about these tactics, I strongly recommend studying the sections on creating a direct-mail piece or ad, placing them in the right media (or to the right list), picking the correct size and frequency for your ad (or ad series), and lowering your costs while increasing your return.

Chapter Seventeen

Sell Rights, Extend the Brand, Make Profits

- *Ways to exploit the full potential of the intellectual property you've created*
- *Sales of rights*
- *Alternative information formats*
- *Brand extensions*

Big publishers understand that simply selling copies of the book doesn't begin to exhaust the market. Often, they make as much or more from selling the rights to the work in different forms as they do on sales of the original book—but the longer you wait to use or sell these rights, the harder it often is to find buyers.

And that's why, whether you're an author or publisher, think from the very beginning of the project about other rights you can either exploit on your own or sell off, and about ways to extend the brand for the book so that each product extension helps sell all the rest.

These types of sales fall into a few major categories:
- Foreign rights
- Subsidiary rights, commonly known as sub rights
- Bulk sales to corporations/organizations (usually referred to as special sales)
- Repurposing (technically a form of sub rights)
- Brand and product-line extensions

There isn't space here to really do these topics justice; whole books have been written. If this is an area that interests you, I strongly suggest the Jud, Kremer, and Woll books listed in the Appendix.

Foreign Rights

There are few things more fun for an author than opening up a package and seeing a few copies of a book published in another country—with *your* name on the cover!

More importantly, if you sell the right to publish your book to another publisher, that validates your book in the marketplace. With hundreds of thousands of titles to choose from, the publisher found yours worthy of the expense of translating the book, getting it designed, getting it printed, and taking it to market. And no matter what publishing model you choose, you can leverage that credential in dozens of ways.

In fact, when my first foreign book was published—*Marketing without Megabucks* in Korean, from the publisher of South Korea's equivalent of *The Wall Street Journal*—I sent out a press release to local media about it, and the local regional daily paper sent out a reporter and photographer. The 30-inch story ran with a picture of me holding the English and Korean editions. This paper had not bothered to review the book when it came out, but here I was, two years later, with a big story.

That was a deal involving a major U.S. publisher and an agent. But I've also sold my self-published *Principled Profit* to publishers in Mexico, India, and Nigeria. Two of these deals were initiated by my exhibiting the book at Book Expo America in the PMA booth and finalized by my agent; the Nigerian publisher came across my website and inked a deal directly with me to buy not only *Principled Profit* but also *Grassroots Marketing*.

For the 2006 BEA, even though the book is three years old, I made appointments ahead of time with one foreign-rights agent and with a publisher who might buy the rights to the book. I also made my usual effort to generate foreign rights and republication interest by walking the floor, as I often do—which led me to several additional good contacts.

What kind of money can you expect for a foreign-rights deal? It's all over the map. I've heard of deals in the five figures, but in my own experience, that's reserved for blockbuster books. After subtracting agent commissions and foreign taxes, the best I've ever netted was $1200 up front (and another $600 when it went into a second edition) and the worst was a paltry $127.50 (and no, that wasn't the Nigerian deal).

Still, it's free money, and of course once you've sold the book in one market, it's easier to sell into others. If you've got a good agent who actively markets you, there's really no downside even if the advances are tiny. If you have to agent the book yourself, you must decide if it's worth it.

And the foreign-rights arena is one where self-published and independently published books can compete with the big dogs. Charles Patterson <http://www.EternalTreblinka.com>, whose book, *Eternal Treblinka*, was rejected by numerous publishers before he decided to self-publish, has had at least 12 foreign-rights sales.

Sub Rights

A magazine wants to run an excerpt of your book. A book club would like to print its own edition. You bring your book out in hardcover and sell off the trade paperback rights to a larger publisher (as Richard Paul Evans did with *The Christmas Box*).

These are all examples of subsidiary rights. And not only that, when you sell these rights, you're able to get paid for your own marketing.

If you sell an excerpt of your novel to a major magazine with 500,000 readers, those half a million people now know about your book and have gotten a "try-before-you-buy" sample that leaves them hanging and wanting more.

If you ink a deal with a book club, your cover and brief description will likely drive about as many sales to bookstores as through the club's catalog and website (at least if your title is widely available)—and even if your book isn't in stores, you could generate significant word-of-mouth. Of course, your book will make it easy for readers to find your website and contact information so you can capture that buzz and turn it into future sales.

The best time to approach a book club is well in advance of publication—six months to a year ahead. Follow *exactly* the procedures outlined on the club's website, write a strong cover letter that not only tells the club's buyer why this book is right for this particular club but also provides at least the outline of your other marketing efforts. In most cases, the club will buy very cheaply and contract to distribute (and sometimes print) a certain number of copies—and these are generally nonreturnable sales. If you're lucky, you'll be able to work out an agreement to print at the same time, which will bring your unit cost down.

Note: Legitimate book clubs do not charge you; they pay you. If anyone offers you a "chance" to pay for inclusion in their club, my best advice is "run away!"

Catalogs

If you're writing or publishing in a niche, there are probably a number of catalogs that serve that market. If your "beat" is outdoor recreation, find the catalogs for RV-ers, hunters and fishers, camping enthusiasts, etc. Books about food can be sold in cookware catalogs. Books about famous musicians could be sold by music clubs. There are catalogs serving knitting and handicrafts, woodworking, birding, health and beauty (including numerous catalogs serving the aging Baby Boomer population), and of course, many catalogs serving genre fiction (science fiction, mystery, romance, etc.). Office-supply catalogs could sell business books. You can believe I'll be shopping this book around to catalogs for writers!

Catalogs typically buy at a deep discount (often as much as 70 or 80 percent off list), or perhaps at cost plus a specified per-unit profit. Usually, they'll test a small order, and if it does well, they come back for more.

There are also a number of organizations that bring books into schools, such as Reading Is Fundamental <http://www.reading-isfundamental.org>, which operate similarly to catalogs, if your book works in the school market.

Special Sales

Many organizations buy a lot of books. Those they buy are non-returnable. And they usually pay within 30 days.

Among the possibilities: Corporations, small businesses, schools, museums, nonprofits, trade associations, professional conferences, military groups, medical services providers...

Diane Pfeifer had a humorous cookbook called *Gone with the Grits*. She approached Quaker Oats, which sells lots of grits. It literally took several years to negotiate a deal, but when the dust settled, the company agreed to promote the book on grits boxes and take 15,000 copies. Even at just a little bit over production cost, that's going to be very nice for the bottom line. If she netted even 25 cents per copy over her cost, that's $3750 of pure profit. If she got a dollar profit per book, that's a cool $15,000, after all the expenses have been taken off. Since many books using distributors may net less than that after expenses, you'd have to sell a whole lot of books at retail to do as well!

For *Principled Profit*, I hired Penny Sansevieri to go after corporate sales (Yes, I could have done it myself, but it's always easier to promote someone else's book). We identified and contacted nine companies for the first special sales push. Only one, Southwest Airlines, was interested, but the 1000 copies the airline bought before the book was published covered *all* my expenses getting the book out: interior and cover design, copy editing, indexing, a single illustration, galley printing, and offset printing in a run of 3000. Which meant that just the relatively few copies I sold to my own list prior to publication made the book profitable the day it was printed.

You can approach companies or organizations directly, work with a special sales consultant, or have an intern identify the companies, and get a professional to write the approach letter. Some agents go after these kinds of deals, too. If you mention any companies positively in the book, start with those. No guarantees in any case, but worth pursuing. The key question to ask yourself is this:

How does this company genuinely benefit from using my book?

There are many possible answers; finding the correct answer may be the key that will turn your prospect into a buyer. Usually, the correct answer will involve drilling down with "so what" questions, until you find ways to either increase sales of the company's products and services and/or increase the company's status in the minds of its customers, prospects, employees, vendors—and in some cases (especially to counterbalance negative publicity) the general public. Among many possibilities, the company might want to:

- Show people how to use the company's product in creative or expanded ways.
- Establish its own expertise.
- Demonstrate a commitment to the community (as when a local bank sponsors a history of the town).
- Overcome bad press.
- Show off the company in time for an important anniversary or milestone.
- Woo lucrative clients or business-venture partners with interesting and useful gifts.
- Use the book for internal training.
- Convey a point of view about a hot-button issue of the day (for instance, a company might give out copies of a book to legislators, regulators, or policy makers).
- Demonstrate that it is a caring and concerned company willing to help.

For Quaker Oats, the answer was obvious: selling a grits cookbook meant turning their customers on to more ways to use their product, and thus selling more grits. Plus the company did it as a "self-liquidator," which means the customer actually paid enough for the book to cover Quaker's cost. Also, the promotion required sending in some proofs-of-purchase, so more grits were sold ahead of time as well.

Southwest Airlines' motivations for buying my book are a little less obvious. What I was told was that the president of the company wanted to give them out to people he wanted to impress, presumably with the company's commitment to high ethics standards and progressive business practices. This was very different from what I was thinking when I decided to approach them. I was expecting the book would be used in sales and customer-service training—but I surely wasn't sorry that the company came up with this more innovative use.

Stacey Kannenberg, coauthor of *Let's Get Ready for Kindergarten*, whom you met in Chapter 7, found a great special sales lead by reading Dan Poynter's free e-mail newsletter.

> He had a lead about a company interested in purchasing large volumes of books, long shot but if you are interested, send an e-mail...this opportunity did not cost us more than postage and two free samples of our book and the potential pay-off could be an order for 75,000–100,000 books.

She found another great lead by watching TV!

> I donated ten books to a nonprofit children's group that I saw on the Jane Pauley Show...They called for a price on 200 books.

This isn't strictly special sales, but Kannenberg also got her book approved for use in 40 school districts and is currently seeking California statewide approval. It cost her all of $35 plus 2 review copies.

PLAN FROM THE BEGINNING FOR SPECIAL SALES

Sheree Parris Nudd, FAHP, of <http://www.DesignsForGiving. com> designed her quotation books to appeal to nonprofits interested in bulk purchases, and potentially willing to buy new books every year. She sold 5000 in 12 months.

Virginia Brucker is the recipient of a national award from the Canadian Cancer Society for her innovative approach to fundraising on their behalf. Her website is <http://www3.telus. net/webelieve/>. She designed her book, *Gifts from the Heart*, specifically to raise money for cancer research, and she knew all along that she wanted an organization as a partner. This is what she did:

> I wrote a book called *Gifts from the Heart: 450 Simple Ways to Make Your Family's Christmas More Meaningful* after our small school lost four parents and our secretary to cancer. I wanted to write a book that encouraged families to spend their time together creating special memories and traditions, and hoped to sell 2500 copies and raise $10,000 for the Canadian Cancer Society. I'd never written a book and knew absolutely nothing about self-publishing.

We sold just over 23,500 copies. Book sales raised $98,000 for cancer research and helped...raise an additional $138,000 for all sorts of wonderful projects. *Gifts from the Heart* has been described as a "gift that keeps on giving...a miracle disguised as a book" (*The Ottawa Citizen*). Its success has indeed been our own small miracle. But behind our success was a carefully designed manuscript, an effective marketing campaign targeting groups that needed to fundraise for their own projects and an endorsement from the Canadian Cancer Society... I "seeded" the book with ideas that would appeal to the groups I planned on approaching as fundraising partners.

When my manuscript was complete, I contacted the Canadian Cancer Society to see if they'd be interested in endorsing the book. The national office put me in touch with the Revenue Development Officer for my province. While the CCS does not directly sell products, the director agreed to provide a very supportive comment for the back cover. I designed a front cover with a small star that let readers know each book sold would support cancer research. Letting readers know their purchase supports a good cause can be an effective strategy for selling books. But it shouldn't be an "add on." You should be *very* committed to the cause you propose to help. What do *you* have to offer your prospective partner? If you are going to work with a nonprofit or charity, you are making a commitment to be an ambassador for them.

To cap Virginia's story, after self-publishing her book for several years, she just sold it off to Insomniac Press, a midsized publisher in Toronto.

If you're really lucky, organizations might come after you. It happened to Rita Toews, author of *The Bully Book* <http://thebullybook.com>, who'd expected that schools would be her primary market.

In January I received a large order (225 copies) from a police department in California who wanted the book for a campaign. In February another large order from a police department in Canada! I have now been contacted by yet *another* police department who would like to know the price for a copy of the book for each grade 3 & 4 student in their city.

For some reason I would have never thought of police departments as a market for these books. I wonder what other market I'm missing out on.

Repurposing

Dan Poynter, author of *The Self-Publishing Manual*, always tells publishers and authors that we're not in the book business; we're in the information business.

You've developed your intellectual property: the ideas and concepts and logical or tested outcomes, the instructions on how to move, physically, psychically, intellectually, emotionally, from point A to point B—or the gripping prose and wild new plot or images that fuel your novel, short stories, plays, or poems.

Certainly, a book is a logical way to serve up this material for an audience. But it's far from the only option. Once you've created the content, there are dozens of ways to use it. It's often not that much work to take the information you've created in one format and repurpose it for another format. Different people like to learn in different ways, and the same people learn differently in different situations. You may really enjoy reading printed books—but when you're driving, a CD audiobook is a lot more practical.

You can sell these additional formats, or give them out for free to promote your paid products. For every informational or entertainment product you create, think about whether you're getting the maximum return, and whether you should be setting up any of these methods of passing on the content. This list is a starting point; it's not intended to be comprehensive.

- Printed books
- Electronic books (e-books, eBooks, ebooks—it's all the same stuff), with or without special features like hyperlinks and/or multimedia
- Short articles or tipsheets
- Individual chapters or sections sold separately
- Compilations

- Web pages
- Blog entries
- Special reports, sold either as downloads or through the mail
- Audiobooks (on CD, cassette, MP3, podcast, website audio, and other formats)
- Solo teleseminars (one voice), both live and recorded
- Interview-format teleseminars
- Teleseminars that include active audience participation
- PowerPoint or other slide/multimedia presentations
- Audio transcripts
- Webinars
- Speeches
- Live readings
- Vlogs (video blogs)
- Boot camps and conferences
- Video seminars
- Full-production videos with special effects, etc.
- Calendars in a variety of formats (tear-a-sheet-per-day, fold-out page-per-month, web-based, etc.)
- Tutorials such as flash cards, Q&A formats, discussion guides for teachers, study guides, or help wheels
- Greeting cards
- Posters
- Movies

The key to success is knowing what your audience prefers and making it available—which may mean producing in multiple formats. If your target audience is in its 80s, large-print books will be a better bet than e-courses and webinars. If you sell to Type A executives who need the most current information and need it instantly, you might want to set up a paid-subscription website or daily e-newsletter, or even a blog where you and your experts post many times per day. If you have a high-value niche product targeting, say, real-estate salespeople selling properties $1 million and above, manuals in three-ring binders, with worksheets and accompanying CD of web-based resources may enable far higher profits than other options.

Paulette Ensign <http://www.tipsbooklets.com> has had tremendous success with small booklets:

> I sold 15,000 individual copies of my booklet, one at a time, by sending a sample copy of the booklet "110 Ideas for Organizing Your Business Life," and a cover letter to numerous magazine editors, specifically inviting them to excerpt from my booklet into articles they would write, as long as they were willing to put my full contact info and the price for a complete copy of the booklet at the end of the article. This marketing method prompted not only single copy sales of the booklet. It also brought the first bulk sales (1000–5000 copies each)... a two-tape audio program, which then led to a 20-minute interview on the in-flight audio programming of one of the major American airlines.

Brand and Product-Line Extensions

You're reading this book because I decided to extend the brand I'd already created with the original *Grassroots Marketing: Getting Noticed in a Noisy World*. I decided the time was ripe to do a companion book for authors and publishers, which happens to be an area I know a lot about. In fact, my original intention was to modify the existing book for this audience, but I discovered when I got started that I had enough new material to fill a book. There is very little overlap between this book and the original.

However, if I expand to write (or commission) books for other niches (and there are a number I'm thinking about), I'd hope to reuse a good portion of my existing material. This is often an easy way to repurpose material and at the same time extend your brand.

So if you've written an information product aimed at, say, chiropractors, you can probably use 80 percent of the same material to talk to dentists, massage therapists, and so on. And then, if these are successful, you can probably use 50 percent of the material to address other small-office professionals, like accountants and real estate agents.

Think about some of the most successful brands in publishing, like the Dummies books and its imitators. Those brands have been extended far, far beyond the original Dummies mission of educating people about their computers. Now, it's hard to think of a niche that doesn't have a Dummies book. Chicken Soup is another example. Now there are Chicken Soup books for golfers, for teenagers, for writers, and on and on it goes.

In my own field, marketing, we have only to look at Jay Conrad Levinson's phenomenally successful Guerrilla books. Not only are there quite a few on various aspects of marketing, but also books like Guerrilla Saving and Guerrilla Publicity. And then there are the conferences, the tape sets, and so forth.

Product line extensions can be anything you can imagine. Ever buy a t-shirt with a Peanuts character? See a Harry Potter or Lord of the Rings movie? Cuddle a stuffed Winnie the Pooh? See a play like "Fiddler on the Roof" or "Man of LaMancha"? All of these started in printed form; in the case of Peanuts, even the books were extensions: reprints of the original newspaper cartoons.

With a strong and well-established brand, the author and publisher have to work a lot less hard to gain sales on these subsequent projects, because each of these works together with the rest to create a unified marketing machine in which each product reinforces all the others—and of course can be bundled easily with various cross-sell marketing offers.

Appendix

Resources

In alphabetical order within each category—not intended to be a comprehensive list. All prices in U.S. dollars, and subject to change.

Supplement to this Book for Publishers and Self-Publishers
How to Write and Publish a Marketable Book

A supplemental e-book to this book, aimed specifically at publishers and self-publishers. Learn how to...

- Identify the right market(s) and gear your book to that identified audience
- Choose among the four primary technologies to produce your book
- Select a title that will attract the right buyers to your book
- Create a book whose cover, interior design, and production values are every bit as good as those of the New York publishers with which it competes
- Understand and use the wholesale and distribution systems that feed the bookstores

If you bought this book directly from me, it was included in the purchase price (contact me if you didn't get the download link). If you bought the book elsewhere, visit <http://www.grassrootsmarketing forauthors.com/buysupplement.html> or call 800-683-WORD (9673)/413-586-2388 to get the five-chapter supplement for just $9.95.

Publishing Consultants and Book Packagers

Accurate Writing & More—Shel Horowitz (me)
413-586-2388 or 800-683-WORD
<http://www.frugalmarketing.com/contactform.shtml>
<http://frugalmarketing.com/publishing-consulting.shtml>

Aeonix—Pete Masterson
510-222-6743
info@aeonix.com
<http://www.aeonix.com/whoaeonix.htm>

Creative Minds Press—Jacqueline Church Simonds
775-827-8654
<http://www.creativemindspress.com/scr/> (contact form)
<http://www.creativemindspress.com/>

Cypress House—Cynthia Frank
707-964-9520
Cynthia@CypressHouse.com
<http://www.cypresshouse.com>

Desktop Miracles—Barry Kerrigan
802-253-7900
barry@desktopmiracles.com
<http://www.desktopmiracles.com>

Elite Books—Dawson Church
707-525-9292
dawson@elitebooksonline.com
<http://www.elitebooksonline.com>

Jenkins Group
800-706-4636
publish@jenkinsgroupinc.com
<http://www.jenkinsgroupinc.com>

PeopleSpeak—Sharon Goldinger
949-581-6190
pplspeak@norcov.com

Pneuma Books—Brian Taylor
410-287-3120
info@pneumabooks.com
<http://www.pneumabooks.com>

The Publishing Game—Fern Reiss
617-630-0945
info@publishinggame.com
<http://www.publishinggame.com>

Sharp Spear Enterprises—Bob Spear
913-772-8253
sharpspear@kc.rr.com
<http://www.sharpspear.com>

Silvercat—Bob Goodman
858-794-1597
info@silvercat.com
<http://www.silvercat.com/>

Books on Book Marketing and Publishing

Disclosure: Some of these are affiliate links, including all the Amazon links. However, I have only listed resources that I honestly think are worth it, whether or not they earn a commission for me—and I have not listed some of my most successful affiliate relationships, because they're not specifically relevant to book marketing. This is not a comprehensive list.

Bowerman, Peter: *The Well-Fed Self-Publisher*
How to turn an instructional nonfiction book into a full-time living—using his own *The Well-Fed Writer* as a case study. Many excellent suggestions, and some I disagree with (mostly because

I'm more frugal and perhaps a better shopper than he is). His section on setting up and fully exploiting your website's media center alone is worth the price of the book.
Order directly from the author: <http://www.wellfedsp.com>
Order from Amazon: <http://snipurl.com/qeq3>

Cole, David: *The Complete Guide to Book Marketing*
Publishing consultant, publisher, and former Marketing Director for Nolo Press has excellent advice for those who have a few thousand dollars in the marketing budget and want to spend it wisely. Particularly strong on profitability analysis, library marketing, and selling direct. In fact, if you want to sell a lot to libraries, buy this book just for the contacts, even if your budget is much smaller.
Order directly from the publisher: <http://www.allworth.com/Pages/PR_WP314.htm>
Order from Amazon: <http://snipurl.com/t7zx>

Gleeck, Fred: Five free e-books on publishing, marketing, speaking, product generation, and sales.
Fred is one of the foremost exponents of the Internet Millionaire style of publishing, and provides a very high ratio of good solid information. His model may or may not be right for you, but you can certainly learn a lot from him. Available directly from the author at <http://www.fredgleeck.com/ebooks>

Horowitz, Shel: *Grassroots Marketing: Getting Noticed in a Noisy World.*
39 very detailed chapters on virtually every facet of marketing. Many examples from publishing, and many from elsewhere. Very little overlap on the specifics with *Grassroots Marketing for Authors and Publishers*; explores different angles and techniques on similar topics. Far more detailed on general marketing principles and nuts and bolts of copywriting, in-person sales, etc. Read this book if you want to learn how to...

- Write profitable ads and direct-mail letters and place/distribute them with the greatest effect for the lowest expenditure

- Develop a comprehensive media list
- Create affordable and effective brochures, sell sheets, business cards, etc.
- Incorporate a telemarketing program that those who answer the phone actually welcome

And much more.

Available directly from the author at <http://www.frugalmarketing. com/shop.html> or 800-683-WORD (9673)/413-586-2388.

Or purchase from Amazon: <http://snipurl.com/qem7>

Horowitz, Shel: *Principled Profit: Marketing That Puts People First.* Taking marketing to a whole new level, this award-winning book looks at how strong ethics, a cooperative attitude, and a true understanding of your own brand prove that nice guys *don't* finish last. Learn to take full marketing advantage of your ethical commitment. Essential reading before doing joint ventures.

Available directly from the author: <http://www.frugalmarketing.com/shop.html> or 800-683-WORD (9673)/413-586-2388.

Or purchase from Amazon: <http://snipurl.com/qem6>

Howard-Johnson, Carolyn: *The Frugal Book Promoter.* Basic introduction to frugal book marketing, worth getting for its huge collection of online resources.

Order from Amazon: <http://snipurl.com/pjs0>

James, Larry: *40+ Ways to Make Your Next Book Signing an EVENT!!* E-book with lots of great ideas for successful bookstore events. Available free at <http://www.AuthorsandSpeakersNetwork. com/booksigningtips.html> and various other sites.

Jud, Brian: *Beyond the Bookstore* A thorough and comprehensive guide to special sales. Published at $49.95, but available directly from the author for $29.95.

<http://www.bookmarketingworks.com> (click on "bookstore" and then click on "books")

Kremer, John: *1001 Ways to Market Your Book*
Extremely comprehensive mix of frugal and more extravagant
book-marketing techniques, from one of the masters in the business. Be sure to get the 6th (2006) edition; a great deal has changed
in book marketing since the previous version. Indexes are on the
web (ugh!)
Buy at Amazon: <http://snipurl.com/vzeh>
Order directly from the author: <http://bookmarket.com/
1001ways.html>

Krupin, Paul (editor): *Trash-Proof News Releases*
How to write news releases and pitch letters that work, plus a
collection of successful examples. Disclosure: Some of my own
work is included. Available as a free e-book (or $37.95 if you want
a physical book) at <http://www.DirectContactPR.com> (this
same URL also gets you to one of my favorite press-release distribution services).

Laties, Andrew: *Rebel Bookseller*
A successful and very unconventional bookseller explains the retail book business. Particularly lucid explanation of how books
destined for bestseller status end up on the remainder table for a
couple of bucks.
Buy directly from the publisher: <http://shop.voxpopnet.net/
product_reviews.php?products_id=35>
Or from Amazon: <http://snipurl.com/qeqe>

Leal, Carmen: *You Can Market Your Book*
Quick hits on a lot of good marketing ideas, in a clear and acces-
sible style but deeply hampered by lack of an index. Many good
resources and case studies. Particularly helpful in the Christian
market.
Order directly from the author: <http://carmenleal.com/WS/
YCMYB/YCMreviews.html>
Order from Amazon: <http://snipurl.com/pjsm>

Levinson, Jay Conrad, Rick Frishman, and Michael Larsen:
Guerrilla Marketing for Writers
A book specifically for writers. Guerrilla Marketing founder Jay
Conrad Levinson, who pretty much single-handedly showed
ordinary people in mass markets how they could compete with
the big dogs at a fraction of the cost, teams up with master PR
maven Rick Frishman (president of Planned Television Arts) and
well-known literary agent Michael Larsen. Emphasis on low-cost/
no-cost methods. And you have to see the Guerrilla Marketing
store (first link below) for a fabulous example of creating and
maximizing a brand.
Order directly from the authors: <http://snipurl.com/pjsz>
Order from Amazon: <http://snipurl.com/pjsu>

Masterson, Pete: *Book Design and Production: A Guide for Authors
and Publishers*
If you self-publish, this book could keep you from making some
very expensive, penny-wise/pound-foolish mistakes. Focusing
both on the technical know-how an author or publisher needs to
work with designers (or to actually become a designer) and also
how design choices influence book marketing, this is another one
for the "must read" list. As far as I know, there simply is no other
book covering these issues in any depth.
Buy directly from the author: <http://www.aeonix.com> (also
an excellent resource site for book production, including a list of
qualified book printers)
Order from Amazon: <http://snipurl.com/qeqi>

Mowday, Bruce: *The Selling of an Author*
While its scope is sharply limited, this book, based on the author's
experience promoting Civil War history books, has some excellent advice about marketing in niche-specific nonbook events (in
his case, Civil War re-enactments and the like), as well as tips on
doing bookstore events.
Order from Amazon: <http://snipurl.com/qeq6>

Poynter, Dan: *The Self-Publishing Manual*
If you read just one book before deciding to publish, make it this one. Provides the best overview of the numerous aspects of publishing and marketing a book. Dan has been at it for about 30 years. The most recent edition is the 15th, published in 2006. Again, don't buy an earlier edition. While you're picking up your copy, spend some time on Dan's website: <http//www.parapublishing.com>; it offers tons of resources, many of them free. Or get the book at Amazon: <http://snipurl.com/pk6l>

Reiss, Fern: *The Publishing Game: Bestseller in 30 Days*
One of a whole series of Publishing Game books covering production, finding an agent, and getting a syndicated column. Forget the 30-day timetable, but buy them because they're very clear and easy to follow, and because Fern is an extremely gifted marketer from whom you can learn a great deal.
Buy directly from the publisher: <http://www.publishinggame.com/books_and_audio.htm>
Buy from Amazon: <http://snipurl.com/p4s6>

Ross, Marilyn, and Tom Ross: *Jump Start Your Book Sales*
Drawing heavily from the archives of SPAN's newsletter—the Rosses used to own SPAN—this book offers many creative approaches, especially in the vast reservoir of markets outside the bookstore.
Buy directly from the authors:
<http://www.communicationcreativity.com/js/>
Order from Amazon: <http://snipurl.com/pk6t>

Sansevieri, Penny: *Get Published Today*
Pretty much the only book on book marketing to treat subsidy publishing as a viable platform, it offers a comparison of some of the subsidy houses—so if your marketing plan means that subsidy publishing makes sense, you may want to read it. Also a good resource on specific major-market media and how to approach them.
Buy directly from the author: <http://snipurl.com/ue86>
Buy on Amazon: <http://snipurl.com/pk6w>

Shelton, Connie: *Publish Your Own Novel*
A beginner-oriented book useful for author–publishers doing fiction or nonfiction. About half the book is a massive resource section, so try to track down the 2004/2005 edition rather than my 1996 copy. The book does not appear on the author's website, and Amazon only shows the 1996 edition. At the moment, you can find it at <http://www.allbookstores.com/book/compare/1890768553>

Shepard, Aaron: *Aiming at Amazon: The NEW Business of Self Publishing* (Shepard Publications, Olympia, Washington, 2007). A successful self publisher's system for making money from nonfiction books with print on demand, desktop publishing, and (about 1/4 of the content) book marketing on Amazon. com. Straightforward, easy to follow, and full of tips you won't find elsewhere, particularly in the Amazon section. Order from Amazon: <http://snipurl.com/wcya>

Silverman, Francine (editor): *Book Marketing from A–Z*
Little nuggets of success stories from authors using a wide range of strategies. Be prepared to write page numbers down for ideas you want to follow, as without an index, you probably won't find the same thing twice. I have a three-page contribution about my amazon.com campaign.
Buy directly from the publisher: <http://snipurl.com/pk4j>
Buy from Amazon: <http://snipurl.com/pk4i>

Walker, T. J.: *Catapulting to the Best-Seller List—One Talk Show at a Time* (audiobook)
A short course in basic media training specifically for authors.
Buy directly from the author: <http://snipurl.com/pk48>
Purchase from Amazon: <http://snipurl.com/qer8>

Woll, Thomas: *Selling Subsidiary Rights*
Essential reading if you're approaching or negotiating with book clubs, foreign publishers, movie studios, magazines, etc. Apparently out of print. Try Amazon Marketplace:

<http://snipurl.com/qerg> The author's site is <http://pubconsultants.com/>

Resources to Contact the Media

Alex Carroll's radio system: List and course focused on getting on to talk shows with large audiences: <http://snipurl.com/qfuw>

Direct Contact PR: Among other things, a very inexpensive service for contacting reporters: <http://www.DirectContactPR.com>

Gebbie Press Directory of Media Contacts: <http://snipurl.com/on56>

William Gordon's radio talk-show list: <http://www.radiopublicity.net>. Frequently updated list of over 1100 talk shows.

PR Leads media query service (less expensive reseller of Profnet): <http://snipurl.com/nv6p>

Radio TV Interview Report, a magazine that goes to several thousand talk-show hosts and producers; prospective guests advertise in the magazine. <http://snipurl.com/oun8>

Joe Sabah's list of 953 talk shows and accompanying how-to kit (including one update): <http://www.sabahradioshows.com/>

Toms Lake Humor Company (e-mail blast to producers and hosts, once per year per guest). <http://www.tomslakehumorcompany.com>

Organizations

American Booksellers Association (ABA): If bookstores are a big part of your marketing plan, you may want to become a member. <http://www.bookweb.org>

Association of American Publishers (AAP), trade association primarily aimed at larger publishers based in the United States (though open to publishers and publishing consultants in all strata). <http://www.publishers.org>

PMA (which once stood for Publishers Marketing Association, now called "PMA, the Independent Book Publishers Association"), the largest organization of independent publishers. Worldwide membership. Many resources, including an excellent newsletter, educational conferences, discounts on freight, etc. <http://www.pma-online.org>

SPAN, a somewhat smaller organization with a similar list of services and benefits to those of PMA. If you're just starting with self-publishing, I recommend joining both, just to get the resource-filled monthly newsletters (more like magazines, really). <http://www.spannet.org>

REGIONAL GROUPS

In many regions, there are regional subgroups, affiliates of PMA and/or SPAN. For example, I founded and have been involved for many years with Independent Publishers of New England <http://www.ipne.org>. Oh, and if you join these local organizations, you get discounts on your membership in the parent organization—in some cases enough to cover the entire local dues.

Complete list of regional affiliates:
<http://www.pma-online.org/affiliat.cfm#affil>
<http://www.spannet.org/partners.htm>

Websites

MY MOST RELEVANT PAGES (OUT OF 1536 ARTICLES ON MY VARIOUS SITES)

Book Marketing Copywriting and Consulting: <http://www.frugalmarketing.com/publishers.shtml>
Frugal and Ethical Marketing Jumpstart Kits: <http://www.frugalmarketing.com/jumpstart.shtml>

Help Creating Your Book: <http://www.frugalmarketing.com/ author-services.shtml> or <http://www.frugalmarketing.com/ publishing-consulting.shtml>
Business Ethics Pledge: <http://www.business-ethics-pledge.org>
Additional Resources Directly Related to this Book: <http:// www.grassrootsmarketingforauthors.com/resources.html>
Website to Supplement this Book:
<http://www.grassrootsmarketingforauthors.com/innerpages. html> (including all URLs listed in the book)

Publishing Resources Websites
Many of these folks also have free newsletters; I strongly suggest subscribing.

Aaronshep: <http://www.aaronshep.com/publishing>
Aaron Shepard's resources page for desktop book publishing, self- publishing, book printing, and print on demand. Includes a handy link to simultaneously check several books' sales ranks at Amazon.

Aeonix: <http://www.aeonix.com>
Pete Masterson's extensive list of printing and production re- sources, including the best list of book printers out there (a list that even notes which printers do on-demand printing).

Bookmarket: <http://www.bookmarket.com>
Site of John Kremer, author of 1001 Ways to Market Your Book
Resources: <http://www.bookmarket.com/files.html>
Self-Publishing Hall of Fame (success stories): <http://www. bookmarket.com/selfpublish.html>

John Culleton's Shortlist: <http://wexfordpress.com/tex/ shortlist.pdf>
Recommended reading list covering every aspect of publishing and marketing, from a professional typesetter/indexer with decades of experience and a great desire to help newbies succeed.

John Culleton's List of Book Packagers, Coaches, and Consultants: <http://wexfordpress.com/tex/packagers.pdf>

Gropen Associates Reference Desk for Publishers: <http://www.gropenassoc.com/TopLevelPages/reference%20desk.htm>
Marion Gropen, proprietor of this site, also offers fee-based accounting and profitability advice for publishers, in increments as small as a single question. She is familiar with small, midsized, and large publishers, and participated in the publication of several best-sellers.

Midwest Book Review's Advice for Authors: <http://www.midwestbookreview.com/bookbiz/advice/advice.htm>
Jim Cox of MWBR, a long-time friend to the small press and self-publisher, compiled this extensive list of helpful articles.

Para Publishing: <http://www.parapublishing.com>
Site of Dan Poynter, author of *The Self-Publishing Manual*. Perhaps the largest collection of publishing resources out there, some for pay and some for free.

Self-Publishers' Frequently Asked Questions (FAQ): <http://www.creativemindspress.com/newbiefaq.htm>
Prepared by Jacqueline Church Simonds of Beagle Bay Books (small publisher and distributor)/Creative Minds Press (book packager/consultant) at the request of members of the Self-Publishing Yahoogroup, which she coadministers. This is a mixture of FAQ answers and useful resources, including direct links to everything you need to register yourself as a publisher, etc.

The Publishing Game: <http://www.publishinggame.com>
Publishing and marketing wizard Fern Reiss offers a substantial selection of her own articles, organized by category. Scroll past the descriptions of her books (unless, of course, you don't have them yet; you'll want at least one).

The Tool Shed in the Cat's Back Yard: <http://hometown.aol.com/catspawpress/ToolShed.html>
Pat J. Bell, who compiled these resources, has been a fixture on the various publishing discussion lists for over a decade. The author

of the now-out-of-print *Pre-Publishing Handbook*, she also served as PMA's liaison to self-publishers for several years.

Discussion Groups

These are the three where I regularly participate; there are many others. Two of the three lists generate a large volume of messages; management strategies include sending all the messages to a designated folder that you set to sort by topic (so you can delete whole threads that don't interest you), receiving a digest of many posts at once, which you can then either quickly scan onscreen or print out and read), or reading in a web browser where you can sort by thread.

Pub-Forum: <http://www.pub-forum.net>
Free-ranging and at times antagonistic discussions by primarily very experienced publishers. Not moderated and frequently wildly off-track, but you can get great answers here if you can "swim with the sharks." Very active.

Self-Publishing:
<http://finance.groups.yahoo.com/group/Self-Publishing/>
A mix of very experienced and patient publishers and a steady stream of newbies/wannabees. Probably the best place for newer publishers to get good advice, and you'll get a lot more benefit if you first read a few of the books on John Culleton's Shortlist. Moderated (posts are reviewed before they get sent to the list) and very active.

Small Pub-Civil:
<http://finance.groups.yahoo.com/group/smallpub-civil/>
Free-ranging and unmoderated, but much more focused discussions than Pub-Forum, also with a very experienced group. Set up specifically to provide a comfortable, non-confrontational, alternative to Pub-Forum. Low to moderate volume. Disclosure: I own this list. When you sign up, be sure to give a reason for joining (e.g., "I'm an author and want to learn about publishing"); this will get you approved immediately. Otherwise, you'd have to respond to a query—this is to keep spammers out.

Major Reviewers, with Submission Guides (follow *exactly!*)

Choice: <http://www.ala.org/ala/acrl/acrlpubs/choice/infoforpub/informationpublishers.htm>

ForeWord: <http://www.forewordmagazine.com/reviews/guidelines.aspx>

Independent Publisher: <http://www.independentpublisher.com/guidelines.html>

Kirkus Reviews: <http://kirkusreviews.com/kirkusreviews/about_us/submission.jsp>

Library Journal: <http://www.libraryjournal.com/info/CA603906.html>

Midwest Book Review: <http://www.midwestbookreview.com/get_rev.htm>

Publishers Weekly: <http://www.publishersweekly.com/index.asp?layout=submissions>

School Library Journal: <http://www.schoollibraryjournal.com/info/CA444296.html>

Awards

Note that some of these pages only have submission information during the entry period.

Ben Franklin Awards: <http://www.pma-online.org/benfrank.cfm>

DIY Book Awards: <http://www.diyconvention.com>

Eppie Awards (for e-books): <http://www.epicauthors.com/eppies.html>

ForeWord Book of the Year Awards: <http://www.forewordmagazine.com/awards/>

Ippy Awards: <http://www.independentpublisher.com/ipaward.lasso>

Writer's Digest International Self-Published Book Awards: <http://www.writersdigest.com/contests/self_published.asp>

Media/Speaking Training/Coaching/Resources

Tom Antion, <http://www.antion.com/beaspeaker.htm>

Shel Horowitz, <http://www.frugalmarketing.com/media-training.shtml>

Brian Jud, <http://www.bookmarketingworks.com> (click on "book marketing" and then click on "media training" immediately below the top menu)

National Speakers Association, <http://www.nsaspeaker.org>
Joel Roberts, 310-441-2560
SpeakerNet News, http://snipurl.com/os23 (free weekly e-zine and many low-cost teleseminars).

Toastmasters, <http://www.toastmasters.org>

Tony Trupiano, <http://www.effectivemediatraining.com>

T. J. Walker, <http://www.mediatrainingworldwide.com>

My E-mail Distribution Service ***URL

Help from Me
- Book packaging/consulting
- Book publicity copywriting and strategic planning: copy for press releases, media pitches, sell sheets, websites,

brochures, etc., marketing plans, overall strategic thinking
about marketing
- Media coaching
- Public-speaking training

<http://www.frugalmarketing.com/shop.html> (order form),
<http://www.frugalmarketing.com/contactform.shtml> (contact
form)

or 800-683-WORD (9673)/413-586-2388.

Endnotes

1. E-mail post from Dee Power to the Pub-Forum discussion list, July 12, 2006.
2. For a good analysis of advances, royalties, and author earnings through traditional publishing, see Rebecca Brandewyne's article, <http://www.brandewyne.com/writingtips/authorspaid.html>.
3. Telphone conversation, July 11, 2006.
4. 2004 figure is from <http://www.bowker.com/press/bowker/2005_1012_bowker.htm>; 1996 figure comes from <http://www.tarakharper.com/faq_pub.htm>, both downloaded March 2, 2006.
5. Personal e-mail to me specifically for accuracy in this book, April 23, 2006.
6. Personal e-mail to me in response to a request for a description of the promotion, August 3, 2006.
7. Personal e-mail to me in response to a fact-checking request, received April 13, 2006.

Index

Just Because You Read My Book: Let Me Say Thanks With These Special (Mostly Free) Invitations

1. Get ongoing marketing support with our free monthly newsletters: Book Marketing Success of the Month, Positive Power of Principled Profit, and Frugal Marketing Tips. Sign up for any or all at
   http://www.frugalmarketing.com/newsletters.shtml

2. See your name in lights! Send in your book marketing success stories. You might get featured in Book Marketing Success of the Month and/or a future edition of this book! (Note that sending in material gives me permission to use it at no cost, with attribution unless you specify that you'd rather be anonymous).

3. If you ordered directly from us, don't forget the free e-book (described on page 21) and bonuses (described at http://www.grassrootsmarketingforauthors.com). If you ordered elsewhere, you can get all of that for just $9.95, at http://www.frugalmarketing.com/shop.html

4. Would you like an ongoing stream of money? You can earn generous commissions on all our products and services: books, other information products, speeches, copywriting and marketing consulting, even our domain-name finding service. Please visit: http://www.frugalmarketing.com/affiliate-program.html to find out the whole scoop.

5. Sign the Business Ethics Pledge—Become Part of the Change You Want to See! http://www.business-ethics-pledge.org

By the way, you can find all our books and information products at http://www.frugalmarketing.com/shop.html

About the Author

Shel Horowitz is an expert on frugal, ethical, and effective marketing—and among the world's leading authorities on frugal fun. He is also a long-time community activist and the founder of the Business Ethics Pledge movement.

The award-winning author of *Grassroots Marketing: Getting Noticed in a Noisy World*, *Principled Profit: Marketing that Puts People First*, and five other books, Shel Horowitz has published with Simon & Schuster, two mid-sized publishers, Infinity, and his own imprint.

Shel and his wife, novelist D. Dina Friedman, have two teenage children. They live in Hadley, Massachusetts, in a farmhouse built in 1743, in the shadow of the mountain they helped protect in 2000.